FLORENCE: A LITERAR

FLORENCE
A Literary Companion

Francis King

JOHN MURRAY

© Francis King 1991

First published in 1991 by
John Murray (Publishers) Ltd
50 Albemarle Street, London WIX 4BD

The moral right of the author has been asserted

All rights reserved
Unauthorized duplication contravenes applicable laws

ISBN 0 7195 4831 4

Photoset by Rowland Phototypesetting Ltd
Bury St Edmunds, Suffolk
Printed and bound in Great Britain by
Biddles Ltd, Guildford and King's Lynn

To the memory of Anita Ryan
first and most entertaining of companions in Florence

Contents

Contents

Illustrations

The author and publishers wish to thank the following for permission to reproduce illustrations: Archivi Alinari, Nos. 2, 17, 23, 24; Bridgeman Art Library, Nos. 1, 3, 10, 11, 12, 13, 14, 19; National Portrait Gallery, Nos. 4, 5, 6, 7, 8, 9, 18, 20, 21; The Royal Collection, No. 15; Secker & Warburg, No. 22; Victoria & Albert Museum, No. 16.

Introduction

O Foster-nurse of man's abandoned glory,
Since Athens, its great mother, sunk in splendour . . .
                    Percy Bysshe Shelley (1792–1822)

I first visited Florence, a young man in the immediate after-math of the last War, in order to fulfil a commission to write a book entitled *The Brownings in Italy*. That book never reached completion. But my research, half-heartedly carried on when I was not gawping at buildings and works of art, chatting with my contemporaries at café tables, or being entertained by members of the 'community', often elderly and often eking out impoverished and improvident lives in once sumptuous but now dilapidated villas, provided, after an interval of more than forty years, the basis for this book. As people reminisced to me, with a typically Florentine mixture of tolerance and malice, not merely about such writers as D. H. Lawrence, Norman Douglas, and Aldous Huxley in the inter-war years, but also about Henry James, E. M. Forster, Anatole France, and even, in the case of one octogenarian Englishwoman, Ouida, I felt the literary past of Florence to be constantly interpenetrating its literary present. With that feeling came another: in some way that literary past – so various, so strenuous, so distinguished – still had the ability to instruct and, far more important, to inspire. Other expatriate writers or would-be writers clearly felt the same. Florence at that period was full of them, from a prematurely aged and drink-sodden Sinclair Lewis, fumbling his way to long-delayed completion of the least successful of his novels, *World So Wide*, to a youthfully ardent Lettice Cooper.

In the first part of this book, I have attempted to describe the lives of these expatriate writers, whether, like the Brownings, Charles Lever, or Fanny Trollope and her son Thomas, as long-time residents, or whether, like George Eliot, Nathaniel Hawthorne, or D. H. Lawrence, as mere transients on whose creativity the city nevertheless exerted a profound influence. In the second part, I have attempted to illustrate how these expatriate writers and such indigenous writers as Dante, Boccaccio, and, in our own times, Pratolini, have viewed the city. As in the case of Michelangelo's *David*, by turns execrated as 'disproportionate', 'brutal', and 'hideous', and lauded as the supreme depiction of youthful masculinity, such writers have often violently disagreed with each other. D. H. Lawrence loved the 'maleness' of Florence; his friend and disciple Aldous Huxley came to hate its maidenly primness. After her turbulent and emotionally ravenous early years, Violet Trefusis found peace and contentment in her villa in Bellosguardo; Dylan Thomas loathed the spot, as he loathed the rest of the city.

Since the fifth century, when Sidonius Apollinaris left his native Lyons on what was in effect a Grand Tour, the things which have lured writers to Florence are generally those which have also lured non-writers. There has always been the beauty of situation, buildings and works of art. Until the nineteenth century there was also the conviction that in culture and civilization Florence was ahead of the cities of northern Europe. As Addison wrote of Italy as a whole:

It is the great school of music and painting, and contains in it all the noblest productions of statuary and architecture, both ancient and modern. It abounds with cabinets and curiosities, and vast collections of all kinds of antiquities. No other country in the world has such a variety of governments, that are so different in their constitutions and so refined in their politics. There is scarce any part of the nation that is not famous in history,

nor so much as a mountain or river that has not been the
scene of some extraordinary action.

Ruskin's hyperboles about Florentine architecture and art
were echoed by innumerable lesser Victorians: for him the
Campanile was 'the last building raised on the earth by the
descendants of workmen taught by Daedalus'; the Bardi
Chapel in Santa Croce 'the most perfect and interesting little
Gothic chapel in all Italy'. If human nature could be redeemed
through beauty, as Ruskin believed, then Florence was the
ideal location for such a miracle.

Increasingly people also came to Florence in search of
health. The fruitlessness of such a search in a climate so cold in
winter, so hot in summer and so damp in every season is
cruelly illustrated by the many nineteenth-century graves of
young foreigners in the Protestant Cemetery. D. H. Lawrence
was one of the last and arguably the most distinguished of
consumptives to discover that, so far from bettering his
condition, Florence merely worsened it. No doubt this high
incidence of premature mortality had much to do with the
foreign community's intense interest in spiritualism during
the nineteenth and the first half of the twentieth centuries.

Many people also settled in the city either because it was so
cheap that they could live there in a style far grander than
would have been possible at home, or because it was so
tolerant of their sexual foibles and practices. Thus, in the first
half of this century, a number of sexual heretics – among them
Radclyffe Hall and Una Troubridge, Vernon Lee, and that old
reprobate Norman Douglas – found it far easier to exist at
peace not merely with their bank managers but with society
and themselves in Florence than in England.

In addition to all these reasons for visiting, even settling in
Florence, there was for expatriate writers yet another one.
When I arrived there in 1947 there was a feeling, as I have
indicated, that Florence was not merely an artists' city but also
a writers' one. Just as in the 1920s and 1930s foreign writers
had flocked to Paris as to some gigantic forcing-house for
literary talent, so for centuries, not merely two decades,
writers had similarly flocked to Florence. All that past striving

and achievement must, they felt, have somehow impregnated the gold of the air, the grey-brown of the Arno, the greenery of the surrounding hills, the ever-changing colours of the stones.

In *Childe Harold* Byron with justice exclaimed 'Ungrateful Florence!' because it had failed to provide a last resting place for 'the all-Etruscan three' of Dante, Petrarch, and Boccaccio. But to a host of subsequent expatriate writers Florence has provided a home in which they have been able to be both happy and creative.

PART ONE

VISITORS

Montaigne, Lassels, Milton, Evelyn, Addison, Gray, Walpole, Mrs Piozzi, Madame de Staël

The first expatriate writer of note to visit Florence – their Italian travels took neither Chaucer nor Cervantes there – was the French moralist and essayist, Michel Eyquem de Montaigne (1533–92) in 1580. A sufferer from calculus, he had heard that the waters of Tuscany were particularly efficacious in curing or at least alleviating this malady. His *Journal du voyage*, first published in France in 1774 after having lain undiscovered for almost two centuries, and published in England in 1842 in a translation by the son of William Hazlitt, also named William, is much taken up with trivialities about health, diet, and the discomforts of travel. There is little about scenery, since a taste for it was then as uncommon in France as in England; and (as Stendhal noted) there is not even a mention of Michelangelo or Raphael.

Richard Lassels (1603–68), an English Roman Catholic, made a number of tours of Italy as tutor and guide to young noblemen. His *The Voyage of Italy*, an invaluable account of his travels, which included Florence, was posthumously published in 1670. The travels themselves took place in the years 1630–40. As when he describes Italian women looking like 'haycocks with armes and heads' or Genoa as looking 'like a proud young lady in a straight bodyed flowered gowne, which makes her look tall indeed and fine, but hinders her from being at her ease and taking breath,' he writes with humour and vivacity.

The first English writer of real note to visit Florence was John Milton (1608–74). An interesting letter from Sir Henry Wotton, poet and diplomatist, close friend of Donne, formerly agent and secretary to the Earl of Essex and at the time Provost of Eton, is printed in the second edition of Milton's *Comus*. Milton received it shortly before his departure for Italy. After having thanked the poet for his 'dainty piece of entertainment,' Wotton tenders some advice: 'I should think your best line will be through the whole length of France to Marseilles, and thence by sea to Genoa, whence the passage into Tuscany is as diurnal as a Gravesend barge.' He goes on to 'tell you a short story from the interest you have given me in your safety.' The story is as follows:

> At Siena I was tabled in the house of one Alberto Scipioni, an old Roman courtier in dangerous times, having been steward to the Duca of Paglioni, who with all his family were strangled, save this only man that escaped by foresight of the tempest. With him I had often much chat of those affairs, into which he took pleasure to look back from his native harbour; and at my departure toward Rome (which had been the centre of his experience) I had won his confidence enough to beg his advice how I might carry myself there without offence of others or of mine own conscience. '*Signor Arrigo mio,*' says he, '*I pensieri stretti ed il viso sciolto* [honest thoughts and guarded looks] will go safely over the whole world,' of which Delphian oracle (for so I have found it) your judgement doth need no commentary.

Wotton was British ambassador in Venice for three separate periods between 1604 and 1624.

Having set out with letters of introduction from Wotton, Milton arrived in Florence in the autumn of 1638. There are rival claims that he stayed at the house of one Jacopo Daddi, 11 Via del Griglio, and at the house of one Vicenzo Viviani, on the Via Sant' Antonio. Then thirty, he received a hospitable reception from the learned Academies, in the minute book of one of which he is described as *molto erudito*. There are a few references to Italy in his prose works and in his poetic works the famous reference to the autumn leaves in Vallombrosa and the hardly less famous one to Galileo – whom he met in 1639. Landor wrote an Imaginary Conversation between the two men.

John Evelyn (1620–1706), whose diaries cover the years 1641–1705, arrived in Florence in 1644. He lodged in the house of a Signor Baritiere in the Piazza di Santo Spirito – now the site of a colourful market during the day and a resort of drug addicts and dealers during the night. Passionately interested in the fine arts, he has left some vivid descriptions of both buildings and objects of *vertu*. Since, at that period, the value of a painting or a statue was usually only assessed in relation to the building of which it formed a decorative detail, he often writes of 'divers good pictures' and leaves it at that. The merit of his observations lies in the fact that he was a man both erudite about the past and passionately interested in the present.

Largely because of the Civil War, there was something of a hiatus in English travel to Italy between Evelyn and Addison. John Addison (1672–1719) was still in his twenties when he spent the two years in Italy which resulted in his *Remarks on Several Parts of Italy*. Dr Johnson summed up this work, so popular in its own day, as follows: 'As his stay in foreign parts was short, his observations are such as might be supplied by a hasty view, and consist chiefly in comparisons of the present face of the country with the descriptions left to us by the Roman poets . . . Of many parts it is not a very severe censure to say that they might have been written at home.' Anyone who has attempted to read the work in question is unlikely to dissent from this judgement.

Thomas Gray (1716–71) and Horace Walpole (1717–97) arrived in Florence on 15 December 1739 as part of a Grand Tour, then obligatory for young men of family and means, which took them away from England for three years. Having descended 'through winding-sheet of mist' (the phrase is Gray's) into the streets of Florence, they were met by their host-to-be Horace Mann, described by Gray as 'the best and

most obliging person in the world.' Mann was later to become
envoy extraordinary at the Court of Tuscany, and with him
Walpole was to carry on a correspondence for almost half a
century. For much of the time they led a pleasurably indolent
existence in Horace Mann's guest house, Casa Ambrogi in Via
dei Bardi, overlooking the Ponte Vecchio. Florence, Gray
wrote,

> is excellent to employ all one's animal sensations in, but
> utterly contrary to one's rational powers. I have struck a
> medal upon myself; the device is thus O, and the motto
> *Nihilissimo*, which I take in the most concise manner to
> contain a full account of my person, sentiments, occu-
> pations, and late glorious successes. We get up at twelve
> o'clock, breakfast till three, dine till four, sleep till six,
> drink cooling liquors till eight, go to the bridge [the Ponte
> Vecchio] till ten, sup till two, and so sleep till twelve
> again.

But he could not have been as idle as he here makes out. While
in Florence, he wrote in Latin the major part of a long poem on
Locke's philosophy and a number of other poems, also in
Latin, about the beauties of Fiesole, the Arno, and so forth.
During the Carnival Walpole wrote: 'I have done nothing but
step out of my domino and into bed and out of bed into a
domino.'

When the two men finally left Florence on 24 April 1741,
they had decided that it was 'one of the dullest cities in Italy'.
By now they were also on increasingly bad terms. Eventually
they quarrelled – precisely for what reason, it has never been
established, although Walpole always accepted the blame for
their rift – and were estranged for many years.

Mrs Piozzi (Dr Johnson's Mrs Thrale, 1741–1821) spent the
summer of 1785 in Florence, writing about it most enter-
tainingly in her *Glimpses of Italian Society*. She, her Brescia-
born husband, and a group of friends stayed in the English
House (later to become the Hotel New York) in the Palazzo
Ricasoli on the Piazza Goldoni.

Exiled from France by Napoleon, Madame de Staël (1766–
1817) went to Italy in 1804, and there wrote a novel, *Corinne*

ou l'Italie, which was to have a considerable success in its day. Corinne, half-English and half-Italian and blessed with a multitude of talents, is often said to be the woman whom Madame de Staël herself would like to have been. Madame de Staël visited Florence and the result is a section in the novel entitled *Le Séjour à Florence*. Byron wrote of Madame de Staël and her novel: 'She is sometimes right, and often wrong about Italy and England; but almost always true in delineating the heart, which is of but one nation, and of no country, or, rather, of all.'

ROGERS, BYRON, SHELLEY, LEIGH HUNT

It was on 20 August 1814 that Samuel Rogers (1763–1855) 'set sail from the beach at Brighton in a crouded boat'. So began the journey which was to result in the most successful of all the poems written by this acerbic bachelor, noted both for the breakfasts at which, for more than forty years, he entertained the famous, and for an appearance so cadaverous that the caption over a caricature of him in *Fraser's Magazine* in 1830 ran: '*De mortuis nil nisi bonum!* There is Sam Rogers, a mortal likeness – painted to the very death.' A wealthy banker, often accused of social climbing, he predictably put up at Schneider's Hotel on the north bank of the Arno near the Ponte alla Carraia in Florence, at that time the most expensive and exclusive of hotels in the city and so much frequented by English travellers that it was also known as the 'Locanda d'Inghilterra' or 'The Arms of England.' No less predictably, he was entertained by the *gratin* of Florence: by the Countess of Albany, widow of Prince Charles Edward Stuart, the Young Pretender, and mistress of the poet Alfieri; by Lord Holland; by Lord Brownlow. To set beside other such memorable aesthetic experiences as visiting Santa Croce, San Lorenzo, and the Carmine, he could record in his *Italian Journal*: 'Ortolans at dinner. White as snow and wonderfully rich and delicate.' He was a man whose love of art was equalled by his love of food and drink.

Byron (1788–1824) spent only a day in Florence on his first

visit in 1816 and only a few days, in the company of Samuel
Rogers, on his second visit in 1821. Despite the briefness of
this acquaintance, he was never in any doubt that he had no
wish to live in the city. The trouble was the English tourists –
'Florence and Naples are their Margate and Ramsgate, and
much the same company too, by all accounts,' he wrote to
Thomas Moore. In a letter to James Wedderburn Lester he
varied this condemnation – 'Florence and Naples are their
Lazarettoes where they carry the infection of their society . . .'
Nonetheless it was Florence which inspired one of the finest
cantos, the fifth, of *Childe Harold*.

Shelley (1792–1822) first saw Florence in 1818, when he and
Claire Clairmont – Mary was in Bagni di Lucca – were obliged
to spend four hours there while waiting for the Austrian
minister to provide them with a passport to travel on to Padua.
Their journey, 'performed in a one-horse cabriolet, almost
without springs, over a rough road' had been 'excessively
fatiguing' [letter to Mary Shelley].

On 20 September 1819, Shelley and Claire again travelled to
Florence together, in search of lodgings, once more leaving
Mary, now heavily pregnant, in Bagni di Lucca. The couple
were back in Bagni di Lucca on 29 September, and then
returned to Florence, with Mary, on 2 October. They put up
at the boarding house of Madame Merveilleux du Plantis in the
Palazzo Marini on the Via Valfonda. On 13 November Shelley
wrote to Leigh Hunt, 'Yesterday morning Mary brought me a
little boy. She suffered but two hours pain, and is now so well
that it seems a wonder that she stays in bed. The babe is also
quite quite well, and has begun to suck. You may imagine that
this is a great relief and a great comfort to me among all my
misfortunes, past, present, and to come.' Like Florence Nightingale, the child was named after his birthplace – Percy
Florence Shelley.

By now Shelley had written 'Peter Bell the Third' and his
'Ode to the West Wind' while resident in the city. In a
prefatory note to the latter he recorded: 'This poem was
conceived and chiefly written in a wood [the Cascine] that
skirts the Arno near Florence, and on a day when the tem-
pestuous wind, whose temperature is at once mild and

animating, was collecting the vapours that pour down the autumnal rains.'

The winter surprised Shelley, as it has constantly surprised visitors, with its severity. 'Tuscany is delightful eight months of the year. But nothing reconciles me to . . . such infernal cold as my nerves have been racked upon for the last ten days,' he wrote to Thomas Medwin on 17 January 1820. In the same letter he describes Italy as 'the Paradise of exiles, the retreat of Pariahs'. Shelley left Florence, with Mary and Claire, for Pisa on 26 January.

It was in November 1820 that, always improvident and usually impoverished, Leigh Hunt (1784–1859) set sail with his wife and family for Italy. In the past Shelley had frequently invited him; and now Byron had added his own invitation, suggesting that, once in Italy, Hunt should collaborate in starting a radical periodical with Shelley and himself. At the time Hunt was in a state near to despair: 'I was ill; it was thought by many I could not live; my wife was very ill too; my family was numerous; and it was agreed by my brother John, that while a struggle was made in England to reanimate *The Examiner* [a periodical edited by Hunt], a simultaneous endeavour should be made in Italy to secure new aid to our prospects, and new friends to the cause of liberty.'

Hunt could usually be relied on to take a wrong decision, and he did so on this occasion, opting, on Shelley's advice, for the hazards, delays, and discomforts of a sea voyage in winter, instead of a journey by land. He ruefully confessed that, had Shelley recommended a balloon, he 'would have been inclined to try it.' It was already mid-summer in Leghorn (Livorno) when the Hunts arrived there, to be met by Trelawny and then to be conducted to Monte Nero, where Byron was staying in 'the hottest-looking house I ever saw'. Hunt hardly recognized Byron because he had become so fat, and Byron hardly recognized Hunt because he had grown so thin. Having returned to Leghorn – 'a polite Wapping' in which, he noted, Smollett lay buried – Hunt was joined by Shelley. Soon after, Byron and the Hunts took up residence in Pisa, the Hunts living on the ground floor of the Casa Lanfranchi, said to have been built by Michelangelo, while Byron occupied the rest of the palatial mansion. There followed the tragedy of Shelley's death in Lerici, and the Hunts' move first to Genoa – 'where we received the first number of the periodical work, the *Liberal*, which Lord Byron had invited me to set up' – and then, in 1823, to Florence, where the first two Italian words which he heard on his arrival were *fiore* [flowers] and *donne* [women] – a good omen, he decided.

After a brief stay in a hotel, they found lodgings at 1 Via delle Belle Donne – 'a name which it is a sort of tune to pronounce'. It was in this street that Hunt, to his delight, heard an alfresco concert, with music-stands with scores on them and amateurs performing as though in a room. From there they moved to lodgings in the Piazza Santa Croce, at the corner of Via Magliabechi, and then to the Villa Morandi in Maiano, at that time no more than an isolated village on one of the hills around Fiesole. Maiano has given its name to one of the earliest of the Italian poets, Dante of Maiano, to distinguish him from his far greater namesake. Living close to the Hunts was another Dante, a badly-behaved little boy, who 'excelled in tearing his clothes and getting a dirty face and hands'. Hunt was always delighted when he heard the boy's mother chide him with some such words as 'Oh, Dante, what a brute beast you are!' The Jewish family with whom the Hunts were lodging were great lovers of both Dante and Alfieri. It was of the latter that Hunt remarked tartly: 'Alfieri loved liberty like a tyrant and the Pretender's wife [the Countess of Albany] like a slave.'

Despite the chronic illness of his wife, whose pulmonary tuberculosis caused frequent haemorrhages, and despite a chronic shortage of money, Hunt had many moments of sheer happiness in Maiano. Sadly, his efforts to start a magazine in succession to the *Liberal*, which had by then expired, met with no success, because of the fear inspired in the Tuscan authorities by his revolutionary reputation. Hunt has left us an account of a conversation which he had with the Italian bookseller whom he had hoped would be his publisher:

'You must submit the publication (said my bookseller) to a censorship.'

'Be it so.'

'But you must let them see every sheet before it goes to press, in order that there may be no religion or politics.'

'Very well: – to please the reverend censors, we will have no religion. Politics also are out of the question.'

'Ay, but politics may creep in.'

'They shall not.'

'Ah, but they may creep in (say the authorities) without your being aware; and then what is to be done?'

'Why, if neither the editor nor the censors are aware, I do not see how any very vivid impression need be apprehended with regard to the public.'

'That has a very plausible sound; but how if the censors do not understand English?'

'There, indeed, they confound us. All I can say is, that the English understand the censors, and I see we must drop our intended work.'

But even if the censors impelled him to drop the periodical, Hunt could declare:

I loved Florence and saw nothing in it but cheerfulness and elegance; I loved the name; I loved the fine arts and the old palaces . . . I loved the good-natured, intelligent inhabitants, who saw fair play between industry and amusements; nay, I loved the Government itself, however afraid it was of English periodicals; for at that time it was good-natured also and could 'live and let live', after a certain quiet fashion, in that beautiful bye-corner of Europe, where there were no longer any wars, nor any great regard for the parties that had lately waged them, illegitimate or legitimate. The reigning family were Austrians, but with a difference, long Italianized, and with no great family affection. One good-natured Grand Duke had succeeded another for several generations; and the liberalism of that extraordinary prince the first Leopold, was still to be felt, in a general way, very sensibly.

CHARLES LEVER

The most boldly coloured literary personality to settle in
Florence in the nineteenth century was the best-selling Irish
nóvelist Charles Lever (1806–72). Although his books are
now only obtainable, with difficulty, in second-hand book-
shops, his death elicited from *The Times* the comment,
'Thousands of readers of all ages are deploring Lever's loss as a
personal misfortune.'

What chiefly brought Lever to Florence in 1847 was what
brought many expatriates to the city throughout the
nineteenth century and in the twentieth century up to the
Second World War: the possibility of living there both in
comfort and cheaply. Lever's had, in general, been a robust,
rackety life, in which he had, with some difficulty, qualified as
a doctor at Trinity College, Dublin; had taken to literature in
order to extricate himself from imminent bankruptcy as a
result of his fondness for gambling; had edited the then
prestigious *Dublin University Magazine*; and had finally wandered about Europe with his wife and ever-growing brood of
children, often all but penniless and yet always cheerful,
ebullient, and lavish in his expenditure both on himself and on
others.

Having briefly inhabited apartments in the Palazzo
Ximines-Panciatichi on Borgo Pinti, the family moved to
more spacious ones in the Casa Capponi at Arcetri. A guest
there, Edward Dicey, has left this description of one of those
nights spent in cards, conversation, and drinking which Lever
so much loved:

> See again the loveliest scene on which one's eyes ever
> gazed. We are standing on a vine-clad terrace on the
> hillside of San Miniato; the faint rose tints of the sun,
> rising behind the Arno valley, can be seen glistening on
> the heights of Fiesole, standing out clear and sharp against
> the deep blue of the sky; and from the sea of white mist,
> billows rolling at our feet, rise the countless domes and
> terraces and belfries of the city of the Medici. It is the
> terrace of Lever's house outside the walls of Florence, and

our host, after one of the long nights he loved, has hardly
consented to let us go as the daylight crept in through the
open windows, and has come with us to the garden gate
to show us the way Florencewards. Not 'Addio' we can
hear him saying, but 'Ariverdersi.'

Soon after this the Levers made another move, to the Casa
Standish (Via San Leopoldo, now Cavour), to which – since he
had a passion for amateur theatricals – he was delighted to find
a small theatre attached. As the capital of Tuscany, Florence
then boasted a British minister, Richard Lalor Sheil, a fellow
Irishman and a fellow writer, of whom Lever became a
confidant and friend, as he did of his successor, Sir Henry
Bulwer-Lytton, later Lord Dalling. Another confidant and
friend was Robert, later Lord, Lytton, transferred as attaché
from Washington to Florence for a period of four years in
1852. In addition to such company, Lever made friends less
elevated. As his nineteenth-century biographer W. J. Fitzpatrick puts it, 'It was Lever's lot [in Florence] to be thrown
equally into the society of *diplomats* and demireps, swells and
snobs, princes and pretenders, wits and worthies, snarlers and
social men!' Lever himself commented that the Florence of
that time, like the Florence of today,

> contained a good sprinkling of well-dressed, well-got-up
> men, who daily rise with the very vaguest conception of
> who is to house them, fire them, light them, and cigar
> them for the evening. They are an interesting class, and
> have this strong appeal to human sympathy, that not one
> of them, by any possible effort, can contribute to his own
> support. They toil not, neither do they spin.

He himself did toil, as he continued to spin out his vigorous,
jolly, episodic novels. But he also spent hours sitting out in
cafés, surveying the passing scene; dancing and fencing; entertaining guests after dinner on the terrace of his villa; driving *en
grande cavalcade* through the Cascine; or playing cards at the
Jockey Club or Il Casino del Nobile. Of the people he met at
these last two resorts, he tended to be dismissive. 'The Club
abroad is a room where men gamble and talk of gambling, and

no more; it is not a Club. . . . Can you find anything less clubbable than a set of men like this? You might as well set before me the stale bonbons and sugar-plums of a dessert for a dinner as ask me to take such people for associates or even companions.'

In 1849, the Year of Revolution, Florence underwent a disagreeable change. Lever wrote:

> The streets, once thronged with gay groups intent on pleasure, or hastening from gallery to gallery, are now filled with beggars, whose demands too plainly evince that the tone of entreaty has given way to open menace. Burglaries and street robberies take place in open day, the utmost penalty for such offences being a few days', sometimes a few hours', imprisonment. . . . Thrice within one week the diligence from Bologna to Florence was stopped, and the passengers robbed of everything, and in one instance, for some imprudent expression of anger, severely beaten.

In his essays 'The Italian Question' and 'The Tuscan Revolution', he expressed strong support for the Grand Duke Leopold, 'whose sincere and single-minded desire for the happiness of his people has been the mainspring of all his actions'.

In 1850, Lever found himself in serious financial difficulties, as the result firstly of two friends defaulting on loans and then of a loss at cards.

> To retrench in Florence, where we have always lived in the best and consequently most expensive set, is impossible. To leave it would incur great expense; and so, horned by the dilemma, I am alternately fretting and hoping, writing, dining, riding and talking away – to all seeming the most easy-minded of mortals, but, as Hood said, 'sipping champagne on a tight-rope'.

But like all his recurrent financial crises, this finally resolved itself when in 1858 he was appointed consul at La Spezia. 'Lever's official labours at Spezzia were not proportioned to the width of its waters,' comments Fitzpatrick. 'He had little

to do but boat and bask on its beautiful Bay.' The historian
William Lecky has a story from this period:

I well remember how a large tableful of Italian naval
officers were electrified by his [Lever's] conversation, and
especially by the fire and vividness with which he told the
story of how he, his daughter, and his poodle dog were
one day upset in the Gulf, and how they swam; Miss
Lever carrying the dog on her back. When Lever left the
table I was greatly amused by the exclamation of one of
the officers, who had known him of old. 'What a wonderful man that is! I have heard that anecdote again and again;
but it always seems fresh – there are always new
incidents.'

The approach of each autumn saw Lever back in Florence,
where he would then spend the next six or seven months. On
one occasion a man who, through the influence of eminent
relations, held a high diplomatic post at the English Legation,
said acidly to Lever: 'Your appointment appears to be a
sinecure. How can you be Consul at Spezzia and live entirely at
Florence? You got it, I suppose, in recognition of your
novels?' Lever replied: 'Yes, sir. I got my position in compliment to my *ante*cedents; you got yours in compliment to your
aunts.' (The jibe has most point if spoken in an Irish accent.)

One of Lever's most welcome guests in Florence was
Thackeray. Together, the two friends would often dine at the
Laura Restaurant, on the corner of Via dei Cerchi and Via della
Condotta. Thackeray, a gourmet, was enthusiastic about the
fish soup for which the restaurant was famous, even writing a
poem about it.

In 1867 Lever, so robust, loquacious, and witty, left
Florence, having been appointed to an even more lucrative
sinecure, a consulship at Trieste. In offering the appointment
Lord Derby said: 'Here is £600 a year for doing nothing; and
you, Lever, are the very man to do it.'

In the failing health of his last decade, Lever always looked
back on his Florence years with nostalgia:

Although no longer a young man, I had not yet felt one
touch of age, nor knew myself other than I was at five and

twenty; and it was this conscious buoyancy of temperament, joined to a shrewder knowledge of life, that imparted to me a sense of enjoyment in society for which I have no word but ecstasy. The unceasing business of life went on before me like a play, in which, if occasionally puzzled by the plot, I could always anticipate the denouement by my reading of the actors. Such a theatre was Florence in those old Grand-Ducal times – times which, whatever the political short-comings, were surrounded with a charm of existence words cannot picture. If it were an obligation on me to re-live any portion of my life, I should select this part, even in preference to earlier youth and more hopeful ambitions.

LANDOR

Walter Savage Landor (1775–1864), then forty-six, first settled in Florence in 1821, after several years of wandering Europe, during which he quarrelled now with his wife and now with anyone, however innocuous, to whom he took a dislike or who happened to get across him. His resolute mother had long since taken over the administration of his estate, Llanthony Abbey, and he was, in effect, a high-class remittance man.

For five years he lived in rooms in the magnificent Palazzo Riccardi, once the Palazzo Medici, on Borgo degl'Albizzi. When Cosimo de' Medici, then a frail old man, was being carried through this palazzo immediately after the death of his favourite son Giovanni, he is said to have murmured fretfully: 'Too large a house for such a small family.' All too soon Landor was on the worst possible terms with his landlord, the Marchese Riccardi. The relationship reached its nadir when Landor accused the Marchese of having lured away his coachman with a mixture of threats and promises of higher wages. Seeking a personal confrontation with Landor, the Marchese failed to take off his hat when entering his tenant's apartment. Landor first struck it off and then gave notice.

On leaving the palazzo, Landor established himself in the

Villa Gherardesca, later called 'Villa Landore', in Maiano. He himself wrote of his Florentine homes:

> From France to Italy my steps I bent,
> And pitched at Arno's side my household tent.
> Six years the Medicean palace held
> My wandering Lares; then they went afield,
> Where the hewn rocks of Fiesole impend
> O'er Doccia's dell, and fig and olive blend.
> There the twin streams in Affrico unite,
> One dimly seen, the other out of sight,
> But ever playing in his smoothen'd bed
> Of polisht stone, and willing to be led
> Where clustering vines protect him from the sun,
> Never too grave to smile, too tired to run.
> Here, by the lake, Boccaccio's fair brigade
> Beguiled the hours, and tale for tale repaid.
> How happy! Oh, how happy had I been
> With friends and children in this quiet scene!
> Its quiet was not destined to be mine;
> 'Twas hard tᵣ keep, 'twas harder to resign.

The reason why 'its quiet was not destined to be mine' was an even more acrimonious quarrel than usual with his wife, at the conclusion of which he resolved to quit both villa and Florence, never to return. But before that he had passed some happy, if also tumultuous, years. In a letter to his sister in 1831, he boasted of having planted two hundred cypresses, six hundred vines, four hundred roses, two hundred arbutuses, seventy bays, and sixty fruit trees 'of the best qualities from France'. He had not had a moment's illness since arriving at the villa and neither had his children. But 'My wife runs after colds' – catching them as a result of her frequent descents into Florence, of which he disapproved. 'We have the best water, the best air, and the best oil in the world. They speak highly of the wine too; but here I doubt . . .'

There were the inevitable rumpuses, however. Accused by a neighbour, secretary at the French Legation, of having interfered with an underground stream which provided the Frenchman's estate with water, Landor pursued a nine-year feud, culminating in a challenge to a duel which an intervention by the British consul fortunately averted. Servants, artisans, and shopkeepers all complained of verbal and even physical assaults – on one occasion, displeased with a dish served up to him, the irate poet hurled his cook out of the window, only to exclaim in horror 'Good God, I forgot the violets!' After a sequence of rows with the local authorities, his deportation was only averted by an appeal to the Grand Duke. The English community, members of which he had often met in Lady Blessington's palazzo on the Lungarno, now began to avoid him, since his aggressiveness was as often directed at them as at the local people.

On his departure – he made over the villa to his son, Arnold, and settled a sum on his wife – Landor wrote his farewell to the place in which he had passed some of his happiest, as well as his most vexatious, hours:

> I leave thee, beauteous Italy! No more
> From the high terraces, at even-tide,
> To look supine into thy depths of sky,
> The golden moon between the cliff and me,
> Or thy dark spires of fretted cypresses
> Bordering the channel of the milky way.
> Fiesole and Valdarno must be dreams
> Hereafter . . .

Clearly he thought that he would never return. But, having been obliged to leave England after a ruinous libel case over some Latin verses lampooning a woman of his acquaintance, he was back at the villa, now eighty-three years old, in 1858. After a succession of volcanic quarrels with his family, he was expelled, another Lear, from the villa by his wife and children, and threw himself on the mercy of Browning. Browning behaved with the utmost kindness. Having failed to achieve a reconciliation between the old man and his family, he arranged for him to board with Mrs Browning's faithful maid Wilson, now married to an Italian, in the Via Nunziatina, a stone's throw from Casa Guidi. By now Landor was suffering from the deafness of old age. Asking for news of Fanny Trollope from her son Thomas, he received the answer that she had grown very deaf. 'Dead? Dead? Well I wish I were too,' he answered. 'No, no,' Tom shouted at him. 'Not *dead*! Deaf.'

In his final domicile Landor was visited by a number of literary admirers, the last of them Algernon Swinburne, who wrote a fine elegy when, soon after this meeting in 1864, the old lion died.

Landor himself had written:

To my ninth decade I have totter'd on
    And no soft arm bends now my steps to steady;
She who once led me where she would, is gone,
    So when he calls me, Death shall find me ready.

FANNY AND THOMAS ADOLPHUS TROLLOPE

It was in 1843 that the strenuous switchback of her life brought Frances Trollope (1780–1863), then sixty-six years old and already the author of a pot-boiling *A Visit to Italy*, to settle in Florence. With her was the older of her two surviving sons, Thomas Adolphus (1810–92), like his mother a novelist of more perseverance than natural talent.

Their first residence was an apartment in the Palazzo Berti in the Via dei Malcontenti – so named because it was at one time the road to the Florentine equivalent of Tyburn. 'Our house was the one next to the east end of the Church of Santa Croce,' Thomas wrote in his memoirs *What I Remember*. 'Our rooms looked on to a large garden, and were pleasant enough. We witnessed from our windows the building of the new steeple of Santa Croce, which was completed before we left the house.'

'Within a few weeks . . . my mother's home became, as usual, a centre of attraction and pleasant intercourse and her weekly Friday receptions were always crowded,' Thomas noted. Among the guests either there, at a subsequent dwelling in the Via del Giglio, or at the Villino Trollope, a sumptuous residence on the huge, ugly Piazza dell' Indipendenza, were the Brownings, Charles Dickens, Harriet Beecher Stowe, Nathaniel Hawthorne, James Russell Lowell, and

George Eliot and G. H. Lewes. (Subsequently the Villino Trollope became an hotel. In the spring of 1887 Thomas Hardy and his first wife, Emily, stayed there, spending much of their time in the company of the writer 'Leader Scott' – Mrs Lucy E. Baxter, daughter of Hardy's friend the Dorset poet William Barnes, and a long-time resident of Florence.)

Not all those who were recipients of the Trollopes' hospitality were always gracious about it. One of Elizabeth Barrett Browning's letters contains the passage:

> Mrs Trollope has recommenced her 'public' mornings which we shrink away from. She 'receives' every Saturday morning in the most heterogeneous way possible. It must be amusing to anybody not overwhelmed by it, and people say that she snatches up 'characters' for her 'so many volumes a year' out of the diversities of masks presented to her on these occasions.

The circumstances which eventually enabled Fanny, Thomas, and the wife, Theodosia, whom he had married when well into his thirties, to live and entertain in such style at the Villino Trollope were piquant enough to provide the expatriate community with ample opportunity for the gossip which then, as now, it so much relished. Theodosia's swarthy father, Joseph Garrow, son of an Indian army officer and a high-caste Brahmin woman, had married a rich, Jewish widow, twenty-five years older than himself and the mother of two grown-up children. At the remarkable age of fifty-nine, this wife was declared to have given birth to a daughter, Theodosia. Since the self-effacing daughter of the previous marriage, also called Fanny, showed her 'step-sister' far more attention than did her generally disagreeable mother, the obvious presumption is that Theodosia was in fact Fanny's daughter. This presumption is enforced by the fact that, on her premature death, Fanny left a surprisingly generous sum of money to Theodosia. It was largely with this money that the Villino Trollope was purchased and financed as a centre of Florentine literary life.

Florentine gossip did not end there. For five years Thomas and Theodosia were childless. Then, despite the fact that during the summer of 1852 Thomas had rarely been in Florence, Theodosia announced that she was pregnant. Since the child, Beatrice or 'Bice', looked so much like her mother and in no way like a Trollope, there were inevitable whispers and smiles – to which Browning was to allude in a letter written many years later to his wife's Florentine friend and confidante, Isabel ('Isa') Blagden.

It is astonishing that, despite Anthony Trollope's employment as a civil servant, despite the constant entertaining in which Frances and Thomas indulged during their years in Florence, and despite the fact that Frances did not begin writing until she was fifty-one, the sum total of the published works of the trio, indomitable mother and sons, should have reached three hundred and six.

At a period when spiritualism was so much the vogue, the Villino Trollope was the setting for many a seance, with the world-famous medium Daniel Dunglas Home staying there, at the invitation of Thomas Trollope, for almost a month. It was Home who was to be the prototype for Browning's 'Mr Sludge the Medium'. Observers have reported that even at the mention of Home's name the usually equable Browning would grow pale with passion. Elizabeth Barrett Browning was far more credulous.

Anthony Trollope made a number of visits to his mother and brother, during the third of which he began to write *Dr Thorne*. But he only once used Florence as a setting – perhaps because he felt that, as novelists, Mrs Trollope and Thomas had pre-empted the city. It is in the last third of *He Knew He was Right* that the leading characters find themselves in Florence, Siena and a fictional 'Casalunga'. One of these characters is the American minister to Florence (the city was, at that time, the capital of the country), whose residence Trollope describes as follows:

Mr Spalding at this time inhabited the ground floor of a large palace in the city, from which there was access to a garden which at this period of the year was green, bright, and shady, and which as being in the centre of the city was large and luxurious. From one end of the house there projected a covered terrace, or loggia, in which there were chairs and tables, sculptured ornaments, busts and old monumental relics let into the wall in profusion. It was half chamber and half garden, – such an adjunct to a house as in our climate would give only an idea of cold, rheumatism, and a false romance, but under an Italian sky is a luxury daily to be enjoyed during most months of the year.

This might be the Villino Trollope itself, as other visitors of that time have described it.

George Eliot

George Eliot (1819–80) and her consort G. H. Lewes paid the first of their visits to Florence in May 1860, putting up, as so many literary visitors did at that period, at the Pension Suisse, situated on the first floor of a house directly opposite the Palazzo Strozzi, at the corner of the Via Tornabuoni and the Via della Vigna Nuova. (The number, then 20, is now 13 Via Tornabuoni.) 'We are at the quietest hotel in Florence,' wrote Eliot to John Blackwood, 'having sought it out for the sake of getting clear of the stream of English and Americans, in which one finds oneself in all the main tracks of travel, so that one seems at last to be in a perpetual noisy picnic, obliged to be civil, though with a strong inclination to be sullen. My philanthropy rises several degrees as soon as we are alone.' Anyone so wishing to escape from his fellow tourists would hardly choose a hotel on this site today.

In a letter to John Blackwood's brother William, written nine days later, Eliot reported that 'There has been a crescendo of enjoyment in our travels; for Florence, from its relation to the history of Modern Art, has roused a keener interest in us even than Rome, and has stimulated me to entertain rather an ambitious project, which I mean to be secret from every one but you and Mr John Blackwood.' This 'rather an ambitious project' had nothing whatever to do with Modern Art or its history, but was the novel about the life and times of Savonarola which eventually appeared in 1863 as *Romola*.

Having first been fired to the theme by a passage about Savonarola in a guidebook, Eliot, aided by Lewes, plunged into research with characteristic perseverance and energy. Since women then, like Romola herself before them, were not admitted to the monastery of San Marco of which Savonarola was elected prior in 1490, Lewes viewed it for his consort, making copious notes. Next they visited the Great Hall or Sala dei Cinquecento of the Palazzo Vecchio, supposedly built at Savonarola's request in 1495 in order to accommodate the Council of the People after the expulsion of Piero de' Medici. With Perrens's *Jerome Savonarola, sa vie, ses prédications, ses écrits* (Paris 1859) and a copy of Savonarola's own poems, Eliot embarked on the kind of hectic course of reading which one associates with an ambitious undergraduate cramming for the First which might otherwise be beyond his or her mental powers.

Eliot and Lewes returned to Florence in May 1861, on this occasion taking up residence at the Hotel della Vittoria, Lungarno Amerigo Vespucci 10 – 'English landlady' notes Baedeker. Despite the influenza to which first Lewes and then Eliot succumbed, the couple bustled about their research, now visiting churches and museums and now holing themselves up in the Maglibechian Library (now the Biblioteca Nazionale) – which, among other treasures, contains Savonarola's Bible, with his written comments in the margin, and his breviary with an inscription by his pupil Fra Serafino. 'Mr Lewes is kept in continual distraction by having to attend to my wants . . . poking about everywhere on my behalf,' George Eliot wrote to John Blackwood, adding: 'I having very little self-help about me of the pushing and enquiring kind.'

Thomas Trollope, whom they had met during their 1860 visit, was absent from the city for much of this second one. 'We have seen no one but Mrs Trollope and her pretty little daughter, Beatrice, who is a musical genius,' Eliot wrote to Lewes's son Charles. 'She is a delicate fairy, about ten years old, but sings with a grace and expression that make it a thrilling delight to hear her.' Once Thomas had returned home, he set about persuading the visitors to postpone their departure and make with him an expedition to the two celebrated Tuscan monasteries of Camaldoli and La Vernia. 'Neither he nor she were fitted by their habits, or indeed by the conditions of their health, to encounter much "roughing", and a certain amount of that was assuredly inevitable – a good deal more than would be the case now. But if the flesh was weak, truly the spirit was willing!' The nature of this 'roughing' becomes more apparent when Trollope records: 'There followed another night in the cow-house for George Eliot and for us in the convent.'

In her Journal, Eliot wrote of this visit, spent in 'looking at streets, buildings and pictures, in hunting up old books, at shops or stalls, or in reading at the Magliabechian Library,' the apprehensive question 'Will it be all in vain?' Such readers of *Romola* as Tennyson, Mazzini, and Gladstone (who was later also to express extravagant admiration for the works of Marie Corelli) were to answer that question by, in effect, vehemently declaring 'No, of course not!' But Thomas Trollope himself was less certain: 'In drawing the girl Romola, her subjectivity has overpowered her objectivity. Romola is not – could never have been – the product of the period and of the civilisation from which she is described as having issued. There is far too much of George Eliot in her.' Twentieth-century critics have tended to take the same view – as they have of Eliot's Savonarola, portrayed as though he were some fiery non-conformist radical of her own time.

THE BROWNINGS, FREDERICK TENNYSON

In April of 1847, having found Pisa intellectually and socially inert, Robert and Elizabeth Barrett Browning (1812–89 and 1806–61) arrived in Florence on a visit in the company of their friend Anna Jameson – famous in her day as the author of a six-volume *Sacred and Legendary Art*. After an unsatisfactory marriage, culminating in a legal separation when her husband took himself off to Canada, Mrs Jameson had increasingly channelled her ardent emotions into friendships with such notable women as Ottilie von Goethe, Lady Byron, and Elizabeth Barrett Browning – the last of whom she had met through an introduction, strenuously pursued, from Mary Russell Mitford. In her search for the Divine as revealed in painting and sculpture, she inevitably spent a lot of time in Florence.

The 'wild poets but wise people' (as Mrs Jameson described them) first found a comfortable apartment in Via delle Belle Donne, near the Piazza Santa Maria Novella. Mrs Browning was delighted, although overcome by the humid heat so characteristic of Florence during the summer months: 'At Pisa we say "How beautiful!" Here we say nothing; it is enough if we can breathe.' In August, in quest of cooler quarters, they moved to a suite of rooms in the Palazzo Guidi, opposite to the Pitti Palace. It was from the famous 'Casa Guidi Window' that Mrs Browning waited on and then watched the liberation and unification of Italy:

> I heard last night a little child go singing
>   'Neath Casa Guidi windows, by the church,
> O bella liberta, O bella! – stringing
>   The same words still on notes he went in search
> So high for, you concluded the upbringing
>   Of such a nimble bird to sky from perch
> Must leave the whole bush in a tremble green,
>   And that the heart of Italy must beat,
> While such a voice had leave to rise serene
>   'Twixt church and palace of a Florence street.

It was here that in 1858 Nathaniel Hawthorne, accompanied by his wife Sophia, visited the Brownings. 'We found a spacious staircase and ample accommodation of vestibule and hall, the latter opening on a balcony where we could hear the chanting of priests in a church close by.' Browning greeted them in the anteroom, as did the only child of the marriage, christened Robert but nicknamed Penini by his adoring parents. 'I never saw such a boy as this before; so slender, fragile and spirit-like – not as if he were actually in ill health, but as if he had little or nothing to do with human flesh and blood. His face is very pretty and most intelligent, and exceedingly like his mother's.' Hawthorne continues: 'I should not quite like to be the father of such a boy, and should fear to stake so much interest and affection on him as he cannot fail to inspire. I wonder what is to become of him – whether he will ever grow up to be a man – whether it is desirable that he should.'

Mrs Browning greeted the Hawthornes at the entry to the dining-room: '. . . A pale, small person, scarcely embodied at all; at any rate, only substantial enough to put forth her slender fingers to be grasped, and to speak with a shrill, yet sweet, tenuity of voice. Really, I do not see how Mr Browning can suppose that he has an earthly wife any more than an earthly child; both are of the elfin race, and will flit away from him some day when he least thinks of it . . .'

At first the life of the Brownings was reclusive – 'as to Italian society,' wrote Mrs Browning, 'one may as well take to longing for the evening star, for it seems quite inaccessible.' But soon the fame of the couple, hers then greater than his, attracted people to them. Some of these people – Charles Lever, the buoyant and sometimes even brash best-selling Irish novelist, for example – proved not to their taste. But soon they had assembled a loyal circle around them, the chief member of which was Isabella ('Isa') Blagden, a woman of uncertain origin, with possible Indian blood, who acted as a universal aunt to anyone in trouble or in need in the expatriate community. Isa wished to emulate the literary achievement of her heroine, Mrs Browning; but her talent for writing was inferior to her talent for friendship. 'A little volume of her poems was published after her untimely death,' Thomas Trollope records. 'They are not such as could take by storm the careless ears of the world . . . and must, I suppose, be admitted to be marked by that mediocrity which neither gods nor men can tolerate. But it is impossible to read the volume without perceiving how choice a spirit the authoress must have been, and understanding how it came to pass that she was especially honoured by the close and warm attachment to Mrs Browning.'

'We are as happy,' wrote Browning in December 1847, 'as two owls in a hole, two toads under a tree-stump; or any other two queer poking creatures that we let live after the fashion of their black hearts, only Ba [Mrs Browning] is fat and rosy; yes indeed.' Mrs Browning in turn wrote that, although Browning could not be induced to go out in the evening – 'not even to a concert, nor to hear a play of Alfieri's' – nonetheless 'we scarcely know how the days go, it's such a gallop on the grass.' 'When all's said and sighed, I love Italy – I love my Florence,' she wrote to another correspondent. 'I love "that hole of a place" as Father Prout called it lately, with all its dust, its cobwebs, its spiders even; I love it and with somewhat of the kind of blind, stupid, respectable, obstinate love which people feel when they talk of "beloved native lands". I feel this for Italy, by mistake for England. Florence is my chimney corner, where I can skulk and be happy.'

In 1848 the Brownings moved from furnished rooms in the Casa Guidi to the brighter, more spacious ones, described by Hawthorne and other distinguished visitors, with which they are now associated. The mosquitoes in the garden might be 'worse than Austrians', but the couple had little else of which to complain. For both it was a period of triumphant creativity. Apart from *Casa Guidi Windows*, Mrs Browning also wrote the major part of *Aurora Leigh*, *Poems Before Congress*, and a number of other pieces in support of the liberation and unification of the country whose cause, in company with so many of her fellow expatriates, she had so ardently adopted. There is a parallel between this ardour and that with which non-Spanish writers supported the Republican cause during the Spanish Civil War. Posthumously collected in the volume *Last Poems*, Elizabeth Barrett Browning's later Italian political poems were dedicated by Browning to 'grateful Florence'. Browning produced two of his finest monologues, each a miracle of impersonation, 'Andrea del Sarto' and 'Fra Lippo Lippi', along with 'The Statue and the Bust', and 'Old Pictures in Florence'. 'We neither of us show our work to one another, till it is finished,' Mrs Browning confided in a letter to a friend. 'An artist must, I fancy, either find or *make* solitude to work in, if it is to be good work at all.'

It was in 1853 that Elizabeth Barrett Browning became truly interested in spiritualism. 'You know I am rather a visionary,' she wrote to Mary Russell Mitford, 'and inclined to knock round at all the doors of the present world to try to get out.'

This interest was shared by many of the expatriate community: the Trollopes, whose villa was the setting for many a seance; Sophia Hawthorne, Nathaniel's wife, who recorded in her Journal 'Mr Browning cannot believe, and Mrs Browning cannot help believing'; and Lord Lytton, the future English ambassador in Paris and Viceroy of India – 'visionary enough to suit me', Mrs Browning wrote.

Lord Tennyson's brother, Frederick Tennyson (1807–98), also a poet but one far less gifted than the Laureate – 'It's the smell of a rose rather than a rose – very sweet notwithstanding,' Mrs Browning wrote of his *Days and Hours* – was another expatriate in Florence (1850–7) who also came to share the interest in spiritualism so common at that time in 'the colony'. At first, admittedly, he was sceptical, writing: 'Browning is a wonderful man with inexhaustible memory, animal spirits and bonhomie. He is always ready with the most apropos anecdote and the happiest bon mot, and his vast acquaintance with out-of-the-way knowledge and the quaint Curiosity Shops of Literature make him a walking encyclopaedia of marvels. Mrs B. who never goes out – being troubled like other inspired ladies with a chest – is a little unpretending woman, yet full of power and, what is better, loving-kindness; and never so happy as when she can venture into the thick of mysterious clairvoyants, Rappists, Ecstatics and Swedenborgians.' But in no time at all, Frederick Tennyson himself had also become the most enthusiastic and gullible devotee of such people.

For a long period he lived in the Villa Torrigiani above Doccia, being visited there by his less genial but more eminent brother, Alfred, in August and September 1851.

In *William Wetmore Story and His Friends*, edited by Henry James, Story (1819–95), a sculptor and writer of talent, gives Browning's moving account of the last hours of Mrs Browning at Casa Guidi on 18 June 1861:

At about three o'clock he was startled by her breathing and woke her, but she said she was better, and reasoned so quietly and justly about her state that his fears were again subdued. She talked with him and jested and gave ex-

pression to her love for him in the tenderest words; then,
feeling sleepy, and he supporting her in his arms, she fell
into a doze. In a few minutes, suddenly, her head dropped
forward. He thought she had fainted, but she had gone for
ever. She had passed as if she had fallen asleep, without
pain, without thought of death. After death she looked, as
Browning told me, like a young girl; all the outlines
rounded and filled up, all traces of disease effaced, and a
smile on her face so living that they could not for hours
persuade themselves she was really dead.

   . . . We [Story and his wife] went immediately to
Florence, and it was a sad house enough. There stood the
table with her letters and books as usual, and her little
chair beside it, and in her portfolio a half-finished letter to
Mme Mario [née Jessie White, an ardent follower of
Mazzini] full of noble words about Italy. Yes, it was for
Italy that her last words were written; for her dear Italy
were her last aspirations. The death of Cavour had greatly
affected her. She had wept many tears for him, and been a
real mourner. This agitation undoubtedly weakened her
and perhaps was the last feather which broke her down.
'The cycle is complete,' as Browning said, looking
around the room; 'here we came fifteen years ago; here
Pen was born; here Ba wrote her poems for Italy. She
used to walk up and down this verandah in the summer
evenings when, revived by the southern air, she first
began to enjoy her out-doors life. Every day she used to
walk with me or drive with me, and once even walked to
Bellosguardo and back; that was when she was strongest.
Little by little, as I now see, that distance was lessened, the
active outdoors life restricted, until walking had finally
ceased. We saw from these windows the return of the
Austrians; they wheeled round this corner and came
down this street with all their cannon, just as she describes
it in "Casa Guidi". Last week when we came to Florence I
said: "We used, you know, to walk on this verandah so
often – come and walk up and down once. Just once," I
urged, and she came to the window and took two steps on
it. But it fatigued her too much, and she went back and lay

down on the sofa – that was our last walk. Only the night she went away for ever she said she thought we must give up Casa Guidi; it was too inconvenient and in case of illness too small. We had decided to go away and take a villa outside the gates. For years she could not give up this house, but at last and, as it were, suddenly, she said she saw it *was* too small for us and too inconvenient. And so it was; so the cycle was completed for us here, and where the beginning was is the end. Looking back at these past years I see that we have been all the time walking over a torrent on a straw. Life must now be begun anew – all the old cast off and the new one put on. I shall go away, break up everything, go to England and live and work and write.'

DOSTOEVSKY

Dostoevsky (1821–81) first visited Florence in August 1861, in the company of the Idealist critic Nikolai Strakhov, whom he had met in Geneva. The two of them put up in the Pension Suisse, opposite the Palazzo Strozzi, in the Via Tornabuoni. This hotel, used three years earlier by George Eliot and G. H. Lewes, was then a favourite with foreigners because of its cleanliness, its quietness, and its comparative cheapness. Literally a minute's walk away, in the Palazzo Buondelmonti, once the home of Ariosto, in the Piazza Santa Trinita, was situated the famous Gabinetto Letterario-Scientifico Vieusseux, later Libreria Vieusseux, to which writers as diverse as Longfellow, Ruskin, Heine, Stendhal, Browning, and Fenimore Cooper would resort in order to read foreign newspapers and borrow foreign books. On this brief visit, little in the museums made a favourable impression on Dostoevsky. Indeed Strakhov records that almost as soon as he had entered the Uffizi, Dostoevsky ran out again. Strakhov also records how, in his passionate xenophobia, the great author, apostle of universal brotherhood, insulted a humble waiter, who eventually chided him: 'Don't you realise that I'm a human being too?'

To the Pension Suisse Dostoevsky returned with his wife Anna in November 1868, in order to escape the damp and cold

of Milan, where they had been living for two months. From
the Pension Suisse they soon moved to No. 8 (now No. 22)
Via Guiccardini, opposite the Pitti Palace, a stone's throw
from the Brownings' Casa Guidi. A plaque, set into the façade
in 1952, announces: *In questi pressi/ fra il 1868 e il 1869/Fedor
Dostoevskij/compi il romanzo 'L'Idiota.'* In her fascinating essay
'Dostoevsky in Florence' [*The Russian Review*, 1964], Katherine
Strelsky describes the apartment as follows:

> The house is of the late seventeenth or early eighteenth
> century, and is not particularly distinguished. The stuc-
> coed brick of its facade is dusky honey-coloured, like all
> Florentine buildings. It has a plain shabby entrance with a
> worn stone staircase. . . . The whole floor [the second] is
> an apartment of eight rooms, four on the front and four
> on the rear looking out on a cluttered service court. Two
> large, high, squarish rooms on the center front are flanked
> by a long narrow one on either side. Today there is no
> means of heating, but there are two sealed-off fireplaces.
> In the rear is a large kitchen and a tiny cubicle of a toilet.
> There is no bath. There has been little or no decorating
> since 1868. The floors are the original reddish-brown
> *mattoni* or tiles. One of the large rooms has a crudely
> painted ceiling. The entire apartment is occupied by a
> philanthropic institution to provide a home for orphaned
> young workers. The Dostoevskys did not inhabit the
> whole of this apartment but two or three rooms, as
> lodgers on demi-pension terms.

Arthur Hugh Clough (1819–61) had put up briefly in the
same house a few years previously.

Dostoevsky was working ferociously on *The Idiot*. But in
her *Reminiscences* his wife Anna has recorded the pleasures of
those first months. 'I remember his ecstatic reaction to the
Cathedral, the church of Santa Maria del Fiore, and the small
Chapel del Battistero, in which infants are usually christened.'
Dostoevsky was also so much delighted by the bronze doors
of the Baptistery that he told Anna that, if he should ever
happen to get rich, he would buy photographs of these doors,
as large as the originals, so that he could hang them in his

study. In the Pitti Palace, he was enthusiastic about Raphael's *Madonna della Seggiola*; and he was also enthusiastic about the same artist's *Saint John in the Desert* in the Uffizi. The Medici *Venus* he considered 'a work of genius'. In the evenings he would read Voltaire and Diderot, borrowed from the Libreria Vieusseux, in their original French.

When Anna became pregnant, Dostoevsky was overjoyed. Such was his concern for her that he concealed from her the part of *War and Peace* – sent out to them by Strakhov – in which the death of Prince Andrei Bolkonsky's wife in childbirth is so poignantly depicted. Since the doctor had prescribed a daily walk for the pregnant woman, she and Dostoevsky would each day go up into the Boboli Gardens where, even in January, there were roses to admire. 'Here we warmed ourselves and dreamed of our happiness to come.'

But dreams of happiness to come were now all too often disturbed for Dostoevsky by three increasingly importunate needs. One of these was for his native Russia. In a letter to his niece Sonya in March 1869, we find him writing: 'I cannot write here. For that I must be in Russia without fail, must see, hear and take a direct part in Russian life; whereas here I am losing even the possibility of writing, since I lack both the essential material, namely, Russian reality (which produces the ideas) and the Russian people.' Intensely xenophobic, he was incapable of using Italy and the Italians as his 'essential material'.

Dostoevsky's second need was for congenial company. As Anna records:

> We did not know a single soul in Florence with whom we could talk, argue, joke, exchange reactions. Around us all were strangers, and sometimes hostile ones; and this total isolation from people was sometimes difficult to bear. I remember it occurred to me then that people living in such complete solitude and isolation might, in the final analysis, either come to hate each other or else draw close together for the rest of their lives. Fortunately it was the latter which happened to us. Our enforced isolation compelled us to come even closer together.

At that period there was not, of course, any dearth of Russians in Florence, many of them consumptives in search of health. But such people tended to be one of two things: either aristocrats or rich merchants, who would no more have dreamed of consorting with this novelist of genius than with their grocer, barber, or tailor; or spies or *agents provocateurs* of the Tsarist regime, which was, as Dostoevsky well knew, keeping him under surveillance even in exile.

Dostoevsky's third need was for money. In his lighter moods, he would call himself and his wife Mr and Mrs Micawber; but there were times when the torment of waiting for something to turn up so much exacerbated his nerves that his epileptic fits became more frequent than usual.

Poverty eventually drove them out to a single, cramped room in an apartment overlooking the Mercato Nuovo, the precise address of which has never been established. In a letter to his niece Sonya about this room in a 'tiny dwelling' owned by 'a family [presumably Italian] with whom we are friendly', Dostoevsky describes a hellish three months in the ever-increasing heat of Florence in summer:

Our windows gave on a market square with arcades and splendid granite pillars; in the square was a municipal fountain in the form of a gigantic bronze boar from whose throat the water flowed (it is a classic masterpiece of rare beauty). Well, now reflect that all those arcades and the masses of stone by which the whole square is surrounded, drank in and accumulated all the heat of the sun, and got as scorching as a stove-pipe in a vapour bath – and that was the atmosphere we had to live in. The real heat, that is, the real hell-heat, we had to groan under for six weeks; it was nearly always 34 or 35 degrees Réamur in the shade. You must know that the air, despite this heat and drought (it never once rained) was wonderfully light; the green in the gardens (of which there are astonishingly few in Florence; one hardly sees anything but stones) – the green neither withered nor faded, but seemed brighter and fresher every day; the flowers and the lemon-tree had apparently only waited for the heat; but what astonished

me most – me, who was imprisoned in Florence
by untoward circumstances – was that the itinerant
foreigners (who are nearly all very rich) mostly remained
in Florence; new ones even arrived every day. Usually the
tourists of all Europe throng, at the beginning of the hot
weather, to the German spas. When I saw in the streets
well-dressed Englishwomen and even Frenchwomen, I
could not conceive why these people, *who had money to get
away with*, could voluntarily stay in such a hell. I was
sorriest of all for poor Anya. The poor thing was then in
her seventh or eighth month, and so suffered dreadfully
from the heat. Moreover, the population of Florence
spends the whole night on its feet, and there's a ghastly
amount of singing. Of course we kept our windows open
at night; then, at about five o'clock in the morning, the
people began to racket in the market, and the donkeys to
bray, so that we could never close an eye.

The only advantage of this almost insupportable heat was
that it appeared to have a beneficial effect on the novelist's
epilepsy.

Eventually the long-awaited funds arrived and, having paid
off their debts to their hosts and others, the couple were able to
quit Florence for first Prague and then Dresden. In Florence
they had endured loneliness, indigence, and extremes of climate; but Dostoevsky could also write of the city 'When the
sun shines, it is almost Paradise. Impossible to imagine anything more beautiful than this sky, this air, this light.' It was in
Florence that he not merely completed *The Idiot* but also began
the gestation of *The Possessed* and *The Brothers Karamazov*.

Although Elizabeth Barrett Browning had died and Robert
Browning had quit the Casa Guidi before Dostoevsky's arrival, Browning continued to frequent the Libreria Vieusseux
on his rare visits to Florence. The great Russian novelist and the
great English poet might therefore have met – although there
is no record of their ever having done so. Here would have
been a wonderful subject for an Imaginary Conversation by
Browning's old friend Landor.

OUIDA

It was in 1871 that Ouida (1839–1908) (born Maria Louise Ramé, of a doting English mother and a wayward French father, but later to call herself, more grandiosely, Louise de la Ramée) arrived in Florence, to remain there for twenty-three years. Described by Max Beerbohm as 'that unique, flamboyant lady, one of the miracles of modern literature', this queen of the circulating libraries is now all too often dismissed as merely another bareback performer on the tosh-horse, for extravagant and wholly undeserved sums, in the circus of literature. Nothing could be further from the truth. There was a great deal of exuberant absurdity in both her life and her novels; but Carl van Vechten was right when he wrote of her, 'Ouida was not an artist, but just as surely she was a genius.'

Used to living and entertaining in hotels – for the previous five years she had made the Langham Hotel her London base, placing in the hall of her suite a notice stating 'Umbrellas and morals to be left at the door' – Ouida, accompanied by her mother, first put up in the Hotel de l'Italie, in the Piazza Ognissanti, which today remains under its new name, Excelsior Italia, the Claridge's of Florence. The sort of luxurious, aristocratic, romantic, and often scandalous life of which she had so often day-dreamed in her novels was now in her grasp as, eager for the company of a writer then as internationally famous as George Sand, the foreign colony hastened to make her welcome. Her biographer Monica Stirling, in her admirable *The Fine and the Wicked*, evokes this life as follows

> There was a fancy dress ball at the Comte de Talleyrand's to which the majority of the guests went dressed as their most distinguished ancestors; there was the famous hunt 'Corso' to which everyone including Ouida wore pink coats, followed by a huge dinner-party at Doney's; there was an expedition to Milan to see Garibaldi make one of his last public appearances; there was a trip to San Rossore Grand Ducal park near Pisa, where could be seen the last of the camels introduced in the seventeenth century by Ferdinand de' Medici; later there was the excitement

generated by visits from Queen Victoria, the Duke and
Duchess of Teck, and Queen Victoria's fourth son, Prince
Leopold, Duke of Albany, who became one of Ouida's
admirers.

In addition to all these pleasures, there was the even more
thrilling one of falling in love with the handsome, intelligent,
charming Marchese Lotteria Lotharinga della Stufa, unmar-
ried scion of a family which had first settled in Florence at the
beginning of the thirteenth century. Sadly, it was this nobleman who was to be the unwitting author of most of Ouida's
subsequent troubles.

For ten years, however, all went well between the two,
as they discussed politics – both were ardent admirers of
Napoleon III – literature, and art, and together made a number
of excursions in and around the city as well as to Rome. By
now Ouida and her mother had moved from the hotel into a
sumptuous villa with extensive grounds, rented from the
Marchese Farinola, in Scandicci, some three miles south of
Florence. At this period, the Cavaliere Faenzi described Ouida
to the young Vernon Lee (Violet Paget) as '37, buxom, tall,
very robust, haughty, and taciturn'. Ouida's mother he described as 'a charming old lady'. In a letter to a friend, Vernon
Lee passed on, with what one takes to be the gleeful malice of a
literary aspirant envious of the success of a world-famous
author, a story told to her by this same Cavaliere Faenzi of a
visit to the Villa Farinola. 'Are you fond of art?' Faenzi asked
Ouida. 'I love it,' she declared. 'Look there! There are all
my works.' Faenzi gazed in horror at 'the terrible daubs' which
hung on the walls. Even more at a loss, he asked Ouida who
her master was. 'Master! I never had a master! I would not take
a master on any account.'

Other visitors were kinder in their recollections. In addition
to Ouida's own oil-paintings, they noted such treasures as the
cinquecento Venetian writing-table at which, with frenzied
energy, she wrote at a speed which even Anthony Trollope or
Arnold Bennett might have envied; the two huge golden
eagles once the property of Napoleon I; the della Robbia in the
sacristy; and the bibelots which, in the fashion of the time,

crowded every available space on occasional tables and chimney pieces. Everywhere there were flowers. Offering extravagant hospitality in such a setting, Ouida had no difficulty in
attracting anyone of any importance in Florence. But she
could be cynical about her social success, remarking: 'The
chief difference between Ouida at home and Jumbo at the Zoo
is that people visit him in order to give him buns and her in
order to receive them.'

Unfortunately, after some ten years an acrimonious rivalry
had developed between Ouida and Janet Ross (née Duff
Gordon), an intellectual *grande dame* long established, with her
ex-banker husband, in the magnificent Villa Gherardo in the
Via Settignanese. The cause was della Stufa, who had combined paying discreet court to the eminent and often unlady-
like lady novelist with continuing to act, as he had long done
before Ouida's descent on the scene, as Mrs Ross's *cavaliere
servente*. Ouida had convinced herself that della Stufa was
eager to marry her; Mrs Ross had convinced herself that this
vulgar upstart of a popular novelist had enmeshed her own
particular friend, an unwilling victim, in her toils. What was
the truth? Ouida put her version of it into an over-heated
roman-à-clef entitled *Friendship*, in which Lady Joan Challoner,
all too clearly Mrs Ross, forces her lover to stick with her
against his will, through the expedient of blackmailing him
over a crooked business transaction into which, in all innocence, he has been lured by her and her complaisant husband.
There was talk of a libel action; of Ouida making unseemly
public appeals to della Stufa when he was emerging from his
club, the most exclusive in Florence; of Mrs Ross being shot at
while standing at her bedroom window; even of Mrs Ross, in
one carriage in the fashionable Via Tornabuoni, attempting to
horsewhip Ouida in another.

Precisely what was the nature of della Stufa's role in this
passionate imbroglio has never been precisely established,
but the most satisfactory explanation seems that advanced to
the author by Bernard Berenson in 1948. It was Berenson's
view that della Stufa, who was never to marry, was a
homosexual. He was not Mrs Ross's lover – her husband
would probably not have countenanced that – but merely her

devoted companion. He subsequently also became Ouida's
devoted companion. The gossip that was aroused by these two
liaisons served to silence for him any gossip of a more unwel-
come kind in the Florence of that time. To that extent he
welcomed such gossip and even encouraged it. But when
Ouida became more and more insistent that he should marry
her, he took fright at the possible sexual demands that she
might make of him. It was safer to stick with Mrs Ross.

The row between these two women divided Florence – so
that, just as in the past there had been Guelphs and Ghibellines, so now there were Ouida-ites and anti-Ouidaites.
Meanwhile, half-demented over her disappointed hopes,
Ouida began to behave with even more recklessness and to
spend money even more extravagantly. For a while she could
appease her romantic yearnings in the company of the fifty-
three year old Robert Lytton, later to become Viceroy of
India, when he came on a visit to Florence. Although his
father, Edward Bulwer-Lytton, had enjoyed far greater fame,
Robert had himself been praised as a poet under the
pseudonym 'Owen Meredith'. At first, the vain, vague, fop-
pish, romantic Lytton enjoyed the company of this well-
known novelist; then he started to be embarrassed by a
devotion which he could not return. Once more Ouida was
courting derision.

Disasters began to close in on her. The bank in which she
had invested much of her money failed. She quarrelled, largely
through her own arrogance, with her landlord and was brut-
ally evicted by his peasants, pitchforks at the ready. She and
her mother took up residence in a dank thirty-room apartment
in the Palazzo Magnani Ferroni (now Palazzo Amerigi) in the
Via dei Serragli, where their extravagant entertaining continued among a host of yapping and often incontinent dogs.
Her creditors eventually drove her out of this haven, to a
succession of hotels and of rented villas and apartments.
Finally, the Villa della Corona (later the Burns Murdoch
Villa) in Bellosguardo became their home. But despite the
frenzy with which she continued to write, debts again
accumulated. Walpurga Lady Paget, one of the most loyal and
long-suffering of Ouida's friends, describes a visit as follows:

Ouida now inhabits the Villa della Corona, which is very large and dilapidated. Her only furniture seemed to be a plaster cast of Gay's bust, for which she asked me years ago. There were only two or three chairs in the many rooms which I traversed, a pink-and-gold paper hung in rags from the wall, there were no fires, no carpets. A troupe of fluffy and rather dirty white dogs barked at me and then rolled themselves under Ouida's feet, amongst the folds of a draggled black-lace skirt. She wore a mantelet of some once bright but now faded colour, out of which her arms and tiny but ugly hands protruded. Her legs were encased in very bright blue stockings, and her feet in very thin white slippers. She insisted on walking through the lanes with me in this costume, with a white-browney hat with many feathers superadded, and a spotty veil.

In another, smaller villa, La Campora, Ouida's sweet-natured, long-suffering mother fell ill and died. Crazed with grief, Ouida would not for a long time allow the body to be moved to the paupers' section of the Allori cemetery. When sympathetic friends sent her cheques, she would often tear them up; when they sent food, she would give it to her dogs. Eventually, once more evicted for non-payment of rent, she took herself off to Lucca, where her tragic situation deteriorated even further. It is in Lucca that she is buried.

According to Lina Waterfield, Janet Ross's handsome and accomplished niece, her aunt placed a copy of *Friendship*, its binding removed, for use in her guest lavatory. On Ouida's death, an English journalist approached her rival for help with an obituary notice. Her by now white hair and her white dress adding to the dignity of her bearing, Janet Ross answered him: 'You want to know about Ouida? But who is Ouida?'

That a woman who led Ouida's kind of existence should have written with greater perspicacity of the Italians than any English novelist with the possible exceptions of E. M. Forster and D. H. Lawrence must be cause for amazement. In her biography, Monica Stirling rightly singles out the 1881 *A Village Commune* as the most remarkable of all her works. How did she acquire such knowledge and understanding of the lives of peasants struggling against an oppressive bureaucracy? One can only wonder at a miracle of empathy.

John Ruskin

Despite its schoolmarmish tone and despite the passing of more than a century since its first publication, Ruskin's *Mornings in Florence* remains a golden key to the city and its treasures. But both his diaries and his autobiography *Praeterita* give the impression that there were many occasions when, fretful or even furious, he had no wish to spend another morning or indeed any other time of day there.

A highly-strung, prudish, talented, and diligent youth of twenty-one, he had embarked in 1840 on a Victorian version of the Grand Tour in the company not of the customary tutor or cicerone but of his doting parents. On his arrival in Florence, he recorded in his diary: '. . . My present feelings are of grievous disappointment. The galleries, which I walked through yesterday, are impressive enough; but I had as soon be in the British Museum, as far as enjoyment goes, except for the Raphaels.' The 'Newgate-like palaces' were 'rightly hateful'; the inside of the Duomo 'a horror'; its exterior 'a Chinese puzzle'. All the sacred art was 'mere zero' – as it was, he concluded, to the Italians themselves – and the surrounding countryside, 'dead wall and dusty olive', was equally unappealing. Everything, in short, was 'a provocation and weariness, except for one master, M. Angelo.'

When he returned five years later, this time with no companion other than a Swiss guide, he was more open to the beauty of the architecture and art. Excitedly 'scribbling notes on my arm in the galleries', he was overwhelmed by such 'wonderful things' as Gozzoli's *Procession of the Magi* in the Medici-Riccardi Chapel and the Ghirlandaios in the choir of Santa Maria Novella. 'Progressive, but much puzzled', he gazed at building and pictures; he thought; he wrote; he drew and painted. But the Florentines themselves precipitated in him a constant undercurrent of irritation, sometimes even hatred. Like visitors today, he was infuriated by the endless restoring that went on – largely as a result of previous neglect: 'They expose their pictures to every species of injury, rain, wind, cold, workmen, and then they paint them over to make them bright again.' The Italians, he concluded in one particularly violent paroxysm of rage, were 'lazy, lousy, scurrilous, cheating, lying, thieving, hypocritical, brutal, blasphemous, obscene, cowardly, earthly, sensual, devilish'. Eventually, in July, he was propelled out of the city and to his beloved Switzerland – so orderly, so calm, so clean – by the 'buzz-buzz-bang-bang' of the innumerable festivals taking place during that month.

Ruskin was to pay other brief visits to Florence during his later years; but these two, in his early twenties, were the decisive ones. From them came his *Mornings in Florence*; and it was as a result of them that he wrote a famous letter to *The Times*, on his return to England in 1845, to urge that no more pictures by Guido Reni or Rubens should be bought by the National Gallery, while it contained not a single work by Ghirlandaio or Fra Angelico and not a single important one by Bellini or Perugino.

James Fenimore Cooper, Nathaniel Hawthorne, James Russell Lowell, Harriet Beecher Stowe, Mark Twain

After a sojourn in England, during which he found at least as much to criticize as to admire, James Fenimore Cooper (1789–1851) and his ailing wife travelled south through Germany and Switzerland to Italy in 1828. Their conveyance was a 'a roomy family carriage, coachman's box in front and rumble behind'. One suspects that it was to escape his womenfolk that Cooper often sat on the box. At her first sighting of Mont Blanc in the distance, Mrs Cooper exclaimed: 'What a beautiful cloud.'

Arriving in Florence in the autumn, they stayed briefly at the English York Hotel on Via de' Cerretani, before settling in the

Palazzo Ricasoli (Piazza Goldoni), its rooms so large and damp
that they shocked their Italians friends by the extravagance
with which they piled wood on every fire. Mrs Cooper wrote
to her father: 'Mr Cooper has almost affronted the Lords, the
Dukes, and Princes by declining their invitations – but after
satisfying Curiosity, we thought it would be quite as wise to
stay at Home, and save Purse for other Purposes.' Nonetheless, Cooper consented to a farewell audience, in court dress,
with the Grand-Duke Leopold. He also met the Count Saint-
Leu, son of King Louis of Holland and husband of Napoleon's
sister Charlotte, and Napoleon's mother, Madame Mère.
Throughout this period, he was constantly comparing the
English and the Italians, to the disadvantage of the former.
The Italians, he commented – as people comment even today –
take a pride in waiting on others, while the English merely
consider that it demeans them; the Italians have a natural
aesthetic sense, the English are philistines. With the coming of
summer, the Coopers moved up into a villa in the hills.

It was on 24 May 1858 that Nathaniel Hawthorne (1804–
64), his wife Sophia, and his three children set off from Rome
to Florence. 'We had a nice old vetturino [coachman], Gaetano
by name,' Sophia recorded, 'who looked like a good New
England farmer, face placid and gentle, and not at all Italian in
colour or expression. Our carriage was of the usual long and
cumbersome fashion, with seats inside for four, and a coupé in
front for two, in the form of a chaise – and in front of the
coupé, a box for the vetturino. Our luggage was bestowed
upon the top, and behind, reaching out many a rood, so that
with four, and sometimes six horses, we have an effect of an
endless arrangement of human affairs.' The journey took eight
days.

The Casa del Bello, 36 Via de' Serragli, found for the
Hawthornes by the American sculptor Hiram Powers, long a
resident of Florence, delighted them with its spaciousness.
'We have the first *piano*,' Sophia wrote, 'which opens at the
back upon a broad terrace, leading down into a garden full of
roses, jessamine, orange and lemon trees, and a large willow-
tree, drooping over a fountain in the midst. We have thirteen
rooms on the one *piano*, beside four kitchen rooms beneath.

The Casa is three rooms wide, and four deep – (*five* in one of the rows) – and we are, each one, perfectly accommodated, and each can be alone and remote from each other.' The price was 'only fifty dollars per month (entirely furnished even to silver and linen)'. She concluded, with good reason: 'It is the very luxury of comfort.'

The next morning, she and her husband visited Powers's studio at 111 Via de' Serragli: 'I had hurried glimpses of a bust of Mr Sparks, of California, and Mrs Ward, as Psyche, with a butterfly as a jewel, clasping the bands of her hair.' That Powers should be plying his vocation in Florence of all cities was rather as though one's favourite American aunt were to be discovered making Brownies in the Tour d'Argent. Despite the heat and despite the increasing boredom and irritability of their daughters, Una and Rose, the family spent day after day in sightseeing. 'Florence', Sophia declared, 'is a place to live and be happy in – so cheerful, so full of art, and so *well paved*.' There were old friends to see. Among new friends there were the Brownings – 'a grasp of Mr Browning's hand gives a new value to life', and Mrs Browning's 'fairy fingers seem too airy to hold'.

On 29 June there was a horse race through the city, to which Sophia took Una and Rose. The royal carriage was obliged to stop for three or four minutes precisely opposite the place where the Hawthornes were seated, so that Sophia was able to 'stare straight into the faces of the Grand Duke and the Duchess'. She did not like what she saw. 'The Grand Duke looked like a monkey, with an evil expression, most ugly and mean. The lady has not a ray of beauty left.' Later she reverts to the Grand Duke's unattractiveness: 'The Grand Duke has that frightful, coarse, protruding under lip, peculiar to the court of Austria, and formerly of Spain. It is worth while to extinguish the race, for the sake of expunging that lip and all it signifies. No man with such a mouth can love liberty or spiritual things.'

For August and September, when the heat would be at its worst, the Brownings' ever-helpful friend Isa Blagden per-suaded the Hawthornes to move up to the Villa Montuato, close to her own villa on the Bellosguardo hill. Here were 'multitudinous halls and chambers – with deeply shaded avenues; clear, smooth lawn and semicircular terraces – a strong, old, gray-stone tower, at one end, where owls do whoop and hoot and sit, "to warm their wit", and in which Savonarola was imprisoned.' This was the 'Monte Beni' of Hawthorne's *The Marble Faun*. At peace, no longer distracted by sightseeing or too many visits and visitors, Hawthorne was at last able to settle down to writing. 'Would that he had been able to stay there for years,' his son Julian was later to remark, 'for had he continued in an atmosphere which so admirably suited him, there might have been not just one more romance to be published but a whole series.'

In his Life of Hawthorne, Henry James estimates what must have been the effect of Italy on a fellow New Englander and a fellow novelist:

> Hawthorne's experience had been narrow. His fifty years had been spent, for much the larger part, in small American towns . . . and he had led exclusively what one may call a village life . . . In other words, and to call things by their names, he was exquisitely and consistently provincial . . . I know nothing more remarkable, more touching, than the sight of this odd, youthful–elderly mind, contending so late in the day with the new opportunities for learning old things, and, on the whole, profiting from them so freely and gracefully.

There then follows the barb, which James administered with all the skill of a master dentist sticking a hypodermic needle into a gum. 'His Italian notebooks are very pleasant reading, but they are less interesting than the others; for his contact with the life of the country, its people and its manners, was simply that of the ordinary tourist – which amounts to saying that it was extremely superficial.'

While Hawthorne pressed on with the novel that was to become *The Marble Faun*, Sophia continued to take the refractory children sightseeing. Finally, on 1 October, the Hawthornes 'threw a parting glance – and rather a sad one – over the misty Val d'Arno' and made their way, once more by easy stages, back to Rome.

James Russell Lowell (1819–91) paid three visits to Florence: in 1851, when he and his first wife, Maria, rented Casa Guidi from the Brownings; in 1856 after his first wife's death, when he stayed for about two months at the Hotel Europe in Piazza Ferroni; and in 1873, with his second wife, Fanny, when he stayed for several months at the Hotel du Nord in the Palazzo Bartolini-Salimbeni, Via delle Terme. This last visit coincided with one by Henry James, so that the two New Englanders were able to take wary stock of each other. Lowell's letters rarely produce a comment of any interest about the city; and his *Leaves from my Journal in Italy and Elsewhere* is equally barren.

Harriet Beecher Stowe (1811–96), as famous in Europe as in America after the success of *Uncle Tom's Cabin*, was in Florence in 1857, staying in a large apartment in the Casa Boccini. The Brownings, who were far from sure whether they would like her or not, at once succumbed to her energy, directness and palpable decency. She disclaimed all credit for her book, saying to Elizabeth Barrett Browning: 'I, the author of *Uncle Tom's Cabin*? No, indeed! The Lord Himself wrote it, and I was but the humblest instrument in His hand. To Him alone be all the praise.'

She and Elizabeth Barrett Browning soon found a shared interest in spiritualism On 16 January 1860, she wrote to her husband in America about the consolation which a medium had brought her for the loss of their son, Henry:

What you said about your spiritual experiences in feeling the presence of dear Henry with you, and, above all, the vibration of that mysterious guitar, was very pleasant to me. Since I have been in Florence I have been distressed by inexpressible yearnings after him, – such sighings and outreachings, with a sense of utter darkness and separation, not only from him but from all spiritual communication with my God. But I have become acquainted with a friend through whom I receive consoling impressions of these things – a Mrs E., of Boston, a very pious, accomplished and interesting woman, who has had a history much like yours in relation to spiritual manifestations.

Mark Twain (1835–1910) paid four visits to Florence, two of them as a transient and two as a resident. The result of his first visit in 1867 was his gruff, bluff, no-nonsense *The Innocents Abroad*. In September 1892 he rented the Villa Viviani (now Belvedere) in Settignano. Both delighted and embarrassed by its twenty-eight rooms – emotions shared by many expatriates when first entering their rented apartments or villas – he named the Grand Salon 'the Sahara Desert'. It was during this stay of a little over a year that, in a manner reminiscent of the characters in the *Decameron*, he entertained Janet Ross's guests at the Villa Gherardo in Settignano with a succession of stories, while an influenza epidemic raged in the city below them.

In 1903 he returned to Florence with his by then seriously ailing wife, in the ineffectual hope that the climate would somehow bring about a cure. He rented the Villa di Quarto and began to write *A Year at Florence*. He was negotiating to buy a villa when his wife died.

HENRY JAMES

Henry James (1843–1916) first arrived in Florence, as a twenty-six-year-old tourist, in October 1869, staying at the Hotel de l'Europe in the Piazza Santa Trinita. He had deliberated about going into a *pensione* but had decided against it, since, with the self-consciousness and shyness of youth, he wished to avoid 'public tables', i.e. being obliged to eat in the company of others. An apartment, he decided, would be 'lonesome' and also too costly for his means.

When not writing enthusiastically to his family about the marvels of the city (the Uffizi and the Pitti Palace were '*incroyables*'), he wrote to complain, in anxiety and depression, about the state of his digestion. To his sister, Alice, for example, he reported: 'I am very sorry to say (if you'll allow me to mention the topic) that in spite of the most religious prudence (and I have learned many things) my digestive organs are the bane of my existence and so long as this state of things continues I must ensure myself the best conditions in the way of food and lodging.' After three weeks of 'communing with the immortals' in picture galleries and churches, he was still no better, writing to his father

> . . . I have been in a very bad way. Shortly after getting here I was so knocked up that I had to take to my bed and have the doctor and have since been in his hands. He plies me with drugs, but to no purpose: I only seem to get worse. . . . I don't know whether to think that the Italian air has anything to do with the matter . . . I feel as if I couldn't live a week longer in my present pernicious condition. I'm not impatient: I have given the thing a fair chance and my present condition, which is all that has come of my patience, is quite unendurable. . . . My malady has done a great deal towards spoiling Florence for me . . . The question is of course what to do, inasmuch as I've pretty nearly exhausted expedience. I've almost made up my mind to depart straight from Italy and take refuge at Malvern again.

From all this, the reader might naturally assume that James had fallen victim to the disorder to which travellers to the Mediterranean countries are most susceptible. The revelation contained in a subsequent letter to his philosopher brother William therefore comes as a surprise: 'My back . . . is so chronically affected by my constipated state that there are times when I can hardly drag myself about. Half the week I can eat not a single meal a day; I can't possibly find room for more – and this in spite of getting very tired and passably hungry with all my poking about.' What William, somewhat heartlessly, referred to as his novelist brother's 'moving internal drama' – perhaps 'unmoving' would have been a more a suitable epithet – was finally solved by a Dr Duffy, who prescribed what sounds like an extraordinarily drastic remedy: 'sulfuric acid' pills.

James was back in Italy three years later in 1872. Initially he settled in Rome, where he began to plan what he habitually called his first novel, *Roderick Hudson*, even though *Watch and*

Ward was written earlier. May 1873 found him once more at the Hotel de l'Europe in Florence. But he was undecided whether to stay in the city or to 'shuffle off'. On the one hand there was 'little heat to speak of'; but on the other the 'obstinately relaxing' atmosphere had resulted in another bout of 'perfect torpor and inaction of the bowels', so that he had become 'as yellow as an orange'. In addition, Rome – 'so wondrous in retrospect' – had murdered Florence for him: 'her great smiting hands have snapt the tender cords to which Florence appeals.' Within two weeks, he had departed for Switzerland.

Back in Florence in October of that same year, he was now delighted with it. Most of the people whom he met were New England friends of his family, either briefly in Florence in the course of a European tour or as temporary residents. Soon his brother William had joined him, their period of cohabitation eventually providing much of the material for one of James's least known novels, *Confidence*. William was as indefatigable a sightseer as his brother, and physically far more robust. His talk about all that he had seen during his expeditions about the city was, Henry declared, 'most suggestive'.

After a few weeks in Rome, the brothers returned to Florence in January 1874. Once again, a comparison with the capital worked to the detriment of Florence, which now seemed 'a vulgar little village', 'the region of chapped lips and chilblains', after the sunshine and warmth of the Pincio, where they had been living.

However, as the memory of the sonorous music which Rome played on his imagination began to fade, James once more succumbed to the smaller city's charms. Among those whom the brothers now saw were James Russell Lowell and his wife. Henry had one bout of illness – 'an affair chiefly of the *head*', 'a strange and mysterious visitation' – but recovered after ten days. In February, Willy left to continue his travels to Germany, but Henry remained, working at his *Florentine Notes*. By now Henry was *contentissimo*: 'The spring is coming on bravely and the lights and shadows on the mountain and the river, the sunsets and the moonlights, the walks in the dim palace-bordered streets whose shadow is now losing its winter chill – are all quite worth enjoying.' Unfortunately the *pensione*, the Corona d'Italia, was 'odiously full of new-comers'.

After a spell in Pisa and Lucca, James returned to an apartment, 10 Piazza Santa Maria Novella, on the corner of the Via della Scala, where he declared that he was 'established *à merveille*'. When not working with his usual industry at *Roderick Hudson* – of which he was later to write to Robert Louis Stevenson that it was the work 'in which my little muse first tried to elongate her little legs' – and also at an amazing profusion of articles, he would make solitary excursions around the city or attend this or that hostess's reception. His favourite eating place was Victor's in the Via de' Rondinelli, where he would escape from his own company by conversing with the flower-girl who, like Florentine flower-girls today, would badger men to buy rosebuds either for their button-holes or for the women who were with them. At that time, he confessed to feeling that James Russell Lowell, of whom he was seeing a lot during the American poet's visit to the city, was unlikely to reveal anything new of mind or character to him, and that their friendship was therefore unlikely to de-velop further. There he was wrong.

In May, he attended 'for information's sake' a 'very brilliant ball' given by the Jockey Club at their Casino in the Cascine. Present was 'a concentration of the elite of Florentine society', with 'more tiaras of diamonds, ropes of pearls and acres of *point de Venise*' than he had ever seen before.

Soon after that, the intense heat of summer had driven away most of the expatriate colony. Looking out through the shutters of his apartment on to the wide, glaring piazza below, he recorded: 'It [the sun] shines so as to scorch the eyes: in the shade on one side is huddled a cab-stand with the drivers all asleep on their boxes and a collection of loungers of low degree and no costume to speak of lying flat on their faces on the stones and courting the siesta.' Within days, fleeing this heat like his American friends before him, he had arrived on Lake Como.

James was briefly back in Florence in the spring of 1880, now staying at the Hotel de l'Arno. Everything seemed to him 'quite too lovely', as he enjoyed 'a holiday pure and simple' before embarking on his long novel *Portrait of a Lady*, for much of which Florence and its environs provide the setting. From his open bedroom window he could look out at the yellow-green Arno and 'the little overhanging cabins of the Ponte Vecchio' directly below him. It was all 'divinely beautiful'. From here he wrote to J. W. Cross, to express his 'sympathy' on his recent marriage to George Eliot. Since Cross, twenty-one years George Eliot's junior, was to attempt to drown himself in a canal during their honeymoon in Venice, the choice of word was perhaps, as so often with James, the right one.

The most enjoyable and, perhaps for that reason, the most productive of all Henry James's journeys to Italy was that which he made from December 1886 to June 1887. For the most part he stayed as the pampered guest or the tenant of friends in their luxurious palazzi or villas. In Florence he was briefly at the Hotel du Sud; but his usual address was the Villa Brichieri in Bellosguardo, in which he had taken a three weeks' let of an apartment belonging to Constance Fenimore Woolson, an 'almost impracticably deaf', fussy American spinster, herself a novelist of indifferent talent, and which he and Miss Woolson were subsequently to share for a brief period. Her shy, yearning involvement with him was far stronger than his decorous, wary involvement with her, and it was no doubt largely because of this disparity that she eventually took her life, leaving him a legacy of puzzlement and remorse. In the Villa Brichieri he wrote *The Aspern Papers* and worked on a number of stories and essays and his study of Robert Louis Stevenson.

Looked after by 'a queer old melancholy male cook', he would 'go out' to be 'lionized' (he himself used the inverted commas) by 'a very thin and flimsy society'. 'My poor clever, tactless and tasteless (intellectually) friend Vernon Lee lives here with a paralyzed step-brother (from the legs down) formerly in diplomacy, and she and he are altogether the best people for talk – and indeed the only ones,' he wrote to one correspondent, Grace Norton. In a later letter to her, he wrote that:

The most intelligent person in Florence is Violet Paget (Vernon Lee) who has lived here all her life, and receives every day from 4 to 7, and as often in the evening as people will come to her. She is exceedingly ugly, not 'well off', disputatious, contradictious and perverse; has a clever, paralysed half-brother, Edward Hamilton [in fact, Eugene Lee-Hamilton (1845–1907), who eventually recovered from a paralysis clearly psychosomatic in origin], formerly in diplomacy – who is always in her salon, bedridden or rather sofa-ridden – and also a grotesque, deformed, invalidical, *posing* little old mother and a father in the highest degree unpleasant, mysterious and sinister, who walks *all day*, all over Florence, hates his stepson, and hasn't sat down to table with his family for twenty years. Yet in spite of all these drawbacks, Miss Paget's intellectual and social energy are so great, that she attracts all the world to her drawing-room, discusses all things in *any* language, and understands some, drives her pen, glares through her spectacles and keeps up her courage. She has a *mind* – almost the only one in Florence.

In 1893, Henry James's brother William was again in Florence on a visit, during which he expressed to Mary Berenson, wife of Bernard Berenson, his disgust at the manner in which Vernon Lee had portrayed his brother Henry in her novel *Vanitas*. Branding Lee 'a most dangerous woman' and seemingly unaware that his brother had similarly used friends as prototypes for characters in his fiction, William James expressed the intention of writing to tell her that he wished to have no more to do with her.

By the time that he came to write the second of his letters to Grace Norton, Henry James was living in the Palazzo Giustinian-Recanati, which formed a kind of guest annexe to the even more sumptuous mansion in which his American hostess, Mrs (Katherine De Kay) Bronson had been living for a decade. Browning had also been a guest of Mrs Bronson in the same guest annexe, so that James could boast of writing at the same desk at which the poet had composed 'crabbed verses'.

Browning and his son Pen were now looking for a Florentine palazzo of their own, James reported.

James's other hostesses – 'rather entertaining women' – included a niece of Byron's Teresa Guiccioli; Janet Ross (1842–1927) at her magnificent Villa Gherardo; and the splendidly named Baroness Zunch, a kind of Florentine Madame Verdurin, whose *salon* attracted people with literary, artistic, and musical aspirations.

In April, James was back at the Villa Brichieri from Venice. He had now made it a rule not to accept luncheon engagements, since 'it is necessary to my salvation to make a *long* morning' and so 'to deny myself the pleasure of a festive noon'. During this second spell in Florence, he took part in the fête to celebrate the unveiling of the completed front of the Duomo. In the course of these festivities, he committed 'the fatuity' of cladding himself in scarlet and black quattrocento dress before attending a ball, given to the King and Queen, in 'a wonderful tapestried hall' of the Palazzo Vecchio. He also met the then highly popular but now almost wholly forgotten English novelist Rhoda Broughton (1840–1920), who was on a visit to Italy. He decided that, in spite of her 'roughness', he liked her – and liked her even more for her liking Florence so much. There is, incidentally, more than a little of Rhoda Broughton in the lady novelist, Miss Lavish, in E. M. Forster's *A Room with a View*.

E. M. FORSTER, D. H. LAWRENCE, NORMAN DOUGLAS

In October 1901, E. M. Forster (1879–1970) and his indomitable mother arrived in Florence during the course of what he was later to call 'a very timid outing' from England to Italy. They stayed briefly at the Albergo Bonciani, Via de' Panzani, before moving on to the Pensione Simi, 2 Lungarno delle Grazie. Of the Cockney landlady of this pensione Forster was to write to the musicologist E. J. Dent: 'She scatters Hs like morsels and calls me "the young gentleman".' Oliver Stallybrass, editor of the Abinger Edition of the works of

E. M. Forster, writes in his notes to *A Room with a View* that the Simi must have been located within the present Hotel Jennings-Riccioli. Forster himself declared of the *pensione* in *A Room with a View:* 'The Bertolini=the Pension Simi'.

Since Forster's three stays in Florence in 1901, 1902, and 1903 can be totalled in weeks and during those years he spent only a few months in Italy as a whole, it is remarkable that his two Italian novels, *A Room with a View*, its first part set in Florence, and *Where Angels Fear to Tread*, much of it set in Tuscany, should have defined the Italian national character for so many English people of his generation and of two or three generations after. *A Passage to India*, the fruit of a not much longer stay in India, did the same thing for that country and its inhabitants.

D. H. Lawrence (1885–1930) and Frieda von Richthofen, then not his wife, had twice lived in Italy before the First World War; but it was not until 1919 that they first visited Florence, putting up at the Pensione Balestri, Piazza Mentana 5, at the suggestion of Norman Douglas, who was already himself living there. In *Aaron's Rod*, the protagonist, Aaron, arrives in Florence to enter, on a whim, the 'pension Nardini', 'a big old Florentine house, with many green shutters and wide eaves' in the Piazza Mentana (Lawrence was little bothered about concealing his literal transcription of his immediate experiences).

Having asked about a room, Aaron is shown by a 'bewildered, wild-eyed servant maid' into 'a heavily gilt, heavily-plush drawing-room with a great deal of frantic grandeur about it.' He there cools his heels for half an hour before the arrival of the proprietress: 'a stout young lady – handsome, with big dark-blue Italian eyes, but anaemic and too stout.' She leads him up the rambling house to the top floor; then along a passageway; and finally into 'a big bedroom with two beds and a red-tiled floor – a little dreary, as ever – but the sun was just beginning to come in, and a lovely view of the river towards the Ponte Vecchio, and at the hills with their pines and villas and verdure opposite.' It is a perfect evocation of the kind of *pensione* – Miss Godkin's, Miss Plucknett's, Mme Jenny Giachino's, the Jennings-Riccioli, the Levelis-Marke, the Bertelli-Scott – in which foreign visitors put up in the days before package tours and 'en suite facilities'.

Aaron is contented with his accommodation, as Lawrence was.

He rather liked the far-off remoteness in the big old Florentine house: he did not mind the peculiar dark, uncosy dreariness. It was not really dreary: only indifferent. Indifferent to comfort, indifferent to all homeliness and cosiness. The over-big furniture trying to be impressive, but never to be pretty or bright or cheerful. There it stood, ugly and apart. And there let it stand. Neither did he mind the lack of fire, the cold sombreness of his big bedroom. At home, in England, the bright grate and the ruddy fire, the thick hearth-rug and the man's arm-chair, these had been inevitable. And now he was glad to get away from it all. He was glad not to have a cosy hearth, and his own arm-chair. He was glad to feel the cold, and to breathe the unwarmed air. He preferred the Italian way of no fires, no heating. If the day was cold, he was willing to be cold too. If it was dark, he was willing to be dark. The cosy brightness of a real home – it had stifled him till he felt his lungs would burst. The horrors of real domesticity. No, the brutal Italian way was better.

Many expatriates in Florence at that period – whether writers and artists, retired folk, or people living on slender unearned incomes – had fled their native countries precisely because, like Lawrence and his Aaron, they had wished to escape 'the cosy brightness of a real home' and preferred 'the brutal Italian way'.

One of Aaron's acquaintances in Florence is a young, upper-class Englishman, Francis, obviously homosexual – although, at that period, Lawrence had to convey this merely by implication. Francis talks, with his over-expressive flamboyance, about the English community: 'Oh, they are such queer people! Why is it, do you think, that English people abroad go so very *queer* – so ultra-English – *incredible!* – and at the same time so perfectly impossible? But perfectly imposs-

ible! Pathological, I assure you. And as for their sexual behaviour – oh, dear, don't mention it. I assure you it doesn't
bear mention. And all quite flagrant, quite unabashed – under
the cover of this fanatical Englishness. But I couldn't begin to
tell you all the things. It's just incredible.'

Francis takes Aaron to a party at which many of the guests
are literary, artistic, or musical. Among them are James
Argyle, based on Norman Douglas; Walter Rosen, based on
Bernard Berenson; and Algy Constable, based on Reginald
(Reggie) Turner, an adoring acolyte at the altar of Oscar
Wilde, to whom he had remained loyal at a period when so
many of those who had once relished his company were either
spitting or turning their backs on him. It was Reggie Turner, a
justly unread novelist, who, when Somerset Maugham was
boasting about the rarity of his first editions, piped: 'It's my
second editions which are so rare. They simply do not exist.'

At the party, Argyle–Douglas launches an attack on
chastity.

> Where's the soul in a man that hasn't got a bedfellow – eh?
> – answer me that! Can't be done, you know. Might as
> well ask a virgin chicken to lay you an egg. But believe
> me, there's far more damned chastity in the world, than
> anything else. Even in this town. Call it chastity, if you
> like. I see nothing in it but sterility. It takes a rat to praise
> long tails. Impotents set up the praise of chastity – believe
> me or not – but that's the bottom of it. The virtue is made
> out of the necessity . . .

When Argyle–Douglas 'lays into' poor little Algy–Turner –
he describes him as one of those 'little old maids who do their
knitting with their tongues' – Aaron–Lawrence cannot help
being charmed by 'a certain wicked whimsicality'. 'He must
have been very handsome in his day,' Aaron–Lawrence decides, 'with his natural dignity, and his clean-shaven strong
square face. But now his face was all red and softened and
inflamed, his eyes had gone small and wicked under his bushy
eyebrows. Still he had a presence. And his grey hair, almost
gone white, was still handsome.'

Anyone who knew Douglas in his later years will at once recognize the accuracy of this portrait.

Lawrence had gone to Florence ahead of Frieda, who joined him a few days later. Meeting her train at four in the morning, he insisted on showing her the city at once. For this purpose he hired one of the open carriages, then so common and so cheap, outside the station. Frieda, far too robust to feel tired despite her long journey, describes the experience as follows:

> I saw the pale crouching Duomo and in the thick moon-mist the Giotto tower disappearing at the top into the sky. The Palazzo Vecchio with Michelangelo's *David* and all the statues of men, we passed. 'This is a men's town,' I said, 'not like Paris, where all the statues are women.' We went along the Lungarno, we passed the Ponte Vecchio, in that moonlight night, and ever since Florence is the most beautiful town to me, the lily town, delicate and flowery.

All the English were kind to the couple: they still had, wrote Frieda, 'a sense of true hospitality, in the grand manner.' Nonetheless, 'it all struck me as being like "Cranford", only it was a man's "Cranford". And the wickedness there seemed like old maids' secret rejoicing in wickedness. Corruption is not interesting to me, nor does it frighten me: I find it dull.'

Almost against her will, Frieda warmed to Douglas. Fluent in her own native language of German, he was transformed when he was speaking it and not English to her. She was 'thrilled at the fireworks of wit that went off' between Lawrence and him.

Frieda was far less thrilled than Lawrence with Maurice Magnus, a European-American friend of Douglas also resident at the Balestri. A sly, persuasive conman, who had been both Isadora Duncan's manager and a journalist, Magnus now lived on his wits and his friends – among whom Lawrence was at once enlisted. Having 'borrowed' money from the impoverished Douglas or Lawrence, on the pretext that otherwise he would starve or be thrown into prison, he would then go off and order a suit from an expensive tailor, eat in one of the best restaurants of the city, or make a journey first class. After Magnus had committed suicide in Malta, Douglas and Lawrence were to quarrel over his *Memoirs of the Foreign Legion*, which Lawrence substantially rewrote and for which he provided a lengthy preface in order to achieve its publication and so to earn money to pay off Magnus's creditors. Douglas unjustly accused Lawrence of having exploited their highly exploitative friend. If Lawrence did, in a sense, exploit Magnus, it was in using him as Mr May, the disreputable and slithery American theatrical manager in his story *The Lost Girl*.

Back in Florence early in the next year, Lawrence met Rebecca West through an introduction by Norman Douglas. West would tell the story of how Douglas had remarked, as they set off to see the younger man, that Lawrence had no sooner to arrive in a place than he would at once set about writing about it. Shown up to Lawrence's room in the Balestri, they found him hammering out an article about Florence on his typewriter. 'There – what did I tell you, my dear?' Douglas demanded of West. Lawrence looked furious.

August 1921 found the Lawrences back in Florence for a visit of three weeks. In her absence in Venice, a friend of theirs, Nellie Morrison, had lent them her roomy flat at 32 Via de' Bardi – the house which, so tradition had it, George Eliot's Romola had inhabited. Although, by his own confession, 'feeling tired and seedy', Lawrence was writing away as feverishly as ever in the 'rather dark and cool' room which he occupied above the din of the street below. J. M. Barrie's former wife, Mary, now married to the novelist Gilbert Cannan, visited them in the flat and fell so much in love with it that she herself wished to rent it. Lawrence was happiest when he, Frieda, and Mary would sit out on the terrace in the evening, as the sun sank behind the Carrara mountains and the hills grew dark. 'On the Ponte Vecchio the windows of the little houses shine yellow, and make golden points on the water.'

In the spring of 1926, Lawrence and Frieda settled in the Villa Mirenda, San Paolo Mosciani, Scandicci, a few miles outside Florence, to make of this 'square big box of a house'

their home for what was, for two such nomads, the unpre-
cedentedly long period of two years. What was then in effect
a village has now become one of the grislier and glummer
suburbs of the city. It was in Scandicci that Lawrence wrote
one of the most famous and feeble of his novels, *Lady
Chatterley's Lover*. It was here that Lawrence's friendship with
Aldous Huxley, whom he first met when they were both
guests of Lady Ottoline Morrell at Garsington during the War,
became close and intense. It was here too that the feud between
Lawrence and Douglas over Magnus was resolved. At the
bookshop of Pino Orioli, the Lawrences were chatting to
Orioli when, to their embarrassment, Douglas, one of Orioli's
cronies, burst in. In no way embarrassed himself, Douglas
held out his snuff-box to Lawrence with the invitation: 'Have a
pinch of snuff, dearie.' Dearie took some snuff.

Frieda has left a vivid account of the journey by tram from
Scandicci into Florence.

> The handsome Tuscan girls with their glossy, neatly done
> hair . . . A chicken, sitting, tenderly held by its owner in a
> red hankie, its destiny either a sick friend or the mercato.
> Bottles of wine are hidden from the Dazio [toll-gate]
> men, men friends embrace each other, somebody sees a
> relation and yells something about the 'pasta' for midday,
> and so on, while we sail gaily on for Florence.

She has also left a no less vivid account of Florentine shopping:

> Shopping in Florence was still fun, not the dreary, large-
> store drudgery . . . There are paper shops, leather shops,
> scent shop, stuffs; one glorious shop sells nothing but
> ribbons, velvet and silk, all colours and sizes, spotted and
> gold and silver. Another shop, all embroidery silks. Then
> to have your shoes made is so comfortable . . .

In June and July Lawrence was severely ill, with a series of
bronchial haemorrhages. When he was convalescing, Osbert
and Edith Sitwell arrived on a visit from their father's Tuscan
mansion of Montegufoni. 'They moved us strangely,' Frieda
wrote. 'They seemed so oversensitive, as if something had
hurt them too much, as if they had to keep up a brave front to

the world, to pretend they didn't care and yet they only cared too much. When they left, we went for a long walk, disturbed by them.' Another, less distinguished writer who at that time wandered, a diminishing planet, into their orbit was Michael Arlen, whom Lawrence met on one of his by now rare descents into the city. He wrote of the Armenian-born author of the best-selling *The Green Hat* that he was 'quite a sad dog, trying to be rakish'.

Although he first resided in Florence in 1917 – declaring in a letter 'I don't much like the place; never did; I don't like the Tuscan character' – it was not until 1919 that Norman Douglas (1868–1952) began to make it the one fixed point in his restless life.

When D. H. Lawrence joined him there, he was at the Pensione Balestri. Subsequently he moved to the top floor of the Nardini Hotel, into 'two microscopic rooms' – too small, Reginald Turner remarked, even to swing a boy in. In 1922 he met the bookseller and publisher Pino Orioli, with whom he was to share a love not merely for food, drink, literature, and talk, but also for what Orioli used fondly to call *pulcinini* ('chickens') and Douglas himself 'crocodiles'. Orioli encouraged Douglas, more scholar than professional author, to write – as he could do superlatively well, when he gave his mind to it; and then, through the issue of limited editions, to ensure that his writing brought the maximum returns.

It was Orioli who eventually found for Douglas a flat in the Via San Niccolo – 'a tumble-down sort of place', with no kitchen and 'prehistoric' plumbing such as might well have deterred anyone more fastidious. Ejected from this, which he was renting, he moved first into rooms, also rented, in the Borgo dei Greci, then a red-light district – not that that worried him – and then into a bought flat at 14 Lungarno delle Grazie. Once there, he was soon again in trouble. 'Florence is taboo to me,' he wrote to Lytton Strachey, having been obliged to flee to Prato. 'I . . . only venture in for an afternoon now and then, thickly veiled and wearing blue glasses and a carroty beard.'

Douglas had little interest in the art and architecture of Florence. 'Isn't all that rather *Cinquecento*, my dear?' he derided

Nancy Cunard, when she began to gush to him about Benozzo Gozzoli, Piero della Francesca, and Signorelli. He had even less interest in the conventional world of expatriates hobnobbing with each other and with anglophile members of the Florentine aristocracy. 'I never go to the British Institute,' he wrote to Edward Hutton, a remorselessly industrious journeyman of letters, who became his friend, occasional collaborator, and unpaid agent. 'It is crowded day and night, with frowsy old pension-cats, who occupy all the chairs and read, each of them, five newspapers at the same time.' The people with whom he consorted could usually be divided into three groups: Italian eating and drinking companions; resident or visiting authors who either shared or were tolerantly amused by his sexual tastes; and a multitude of youths, some of whose parents could become so censorious and even financially demanding that he would have to flee from them to other parts of Italy or abroad.

Eventually, what drove Douglas from Florence in 1937, never again to become a permanent resident, was a scandal involving not a boy but a young girl, Renata. 'They always turn to little girls in the end,' Compton Mackenzie remarked, when hearing news which clearly did not surprise him, although it surprised almost all of Douglas's other friends. In fact, Renata was eventually found to be still a virgin; but there seems little doubt that Douglas must have indulged in some kind of affectionate love-play with her.

Through all these years Douglas suffered, Job-like from an extraordinary assortment of painful ailments, ranging from toothache to erysypelas. But, as in the case of his many brushes with irate parents or the police, his pagan robustness and stoicism always enabled him to surmount them.

Aldous Huxley

At first Aldous Huxley (1894–1963) had no reason to feel affection for Florence. In June 1916, while still an undergraduate at Balliol College, Oxford, he had written to his brother Julian that he had 'at last discovered a nice Belgian: wonders will never cease.' This 'nice Belgian' was Maria Nys, despatched by her parents to England to escape the worst of the First War. Initially she had lived at Garsington Manor as the guest of Philip Morrell and his flamboyant wife Lady Ottoline, and it was there that Huxley had met her. But at about the time that Huxley, classified as physically unfit for military service, had himself taken up residence at Garsington, Maria had moved to London, where she gave French lessons to support herself. In 1917, Maria – with whom Huxley had fallen in love – was (as he put it in a letter to Lewis Gielgud, uncle of the actor John Gielgud and a writer of modest talent) 'hustled out remorselessly to her ghoulish mother in Florence', with the result that two years were to pass before the lovers were once more to meet.

In March 1921, by now married for two years and the parents of a baby son called Matthew, Maria and Aldous arrived in Florence to stay in the wing of the Villa Minucci, 4 Via Santa Margherita a Montici, almost opposite to Castel Montici, the residence of the Fasolas, an Italian family who had offered hospitality to Maria and her mother during the war. The flat was 'hideously', albeit adequately, furnished, there was no electricity, all cooking had to be done on a tiny range fed with charcoal, and prices in the immediate aftermath of the war were 'fantastic'. But the great consolation was the view from the western windows: 'A valley sloping away from the house in the foreground, planted with olives and vines, with the church of San Miniato on the opposite side; to the right, looking down the valley, we see almost the whole of Florence lying in the plain, a sort of Oxford from Boar's Hill effect, only very much more so.' [Letter to Leonard Huxley].

After this stay of three months, the Huxleys returned to Florence in 1923, this time for a stay of only one month, at the Castel Montici itself. Once again Huxley complained of the discomforts: because of a failure of the electric water pump, all water had to be laboriously carried in pails to the kitchen and bathroom; the architecture was ugly; recent decoration had been shoddily carried out. But once again there was the compensation of a 'marvellous position', with extensive views down over Florence, up the Arno Valley, and on to the Appenines. With four living rooms, six bedrooms, a tower room, and a fifty-foot balcony terrace, running the whole length of the house, the family had ample space. [Letter to Leonard Huxley]. It was here that Huxley began *Antic Hay*, completed in Siena and the seaside resort of Forte dei Marmi. Sharing Dr Johnson's contempt for those authors who write more than they read, Huxley read strenuously through this month of increasing heat; but he also wrote strenuously, often putting in eight hours a day – which he would compare, unfavourably, with Balzac's 'herculean' eighteen.

In June, the Huxleys returned to the Castel Montici, to remain there, with breaks for visits to London, Tunis, and other parts of Italy, until June 1926. Florence was, he recorded in a letter to his father Frederick on their arrival, packed with English visitors; but he and Maria rarely ventured down from their eyrie to see them. Among those whom they did see were 'funny old' Vernon Lee (Violet Paget), John Mavrogordato (later to achieve fame as the translator of Cavafy into English), Norman Douglas (then lodged at 24 Via dei Benci), and Geoffrey Scott, author of *Portrait of Zélide*, and his wealthy American wife Lady Sybil Scott (Cutting), mother of the writer Iris Origo. This last couple lived in luxurious splendour in the Villa Medici in Fiesole. Of *Portrait of Zélide* Huxley was to write that 'it is full of that kind of exquisitely good writing that is, one feels instinctively, only another kind of bad writing.'

Huxley was now working on the short stories which make up the collection *Little Mexican* and also cogitating *Those Barren Leaves*. Of the latter he wrote to his father that the mere business of telling a story interested him less and less. 'The only really and permanently absorbing things are attitudes towards life and the relation of man to the world.'

Through these eighteen months he was for the most part grateful: 'the greatest luxury of this existence is the feeling and being well – *unberüfen*.' But by 25 April he was beginning to fret. He and Maria would probably look for something in Rome in the autumn, he wrote to his brother Julian – 'After a third-rate provincial town, colonized by English sodomites and middle-aged Lesbians, which is, after all, what Florence is, a genuine metropolis will be lively.'

Shortly before their departure, the Huxleys had 'a curious taste of fascist methods.' Huxley had already had cause to complain of the officiousness of the Italian police over speeding; but this was far more disagreeable. 'Four of the most sinister looking gallows' birds you ever saw' burst into the house and insisted on searching it for either the person of, or documents belonging to, Professor Gaetano Salvemini, an eminent historian and an opponent of Mussolini, who was a friend of friends of the Huxleys. In the event, the police found neither professor nor documents and left with embarrassed apologies.

In October 1926, Huxley was once more back briefly in Florence, from the mountain resort of Cortina d'Ampezzo, in order to have treatment for a painfully abscessed tooth. Once again he was overwhelmed by the beauty of the city:

> . . . I regret having to go up again to the mountains, where I shall miss the delicate colouring of the Tuscan landscape, the grand yet noble forms of the hills, the white villas with their gardens, the patiently elaborated terraces on the slopes with their grey olives, their vines and strips of ploughland, and here and there the black cypresses and the clumps of ilex and bay tree.

In February 1929 the Huxleys paid a last brief visit to Florence. On this occasion, they stayed at the Hotel Moderno, which Huxley warmly recommended in a letter to his brother Julian: 'No nonsense about having to take half pension with your room . . . and the water's hot, the radiators work.' Most of Huxley's novel *Time Must Have a Stop* (1944) is set in Florence. But, like so many expatriate novels set there, it contains virtually no Italian characters who are not either aristocratics or menials.

HAROLD ACTON, BERNARD BERENSON, SINCLAIR LEWIS, VIOLET TREFUSIS

The doyen of expatriate writers in Florence has, for the past half-century, been Sir Harold Acton (1904–   ). For a long

period he and Bernard Berenson (1865–1969) were the twin
peaks to be scaled by any energetic social or cultural climber on
a visit to the city. Now he stands alone.

Having amassed a vast fortune by acting as adviser, in an
increasingly uneasy relationship, to that black prince of art
dealers, Lord Duveen, Berenson settled in his magnificent
villa, I Tatti, in Settignano. There he was surrounded by a
small but obsequious court to which museums, libraries, and
dealers would send their reverential ambassadors. An increasingly frail octogenarian and then nonagenarian, he would
rouse himself to totter forth, a living relic of aestheticism
sought out in worship, to greet yet another busload of tourists
who would wave, stare, and click their cameras at him. Sadly,
this supreme proponent of style – according to one story, his
manservant would be obliged each morning to warm his
wristwatch so that the touch of metal should not administer
too violent a shock to his skin – was cruelly fretted by the
consciousness that, despite his friendships with such writers as
Edith Wharton, often a visitor at I Tatti, and Logan Pearsall
Smith, whose sister he married, and despite the help which he
received from such of his colleagues as Kenneth Clark and
Raymond Mortimer, his own literary style remained turgid
and graceless.

Acton, at once far more kindly, despite his sometimes
abrasive tongue, and far less ruthless, despite an energy and a
drive amazing for a man of his years, has extended the
hospitality of his Villa La Pietra to innumerable writers over
the years, so that it is rare for any book about Florence not to
contain at least one grateful and admiring reference to him.

In the late forties, at the same time as myself, Sinclair Lewis
(1885–1951) was resident in Florence. By then saturated in
alcohol and puffing asthmatically at the fag-end of what had
once been a brilliant career, he had grown so crude and
irascible that, so far from seeking him out, people now
avoided him.

In 1927 the parents of Violet Trefusis (1894–1972) bought
the Villa dell'Ombrellino in Bellosguardo. Described by
Trefusis herself as having 'quality, beauty, spaciousness, but
no intimacy,' the house enjoys magnificent views, over-

looking both the city and the countryside. It was the latter view that Trefusis preferred – 'just like a Florentine primitive' her guests would remark.

Trefusis's mother, Mrs Keppel, had been the mistress of Edward VII. Of this fact Trefusis was inordinately proud. Summoned, an ingenuous and timid young man, to the Villa dell'Ombrellino to meet Trefusis, I was asked as soon as I had seated myself: 'Do you know who I am?' I was about to stammer in bewilderment: 'You're Mrs Trefusis, aren't you?' when she announced, 'I am the illegitimate daughter of Edward VII.' When I recounted this to Harold Acton, he said that it was 'bosh': the dates did not fit. It was no doubt because she so often talked 'bosh' that Harold Acton subsequently wrote of her, in the course of a review in the *Spectator* of *Violet to Vita: The Letters of Violet Trefusis to Vita Sackville-West*: 'In a spacious villa on the hill of Bellosguardo she bombinated in her aura of luxurious fantasy.'

Trefusis's first acquaintance with Florence in 1921 had not endeared the city to her:

> This is a pestilential place, smug little hills domed over with villas, and museums and churches that have been so much photographed and written about that one is fed up to the eyes with them long before one sets foot inside. It amuses me that I have been brought here to be 'reformed'. The Italian Society here is the most corrupt I have ever run across, except perhaps Rome. They are mercenary, vicious, lewd, stupid. If one lived here long enough, I tremble to think what one would become. So much for the *Italian* set. The *foreign* set – Russian, Greek, French, American, English – is worse.

Yet eventually the city so much won her over that she would spend long periods of her life there.

In 1944, when the Second War was drawing to a close, an English major, Hamish Erskine, hurried round to the Ritz in London, where Mrs Keppel was then staying, to tell her excitedly that the Villa dell'Ombrellino was safe. 'Everything is intact, even the Chinese pagodas!' he assured her.

Mrs Keppel replied with frigid hauteur: 'Those, my dear Hamish – those were the *common* pagodas!'

Like many of the English expatriates, Mrs Keppel had a passion for gardens; and for her, as for them, a garden, even in Italy, meant an English garden. She would first point with her parasol in this or that direction and then prod with its ferrule at her aged gardener. '*Bisognia begonia!*' she would command. Eventually the Villa dell'Ombrellino was surrounded with as many begonias as had been any of the palaces once inhabited by her royal paramour.

PART TWO

PLACES

A Distant Prospect

The most distant of all distant prospects of Florence is that of
the adolescent narrator of Proust's *A la recherche du temps perdu*.
His father has proposed an Easter journey to Florence, and at
once, so vivid is his imagination, the boy sets off for the city in
his mind. Since, never having been there, he is unable to
'introduce into the name of Florence the elements that ordinarily constitute a town', he is obliged to 'let a supernatural
city emerge from the impregnation by certain vernal scents of
what I supposed to be, in its essentials, the genius of Giotto'.
The vision is, as it were, a diptych. In one half of this diptych,
he is gazing at a fresco, over part of which 'a curtain of
morning sunlight, dusty, aslant,' is slowly spreading. In the
other half, he is hurriedly moving – so as to arrive at a table laid
out for him with fruit and a flask of Chianti – 'across a Ponte
Vecchio heaped with jonquils, narcissi and anemones.' This
imaginary Florence is so near and yet so inaccessible: a paradox
which never fails to move him as he contemplates it.

In fact, the plan of an actual journey to Florence has to be
abandoned when an over-cautious physician fears that it will
be bad for the ailing boy's health. Years later, grown up, still a
stranger to Florence and now in love with the Duchesse de
Guermantes, the Narrator recalls his unassuaged longing for
the city. Florence for him is forever associated with Easter,
since it was for the Easter holidays that the journey was
planned. 'I could not prevent my memory of the time during
which I had looked forward to spending Easter in Florence

from continuing to make that festival the atmosphere, so to speak, of the City of Flowers, to give at once to Easter Day something Florentine and to Florence something Paschal.'

(The fastidious and accomplished translator of these passages, C. K. Scott Moncrieff, was one of the many *stranieri inverti* – as the Florentines called them – who could be found in Florence in the period between the wars).

One of the most vivid of real evocations of a distant prospect of the city is that of Shelley, in a letter to Mary Shelley, on his first arrival:

As we approached Florence, the country became cultivated to a very high degree, the plain was filled with the most beautiful villas, and, as far as the eye could reach, the mountains were covered with them; for the plains are bounded on all sides by blue and misty mountains. The vines are here trailed on low trellises or reeds interwoven into crosses to support them, and the grapes, now almost ripe, are exceedingly abundant. You everywhere meet those teams of beautiful white oxen, which are now labouring the little vine-divided fields, and their Virgilian ploughs and carts. Florence itself, that is the Lung'Arno (for I have seen no more), I think is the most beautiful city I have ever yet seen. It is surrounded with cultivated hills, and from the bridge which crosses the broad channel of the Arno, the view is the most animated and elegant I ever saw. You see three or four bridges, one apparently supported by Corinthian pillars, and the white sails of the boats, relieved by the deep green of the forest, which comes to the water's edge, and the sloping hills covered with bright villas on every side. Domes and steeples rise on all sides, and the cleanliness is remarkably great. On the other side there are the foldings of the Arno above; first the hills of olive and vine, then the chestnut woods, and then the blue and misty pine forests, which invest the aerial Appenines, that fade in the distance. I have seldom seen a city so lovely at first sight as Florence.

Dickens was equally overwhelmed by the beauty of the far-off vista:

Oh! How much beauty, when on a fair, clear morning, we look from the summit of a hill, on Florence! See where it lies before us in a sunlighted valley, bright with the winding Arno, and shut in by swelling hills; its domes, and towers, and palaces, rising from the rich country in a glittering heap and shining in the sun like gold!

Entering Florence, Thomas Gray commented, like Shelley, on the vines, but this time in a December bareness which, as he put it, revealed the skeleton of Italy. 'I was able to observe very public and scandalous doings between the vine and the elm-trees, and how the olive-trees are shocked thereon.' Gray was rarely so skittish either in his conversation or in his writing.

The 'shocked' olive-trees were what Lord Macaulay chiefly noticed at his approach:

The sight of the olive-trees interested me much. I had, indeed, seen what I was told were olive-trees, as I was whirled down the Rhone from Lyons to Avignon; but they might, for anything I saw, have been willows or ash-trees. Now they stood, covered with berries, along the road for miles. I looked at them with the same sort of feeling with which Washington Irving says that he heard the nightingale for the first time when he came to England, after having read descriptions of her in poets from his childhood. I thought of the Hebrews, and their numerous images drawn from the olive; of the veneration in which the tree was held by the Athenians; of Lysias's speech; of the fine ode in the Oedipus at Colonus; of Vergil and Lorenzo de' Medici.

Like so many travellers at a time when Florence was free of industry and therefore of pollution, Stendhal, approaching the city, remarked on two things above all: the small green hills, covered not, as now, by houses and factories but by agriculture; and the blueness of the sky.

While Milan is a circular town, without a river, a town that lies in an unbroken plain except for its many brooks of running water, Florence is built entirely differently in a fair-sized valley that is bounded by rugged mountains.

The town is right against the hill which limits it to the south, and by the disposition of its streets is not unlike Paris, being also situated on a river, the Arno, as Paris is on the Seine . . . If we go to the southern hill in the garden of the Pitti Palace and then walk around the walls as far as the Arezzo road, we shall get an idea of the infinite number of little hills of which Tuscany is made up, and which, covered with olives, vines and small patches of wheat, are cultivated like a garden . . . As in the pictures of Leonardo and of the early manner of Raphael, the horizon is often bounded by dark trees relieved against a blue sky.

A half century later, in 1895, André Gide, a French novelist scarcely less distinguished than Stendhal, provided his own distant prospect from the Viale dei Colli, San Miniato, 'in the most radiant weather':

A sky now but softly overcast, now almost azure, which deepens towards evening because of the abundant mists: the whole city melts in a golden bake-oven. The roofs are plum-coloured; the Duomo with its campanile, the tower of the Palazzo Vecchio rise above the rest; the hills seem remote; the high mountain opposite Fiesole stands out. The wonderful Arno appears in places, as it enters and leaves the city. The sun is setting, bathing with soft and veiled glory this whole scene that we can see from the marble terraces of the cemetery, framed in by mortuary cypresses, almost black, severe and most appropriate to Florence.

In Somerset Maugham's *Then and Now*, his hero Machiavelli is similarly bewitched by the distant view:

'Look, Messere,' cried his servant Antonio, riding up to come abreast of him. 'Florence.'
Machiavelli looked. In the distance against the winter sky, paling now with the decline of the day, he saw the dome, the proud dome that Bramante had built. He pulled up. There it was, the city he loved more than his soul . . . Florence, the city of flowers, with its campanile

and its baptistery, its churches and palaces, its gardens, its tortuous streets, the old bridge he crossed every day to go to the Palazzo, and his home, his brother Toto, Marietta, his friends, the city with its great history, his birthplace and the birthplace of his ancestors, Florence, the city of Dante and Boccaccio, the city that had fought for its freedom through the centuries, Florence the well beloved, the city of flowers . . . Spring had come early that year and the countryside, with the trees bursting into leaf, the wild flowers, the fresh green of the grass, the rich growth of the wheat, was a joy to the eye. To Machiavelli the Tuscan scene had a friendly, intimate delight that appealed to the mind rather than to the senses. It had none of the sublimity of the Alps, nor the grandeur of the sea; it was a patch of the earth's surface, classical without severity, lightly gay and elegant, for men to live on who loved wit and intelligent argument, pretty women and good cheer. It reminded you not of the splendid solemn music of Dante, but rather of the light-hearted strains of Lorenzo de' Medici.

In his *World So Wide*, matching cliché for cliché, Maugham's American near-contemporary Sinclair Lewis shows his hero, Hayden, at first disappointed but soon equally in thrall to the city:

The railway station at Florence had a fine, flaring Mussolini touch, very spacious and inclined to marble and wood panels, but the piazza in front of it was of a suburban drabness, and the back of the church of Santa Maria Novella was a mud-coloured bareness, sullen with evening. He would not be staying here long! His taxi-driver was learning English, and he was willing to make it a bilingual party, but as Hayden's Italian was limited to *bravo*, *spaghetti*, *zabaglione* and the notations on sheet music, this promising friendship did not get far, and he went to bed blankly at the Hotel Excelsior.

But in the bright morning of late autumn he looked from his hotel and began to fall in love with a city.

He saw the Arno, in full brown tide after recent

mountain rains, with old palaces along it and cypress-waving hills beyond. On one side was the Tower of Bellos-guardo and a fragment of the old city wall, and on the other the marvel of the church of San Miniato, white striped with a green that seemed black from afar. Hayden saw a city of ancient reticences and modern energy, with old passageways, crooked and mysterious, arched over with stone that bore carven heraldic shields.

'I like this! Maybe I'll stay out the week.'

It was this city that Coleridge apostrophized as 'Thou brightest star of star-bright Italy!', and of which, more pro-saically, Elizabeth Barrett Browning wrote: 'If you take one thing with another, there is no place like Florence, I am persuaded, for a place to live in – cheap, tranquil, cheerful, beautiful, within the limits of civilisation, yet out of the crush of it.'

The Arno and its Bridges

In his *The Innocents Abroad* (1869) Mark Twain views the Arno with typically Yankee robustness and realism:

> It is popular to admire the Arno. It is a great historical creek with four feet in the channel and some scows floating around. It would be a very plausible river if they would pump some water into it. They all call it a river, and they honestly think it *is* a river, do these dark and bloody Florentines. They even help out the delusion by building bridges over it. I do not see why they are too good to wade.

For Arnold Bennett in 1912, however, the Arno was 'a surging, yellow-brown flood.'

During his stay in Florence in 1895, André Gide was more appreciative. After one of many walks along the Arno, he wrote in his Journals:

> Beautiful hills along the Arno from San Miniato to those opposite the Cascine. I am becoming more and more familiar with their contours of stern softness and their hues of green and grey.
>
> On the edge of the Arno I like to observe at length the powerful wave made by the rolling water of the weir; the weir is on an angle in the river so that the water piles up rather on one side. Against the wall is a fold that hollows out the wall's edge; the water then rolls over itself like a

propellor, forming a constant unmoving wave. Wonderful to look at that fixed form with a fleeting and fluid matter always passing through it . . .

Even more rhapsodic is one of Gide's subsequent descriptions, this time of the Arno at sunset on 31 December:

> . . . Return along the shores of the Arno – setting sun; water losing itself in golden sands; in the far distance, some fishermen; the smoke rising from the roofs, at first gray, becomes gilded when the sun touches it. That radiance lasts for a long time; the roofs near San Miniato, the white walls of the villas become the colour of unripe apricots; the cypresses around them seem all the darker. The fall of the Arno has as it were some mother-of-pearl glints of an extremely pale green and, lower down, of that same colour with a tint of orange.
>
> The fishermen in the distance are carrying their bownets and returning to their boats . . . The wonder of these lengthening days . . .

But the Arno is not always beautiful and benign. In 1269 there was a flood so severe that it swept away both the Ponte a Santa Trinita and the Ponte alla Carraia and spread so far that – as Giovanni Villani put it in his *Croniche Fiorentine* – 'the great part of the city of Florence became a lake.' It was in response to a similar flooding of the city in 1557 that Cosimo set about beautifying the city, instead of merely restoring it.

In 1740 Horace Walpole witnessed another, less disastrous flood:

> If you have had a great wind in England, we have had a great water in Florence. . . . Yesterday, with violent rains, there came flouncing down from the mountains such a flood, that it floated the whole city. The jewellers on the Old Bridge removed their commodities, and in two hours after the bridge was cracked. The torrent broke down the quays, and drowned several coach horses, which are kept here in stables underground. We were moated into our house all day, which is near the Arno, and had the miserable spectacles of the ruins that were

washed along with the hurricane. There was a cart with two oxen not quite dead, and four men in it drowned: but what was ridiculous, there came along a fat hay-cock with a hen and her eggs and a cat. The torrent is considerably abated; but we expect terrible news from the country, especially from Pisa, which stands so much lower and nearer the sea. There is a stone here, which when the water overflows, Pisa is entirely flooded. The water rose two ells yesterday above that stone. Judge! [Letter to Richard West]

Of 'a terrible and unprecedented flood' (the second adjective is inappropriate since there had already been the precedents above), which occurred in 1844, Thomas Trollope has left us an account. Having climbed to the top of Giotto's tower on the morning after a night of torrential rain, Trollope was appalled to find that one-third at least of Florence was under water.

Having descended from the tower, he made his way to the Lung'Arno, where 'the sight was truly a terrible and a magnificent one.'

The river, extending in one turbid, yellow, swirling mass from the walls of the houses on the quay on one side, to those of the houses opposite, was bringing down with it fragments of timber, carcasses of animals, large quantities of hay and straw; – and amid the wreck we saw a cradle with a child in it, safely navigating the tumbling waters! It was drawn to the window of a house by throwing a line over it, and the infant navigator was none the worse.

But very great fears were entertained for the very ancient Ponte Vecchio, with its load of silversmiths' and jewellers' shops, turning it from a bridge into a street – the only remaining example in Europe, I believe, of a fashion of construction once common. The water continued to rise as we stood watching it. Less than a foot of space yet remained between the surface of the flood and the key-stone of the highest arch; and it was thought that if the water rose sufficiently to beat against the solid superstructure of the bridge, it must have been swept away. But at last came the cry from those who were watching it close at hand, that for the last five minutes the surface had been stationary; and in another half hour it was followed by the announcement that the flood had begun to decrease. Then there was an immense sensation, of relief; for the Florentines love their old bridge; and the crowd began to disperse.

Trollope and the friend accompanying him now decided to go to Doney, in the Via Tornabuoni, for a cup of coffee, to make up for the breakfast which they had missed. But since the Via dei Malcontenti and the Piazza di Santa Croce were both still under water, they had to get a lift aboard a large barge, which was carrying bread to people in the most deeply flooded part of the town. This barge took them to the Palazzo Berti, on the second floor of which the Trollopes were then lodged. Trollope was obliged to ascend to this floor by a ladder, placed on the deck of the perilously rocking boat. For years after, as Trollope records, social events in Florence were dated as having occurred before or after the flood.

In her *Diary of Florence in the Flood*, the American novelist Katherine Kressman Taylor recorded the not dissimilar events of 1966, which resulted in an invasion of water-carried mud and silt bearing off the marble revetments of the Duomo, panels from the great doors of the Baptistery, and statues from the Arno bridges.

A tumultuous mass of water stretches from bank to bank, perhaps four feet below the tops of the twenty-five-foot walls, a snarling brown torrent of terrific velocity, spiraling in whirlpools and countercurrents that send waves running backward; and its colour is a rich brown, a boiling *caffè-latte* brown streaked with crests the colour of dirty cream. This tremendous water carries mats of debris: straw, twigs, leafy branches, rags, a litter that the river sucks down and spews up again in a swelling turbulence. Its thunderous rush holds me tense at the window, as any movement of great force can lay a spell on the eyes. All I can think of is that it is as magnificent as it is threatening, a river in spate moving at full stress, its surface twisting with curling ropes of water that smack together and go up in spouts of foam. The flood is as absolute as a forest fire is absolute or a full gale stripping the countryside and bending down all the trees.

Eventually there are three meters of water in the Piazza Duomo, and stranded families are calling for help from second-floor windows. Army helicopters arrive, rescuing the women and children but leaving the men to wait either for a subsidence of the floods or for future rescue.

As always on such occasions of natural disaster, people alternated between feelings of horror and exhilaration; between wanting the waters to subside and wanting them to sweep everything before them. In 'A Letter from Florence' Francis Steegmuller has recorded the behaviour of onlookers by the Ponte Vecchio:

. . . The wife of one of the jewellers [shop-owners on the Bridge] had said that when she and her husband arrived they found a number of noctambulous Florentines – some of them apparently hoodlums, some in cars with head-lights pointed towards the scene – gathered at the end of the bridge, watching, as though hoping to see it break and collapse. The arrival of the jewellers with their suitcases [to carry away the most valuable of their merchandise] was greeted with jeers . . . The water continued to rise and about half the jewellery shops on the Ponte Vecchio are now gaping open – gutted by the tremendous force of a torrent that passed right through them.

Someone has rightly said that the only sure way of avoiding Florentine floods would be to move the city itself.

In his *Mornings in Florence* Ruskin calls the Ponte Vecchio 'the old treasure bridge', adding that it is 'the most precious historical link of all, tottering under the weight of shops and galleries.' The first of these shops belonged, unromantically, to butchers; but by 1644, when the young John Evelyn paid his visit, the jewellers had already taken over. There is a reference to their presence in the twelfth line of Longfellow's sonnet 'The Old Bridge of Florence':

Taddeo Gaddi built me. I am old,
　　Five centuries old. I plant my foot of stone
　　Upon the Arno, as St Michael's own
　　Was planted on the dragon. Fold by fold
Beneath me as it struggles, I behold
　　Its glittering scales. Twice hath it overthrown
　　My kindred and companions. Me alone
　　It moveth not, but is by me controlled.
I can remember when the Medici
　　Were driven from Florence; longer still ago
　　The final wars of Ghibelline and Guelf.
Florence adorns me with her jewelry;
　　And when I think that Michel Angelo
　　Hath leaned on me, I glory in myself.

In 1868, when he wrote this poem, Longfellow was staying at the Hotel Arno – as he put it, 'within a stone's throw of the Arno.' Foreign visitors of that period constantly expressed delighted surprise at the size of their rooms, whether in hotels or in rented apartments or villas, and Longfellow was no exception: 'My bedroom looking over the river is thirty-two feet by thirty, and high in proportion, I feel as if I were sleeping in some public square.'

Today the Ponte Vecchio totters even more than when Ruskin saw it, under the weight not merely of its shops, galleries, and the passage built by Cosimo to connect the Palazzo Vecchio with his newly completed Palazzo Pitti, but of the tourists who at the height of the season tend to turn it into a squalid mixture of souk, airport lounge, and dormitory.

In his *Pictures from Italy*, Dickens left a vivid picture both of the bridge and of Cosimo's passage:

Among the four old bridges that span the river [the Ponte a Santa Trinita, the Ponte alla Carraia and the Ponte alle Grazie were the other three], the Ponte Vecchio – that bridge which is covered with the shops of Jewellers and Goldsmiths – is the most enchanting feature of the scene. The space of one house, in the centre, being left open, the view beyond is shown as in a frame; and that precious glimpse of sky, and water, and rich buildings, shining so quietly among the huddled roofs and gables on the bridge, is exquisite. Above it, the Gallery of the Grand Duke crosses the river. It was built to connect the two Great Palaces by a secret passage; and it takes its jealous course among the streets and houses, with true despotism: going where it lists, and spurning every obstacle away, before it.

Writing in her *Italy* (1821) the now-forgotten novelist Lady Sydney Morgan (1783–1859) has left an entertaining account of her tribulations when ordering a *bandeau* from a dilatory jeweller on the Ponte. Today these jewellers are quite as prompt and efficient as any English or American ones.

Having explained most circumstantially the nature of the ornament I bespoke, sketched it with my pencil, and cut it out with my scissors, I left him with the full conviction that my order was understood, and would be well executed – a conviction impressed by the manner in which it was received; for while I stood before him, in all the eagerness of detail suited to the importance of the subject, he was squatted in an easy chair in a fine breathing heat after his siesta! – his thumbs twirling, his eyes closing and his answers laconically confined to '*Sarà fatto!*' (It shall be done!) repeated every second. Calling on the following day to see how '*sarà fatto*' was going on; to my enquiries the only answer I could obtain was, '*Veramente non mi ricordo di niente, Signora mia,*' ('Truly I remember nothing of all this, my lady.') To stimulate his memory for the future, I wrote down the order in the best Italian I could muster; and the day was fixed for the delivery of the article, with a promise of punctuality, which all the saints were called on to witness; but that day, and many a following one passed, and the answer to all enquiries was '*Sarà fatto,*' and '*Pazienza, Signora cara mia!*' My *pazienza* and residence at Florence had nearly however expired together, when, a day or two before our departure, '*sarà fatto*' entered my room with the long-expected *bandeau* glittering between his finger and thumb; and with a look of the most obvious triumph distending his apoplectic

face, he exclaimed, '*Mirate, Signora! che gran bella cosa!!
Questa è cosa per far stupire! veramente è degna di nostro
divino Benvenuto Cellini!!!* ('See, Madam, what a beautiful
thing! – a marvellous work! and worthy of our divine
Benvenuto Cellini.') His self-approbation had now
banished the languour of his habitual indolence; and the
naivete and hyperbole with which he applauded his own
work, resembled the very manner, in the self-same
dialect, with which '*Nostro divino Benvenuto*' charms his
readers, and leads them back to the frank simplicity of
the sixteenth century.

Stendhal also had an encounter with one of the jewellers on
the Ponte Vecchio.

This Nathan [the jeweller, like many of those then and
now plying their trade there, was Jewish], besides being a
fervent devotee of his persuasion, has perfected to an
astonishing degree a sort of philosophy of impassivity,
together with the most useful art of paying as little as
possible for all his daily needs. The accident of our
encounter afforded us sincere delight on either side. Upon
the instant, fearing to lose my company, he promoted me
to the status of a business associate, and bade me follow
him to the house of a client, to whom he proceeded to sell,
for the sum of ten *louis*, an exquisite graved stone by
Pickler. No less than three-quarters of an hour was spent
in bargaining; yet to me the time seemed short. Except for
the actual formulation of an offer, not one single word
was uttered of those which a Frenchman would have
employed in similar circumstances.

Stendhal then comments on the difference between the Italian
and the French collector: the Italian is interested in building a
collection for his descendants; the Frenchman in buying an
object which may eventually be resold at a profit.
Stendhal's jeweller friend later introduced him 'into the
society of a group of wealthy merchants and their wives', so
that he could watch a marionette show. Measuring no more

than five feet across, the theatre was an exact copy of La Scala in Milano.

> There were tiny lamps proportionate to all the rest, and each change of set was carried out rapidly . . . I can conceive nothing more enchanting. A company of four-and-twenty marionettes, each eight inches tall, equipped with leaden legs and costing a *sequin* apiece, performed a delicious, if somewhat indelicate, comedy which proved to be an abridged version of Machiavelli's *La Mandragola*. Subsequently these same marionettes proceeded to dance a miniature ballet, with considerable style and elegance.

In 1513 Ariosto stayed for six months in a Hospice of the Knights at the end of the bridge, and fell in love with the beautiful Alexandrina Benucci. Near the Hospice stood the statue of Mars beneath which, in 1215, the body of Buondelmonte dei Buondelmonti was left by members of the Amadei family and their *consorzeria* or allies, who had clubbed and stabbed him to death because he had jilted an Amadei girl in order to marry a Donati one. With an extreme lack of tact, he was crossing the bridge to celebrate his marriage to the second girl on the precise day fixed for his marriage to the first one. In *Il Paradiso* (XVI.140) Dante writes of the tragic incident:

> O Buondelmonte, ill dids't thou to flee
> Those nuptials when another prompted it!
> Glad had been many, who now most mournful be,
> If God thy body had into Ema thrown
> The first time that the city welcomed thee.
> Yet fit it was that to the battered stone,
> Which guards the bridge, our Florence should present
> A victim in the last peace she hath known.

The murder of Buondelmonte in what at first appeared to be no more than an act of private vengeance for a slight to a single family's honour soon embroiled the whole city, some noble families siding with the youth's family and others banding together in opposition to it. The first faction declared themselves Guelphs, the second Ghibellines. Thus, but for

Buondelmonte's fickleness and tactlessness, it is possible
that the history of Florence would have been much less
bloody and Italian literature much less rich.

The original Ponte alla Carraia, made of wood, was erected
in 1218 to accommodate an increase in traffic caused by the
growth of the wool and silk industry in the area it served,
Borgo Ognissanti. In 1304 a dense crowd assembled on it to
watch a mystery play enacted on boats in the river. The bridge
collapsed beneath their weight, drowning many of the spectators in what Dante called now *il bel fiume* (the beautiful
river) and now *la maladetta e sventurata fossa* (the cursed and
luckless ditch). By a grim irony, the work being presented was
entitled 'Inferno'.

The prolific Scottish novelist Mrs Oliphant (1828–97) –
who, with her dying artist husband, spent the winter of 1859
in Florence on the second floor of the Palazzo d'Elci, 28 Via
Maggio – has vividly described the scene in her *The Makers of
Florence*. Messengers had been sent far and wide to announce
that 'whosoever would have news of the other world was to
go on the kalends of May to the Ponte alla Carraia and to the
banks of the river.' When the day dawned, the Arno was
already packed with boats and rafts carrying the performers in
the spectacle, disguised either as demons or as their victims. At
the collapse of the bridge, many received only too literally
'news of the other world.'

Was this strange scene an unconscious reflection from
Dante's *abozzo* [rough draft of the *Inferno*] then reposing
in darkness and secrecy in one of Madonna Gemma's
strong-boxes? [Gemma, Dante's wife, looked after his
papers in Florence when he was in exile.] Or is it merely
an indication how the mind of the time was turning,
occupying itself with such dramatic guesses into a vivid
revelation under the poet's touch? Between the blue skies
of May and the glimmering of the Arno, overshadowed
by its bridges, what strange phantasmagoria it was which
bewildered the crowded spectators on the banks! the red
gleams of the fires floating on the dark river, the cries of
the fictitious victims, the shouts of the demon-actors, the

smoke and burning that figured hell; and then all at once a real hell of terror and suffering – the crash, the plunge, the wild dismay, the fantastic horror come true. Must not the exile, straining his eager ears outside, have heard some echo of the great outcry? and felt with characteristic pride and scorn that nothing less than some unconscious rever- berations from the visionary world which he alone had revealed could have conjured up this extraordinary scene?

A week after their arrival in Florence, the Hawthornes walked beside the Arno in the early evening, after a day of hectic sightseeing. As so often, it is Sophia Hawthorne, rather than her novelist husband, who vividly recreates the scene for us:

As we issued from the dim shade of the court, the golden light and the transparent mirror of the Arno burst upon us like a symphony, and now our way was toward the west, still glowing, with one star brilliant over the central arch of a bridge, making the apex of an invisible pyramid. All being reflected, there was also a pyramid below, each pointed by the star, so that the ovals of the arches and the pyramids were in lovely struggle together.

The Lung-Arno was lighted with gas along its whole extent, making a cornice of glittering gems, converging in the distance, and the reflection of the illuminated border made a fairy show. No painting, and scarcely a dream could equal the magical beauty of the scene.

Two weeks later, the Hawthornes drove in an open barouche beside the Arno to view the illuminations in celebra- tion of the Eve of St John. 'It was,' recorded Sophia, 'a scene of enchantment', with the Ponte a Santa Trinita and the Ponte alla Carraia 'hung with globes of light, like huge bubbles' and everything reflected in the waters.

The parapets, on both sides of the river, were studded with the same delicate globes, making a glittering cor- nice, doubled beneath; and lighted boats floated quietly in every direction, each one a moving constellation of stars, on the surface of the water, as well as in the pictured

world below. The palaces on the Lung'Arno were
kindled up over the facades, and, afar off, the mountains,
a dark, waving outline, and above, a black sky, with
heavy, windy clouds, were the frame of this radiant
pageant.

At that period to walk beside the Arno was not to be jostled
by crowds and deafened by traffic. The most sought-after
hotels and *pensione* would have at least some rooms with a
view of the river, as did the Bertolini in E. M. Forster's *A
Room with a View*:

> 'The Signora had no business to do it,' said Miss
> Bartlett, 'no business at all. She promised us south rooms
> with a view, close together, instead of which here are
> north rooms, looking into a courtyard, and a long way
> apart. Oh, Lucy!'
> 'And a Cockney, besides!' said Lucy, who had been
> further saddened by the Signora's unexpected accent. 'It
> might be London.' She looked at the two rows of English
> people who were sitting at the table; at the row of white
> bottles of water and red bottles of wine that ran between
> the English people; at the portraits of the late Queen and
> the late Poet Laureate that hung behind the English
> people, heavily framed; at the notice of the English
> church (Rev. Cuthbert Eager, M. A. Oxon.), that was
> the only other decoration on the wall. 'Charlotte, don't
> you feel, too, that we might be in London? I can hardly
> believe that all kinds of other things are just outside. I
> suppose it is one's being so tired.'
> 'This meat has surely been used for soup,' said Miss
> Bartlett, laying down her fork.
> 'I wanted to see the Arno. The rooms the Signora
> promised us in her letter would have looked over the
> Arno. The Signora had no business to do it at all. Oh, it is
> a shame!'
> 'Any nook does for me,' Miss Bartlett continued; 'but
> it does seem hard that you shouldn't have a view.'
> Lucy felt that she had been selfish. 'Charlotte, you
> mustn't spoil me: of course, you must look over the

Arno, too. I meant that. The first vacant room in the front –'

'You must have it,' said Miss Bartlett, part of whose travelling expenses were paid by Lucy's mother – a piece of generosity to which she made many a tactful allusion.

'No, no. You must have it.'

'I insist on it. Your mother would never forgive me, Lucy.'

'She would never forgive *me*.'

The ladies' voices grew animated, and – if the sad truth be owned – a little peevish. They were tired, and under the guise of unselfishness they wrangled. Some of their neighbours interchanged glances, and one of them – one of the ill-bred people whom one does meet abroad – leant forward over the table and actually intruded into their argument. He said:

'I have a view, I have a view.'

Miss Bartlett was startled. Generally at a pension people looked them over for a day or two before speaking, and often did not find out that they would 'do' till they had gone. She knew that the intruder was ill-bred, even before she glanced at him. He was an old man, of heavy build, with a fair, shaven face and large eyes. There was something childish in those eyes, though it was not the childishness of senility. What exactly it was Miss Bartlett did not stop to consider, for her glance passed on to his clothes. These did not attract her. He was probably trying to become acquainted with them before they got into the swim. So she assumed a dazed expression when he spoke to her, and then said: 'A view? Oh, a view! How delightful a view is!'

The real Pension White, at which Arnold Bennett put up at about the same period, is an establishment remarkably similar to Forster's fictional one:

Little tickets in each bedroom stating day of week when room is 'cleaned'. Little bookshelves about, in any case hanging in the worst possible place in the room – just over the washstand so that the books can be well splashed.

Embroidered or chintz covers for things. Everything little, and neat in the arrangements. No provision of writing materials. No spectacular quality at all anywhere. The Italian manageress has become almost English in her very soul. The great quality of the place is the meals. A really A1 dinner last night when we came home at 11 p.m.

Whether a glittering trickle or an opaque flood, the Arno always remains the backbone of the city. As C. Day Lewis put in his 'Florence: Works of Art':

> . . . Where rode Lorenzo, panoplied and plumed,
> Where Savonarola burned, and Ruskin fumed,
> The lady artist sets her easel up,
> The tourist with mild wonder is consumed.

> Yet still the Arno navigably flows
> And saunterers past the Ponte Vecchio's
> Jewel shops cast a shadow: here is still
> A taste for life, a market for the rose.

From the Piazza della Signoria to Santa Croce

PIAZZA DELLA SIGNORIA AND PALAZZO VECCHIO

Just as, today, the Acropolis best evokes the whole history of Athens and the Capitol the whole history of Rome, so the Piazza della Signoria performs a similar service for Florence. Many of the approaches to the great square are streets so tall and narrow that one has a feeling of claustrophobia walking up their dimness and dankness. This feeling is succeeded by one of liberation as one emerges into the amplitude and brilliance of the Piazza. It is easy to see this change as symbolic of the emergence of Florence from the artistic and intellectual constriction of medieval times into the freedom of the Renaissance.

Dominating the Piazza, as indeed it dominates the whole of Florence, is the looming bulk of the Palazzo Vecchio – or the Palazzo dei Priori, as it was originally called. At once strong and graceful, it too seems symbolic of a historical transition: its strength, as of a fortress, was necessary in a city where dissension within once posed quite as many dangers as attacks from without; its elegance was desirable in a city that was, at the time the Palazzo Vecchio was erected in the thirteenth century, already setting itself the classical ideal not merely of *mens sana in corpore sano* but of *mens* and *corpus* at perfect ease in surroundings ideally fitted for them. The American novelist W. D. Howells (1837–1920) summed up the qualities of the Palazzo when he wrote of it that it was 'a great, bold, irregular mass, beautiful as some rugged natural object is beautiful, and with the kindliness of nature in it.'

Stendhal was more rhapsodic:

> . . . This stark, contrasting incarnation of the stern re-
> alities of medieval times, set square amid the artistic
> glories of the past and the insignificant throng of modern
> *marchesini*, creates an impression of unparalleled grandeur
> and truth. Here, for the instruction of the philosophic
> mind, stand the masterpieces of those arts, whose genius
> was fired by violence of passion and bore fruit, only to
> wither in a later century and fade, becoming petty,
> insignificant and misshapen when the tempest of desire
> ceased to swell the sails by which alone that frail craft of
> the human soul, so impotent when passion falters and
> evaporates, leaving it bereft alike of vice and virtue, is
> driven across the stormy seas of life.

One evening Stendhal sat out 'on a cane chair in front of the coffee-house in the centre of the great *piazza* facing the *Palazzo Vecchio*.'

> Neither the crowd nor the cold – the one as inconsiderable
> as the other – could prevent my eye from beholding the
> whole tapestry of incident which had been unfolded on
> this same *piazza*. Here, on these very stones, Florence had
> risen a score of times in the name of *liberty*, while blood
> had flowed in the cause of an unworkable constitution.
> And now the rising moon, by imperceptible degrees,
> began to print the massive shadow of the *Palazzo Vecchio*
> upon the scoured flagstones of the *piazza*, and to lend her
> magic touch of mystery to the colonnades of the Uffizi,
> beneath whose arches gleamed the lights of houses, dis-
> tant beyond the Arno.

Eventually Stendhal had to drag himself away from 'this awesome sight' in order to make his way to *il Cocomero*, the theatre in which he was to see a performance of *The Barber of Seville*.

It is at night that the American hero of Henry James's 1873 short story 'The Madonna of the Future', having arrived for the first time in Florence, wanders by accident into the Piazza:

A narrow passage wandered darkly away out of the little square before my hotel, and looked as if it bored into the heart of Florence. I followed it, and at the end of ten minutes emerged upon a great piazza, filled only with the mild autumn moonlight. Opposite rose the Palazzo Vecchio like some huge civic fortress, with the bell-tower springing from its embattled verge like a mountain-pine from the edge of a cliff. At its base, in its projected shadow, gleamed certain dim sculptures which I wonderingly approached. One of the images, on the left of the palace door, was a magnificent colossus shining through the dusky air like some young god of defiance. In a moment I recognized him as Michael Angelo's David. I turned with a certain relief from his sinister strength to a slender figure in bronze, stationed beneath the high, light *loggia*, which opposes the free and elegant span of its arches to the dead masonry of the palace; a figure supremely shapely and graceful; gentle, almost, in spite of his holding out with his light, nervous arm the snaky head of the slaughtered Gorgon. His name is Perseus . . .

John Addington Symonds also admired Benvenuto Cellini's masterpiece, writing of it: 'It has something of a fascination, a *bravura* brilliancy, a sharpness of technical precision, a singular and striking picturesqueness which the works of elder masters want. It soars into a region of authentic, if not pure and sublime, inspiration.'

Writing of the Palazzo Vecchio, Dickens noted 'its enormous overhanging battlements and the Great Tower which watches over the whole town.'

In its courtyard – worthy of the Castle of Otranto in its ponderous gloom – is a massive staircase that the heaviest wagon and the stoutest team of horses might be driven up. Within it, is a Great Saloon, faded and tarnished in its stately decorations, and mouldering by grains, but recording yet, in pictures on its walls, the triumphs of the Medici and the wars of the old Florentine people.

Inevitably, his attention was attracted by the Tetto de'
Pisani, a gaol built by Pisan prisoners in 1364 but demolished,
in an act of unforgivable vandalism, near the close of the
nineteenth century.

The prison is hard by, in an adjacent courtyard of the
building – a foul and dismal place, where some men are
shut up close, in small cells like ovens; and where others
look through bars and beg; where some are playing
draughts, and some are talking to their friends, who
smoke, the while, to purify the air; and some are buying
wine and fruit of women-vendors; and all are squalid,
dirty, and vile to look at. 'They are merry enough,
Signore,' says the Jailer. 'They are all blood-stained here,'
he adds, indicating with his hand three-fourths of the
whole building. Before the hour is out, an old man,
eighty years of age, quarrelling over a bargain with a
young girl of seventeen, stabs her dead, in the market-
place full of bright flowers, and is brought in prisoner to
swell the numbers.

If the Palazzo Vecchio represents a period of transition from
feudalism to oligarchy and from war to peace, the magnificent
arcade of the nearby Loggia dei Lanzi – so called from the Swiss
lancers placed there in attendance on Cosimo I – represents one
of stability and calm. The mixture of round arches with Gothic
design and ornament, so typical of buildings in Florence, has
about it no suggestion of conflict or stress. Indeed, there is an
assurance about the very openness of the structure to every
comer.

As many a tourist soon learns to his surprise, rain is by no
means uncommon in Florence, so that the original reasons for
building the Loggia was to provide a covered space where
public ceremonies could be conducted without any fear of the
elements. But since then the Loggia has fulfilled a variety of
other functions. Less than half a century after its completion,
Leon Battista Alberti, one of those 'universal men' in which
the Renaissance was so rich, commented that its portico
provided a refuge under which old men might pass the heat of
the day. In a letter, Elizabeth Barrett Browning recorded: 'I

often go out after tea in a wandering walk to sit in the Loggia and look at the Perseus' – another reference to Cellini's masterpiece. Some forty years later, in 1896, the Victorian traveller Augustus Hare saw the Loggia as a listening post:

> The predominance of males is striking. Hundreds of men stand here for hours, as if they had nothing else to do, talking ceaselessly in deep Tuscan tones. Many who are wrapped in long cloaks thrown over one shoulder and lined with green, look as if they had stepped out of the old pictures in the palace above.

Arnold Bennett had also remarked, in 1912, on these lounging, loitering men – many of them 'dressed in the most amusing fur-coats.' The Loggia has constantly been a market, whether for flesh, for lottery tickets or, in the years immediately after the Second War, for black market cigarettes sewn into the voluminous overcoats of the sellers.

It was in the Piazza della Signoria that, in 1498, Savonarola presided over his famous Bonfire of the Vanities. In *Romola* George Eliot brilliantly evoked the scene:

> She [Romola] chose to go through the great Piazza that she might take a first survey of the unparalleled sight there while she was still alone. Entering it from the south, she saw something monstrous and many-coloured in the shape of a pyramid, or, rather, like a huge fir-tree, sixty feet high, with shelves on the branches, widening and widening towards the base till they reached a circumference of eighty yards. The Piazza was full of life: slight young figures, in white garments, with olive wreaths on their heads, were moving to and fro about the base of the pyramidal tree, carrying baskets full of bright-coloured things . . .

These 'bright-coloured things' are the objects doomed to incineration.

> There were tapestries and brocades of immodest design, pictures and sculptures held too likely to incite to vice; there were boards and tables for all sorts of games,

playing-cards along with the blocks for printing them, dice, and other apparatus for gambling; there were worldly music-books, and musical instruments in all the pretty varieties of lute, drum, cymbal and trumpet; there were masks and masquerading-dresses used in the old Carnival shows; there were handsome copies of Ovid, Boccaccio, Petrarca, Pulci, and other books of a vain or impure sort; there were all the implements of feminine vanity – rouge-pots, false hair, mirrors, perfumes, powders, and transparent veils intended to provoke inquisitive glances: lastly, at the very summit, there was the unflattering effigy of a probably mythical Venetian merchant, who was understood to have offered a heavy sum for this collection of marketable abominations, and soaring above him in surpassing ugliness, the symbolic figure of the old debauched Carnival.

A year later it was in the Loggia dei Lanzi that, as a test of Savonarola's saintliness, an ordeal by fire was arranged between one of the most faithful of his Dominican disciples, Fra Domenico da Pescia, and a friar of the rival Franciscan order. A bonfire, similar to that which had consumed the Vanities, had been raised. The idea was that, when it had been lit, each contestant would walk through it. Not surprisingly, there were repeated delays, as each side found fault with the procedures of the other. As the nineteenth-century novelist Mrs Oliphant (1828–97) describes it:

From half-past twelve to the hour of vespers, this tragicomedy went on . . . A thunderstorm swept across the Piazza, then a tumult arose; but neither storm nor tumult was enough to disperse the crowd or make a natural end to the situation. At last, as the day waned, the Signoria finding it impossible to screw the contestants to the sticking-point, put a stop to the ordeal altogether and sent word to Savonarola to depart with his brethren.

On 23 May 1498, Savonarola's hanged body was incinerated, along with those of two of his closest companions, in the Piazza.

The Festa degli Omaggi (The Feast of St John) was an annual
event in the Piazza della Signoria for several hundred years; in
1581 Montaigne described the celebrations:

It being St John's eve, the roof of the cathedral was
surrounded by two or three rows of lamps, and a number
of rockets were let off. They say, however, that it is not
the general custom in Italy, as in France, to have fireworks on St John's day. The festival came round in due
course, on the Sunday, and being, of all the saints' days,
the one observed with the greatest solemnity and rejoicing, everybody was from an early hour abroad to take
part in it, dressed in their best. I had thus an opportunity
of seeing all the women, old and young; and I must
confess that the amount of beauty at Florence seemed to
me very limited. Early in the morning the grand duke
took his seat in the palace square, upon a platform which
occupied the whole front of the palace, the walls of
which, as well as the platform, were hung with rich
tapestry. He was seated under a canopy, with the Pope's
nuncio at his side on the left, and the Ferrarese ambassador on his right, but not so near him by a good deal as the
nuncio. Here there passed before him a long procession of
men in various guises, emblems of the different castles,
towns and states dependent upon the archduchy of
Florence, and the name and style of each, as its representa-
tive passed, were announced to the assembled multitude
by a herald, who stood in full costume. Representing
Siena, for instance, there came forward a young man
habited in white and black velvet, bearing in one hand a
large silver vase, and in the other an effigy of the she-wolf
of Siena. These offerings he laid at the feet of the duke,
accompanying them with a suitable address. When he had
passed on he was followed, in single file, and as their
names were successively called out, by a number of
ill-dressed men, mounted on sorry hacks or on mules,
some carrying a silver cup, others a ragged banner. These
fellows, of whom there were a great number, went
on through the streets, without any sort of form or

ceremony, and indeed, without exhibiting the slightest gravity or even decency of demeanour, but rather seeming to treat the whole thing as a jest. They took their part in the affair as representatives of the various castles and other places in immediate dependence upon the state of Siena. . . .

By and by, advanced a car, bearing a great wooden pyramid, with steps all up to it, on which stood little boys dressed in different fashions, to represent saints and angels. The pyramid was as high as a house; and at the top of it was St John, bound to an iron bar. Next after this car came the public officers, those concerned with the revenue occupying the first rank. The procession was closed by another car, on which were several young men with three prizes, which were afterwards run for in different sorts of races. On each side of the car were the horses that were about to take part in the races, led by the jockeys, wearing the colours of their different masters, among whom were some of the greatest nobles of the country. The horses were small, but exquisitely formed.

. . . After dinner, everybody went to see the horse-racing. The Cardinal de' Medici's horse won; the prize was worth about 200 crowns. This spectacle is not so agreeable as the chariot-race, for it takes place in the street, and all you see is the horses tearing past where you stand, at the top of their speed, and there is an end of the matter as far as you are concerned . . .

On the preceding Saturday the grand duke's palace was thrown open to all comers, without exception, and was crowded with country people, who by and by nearly all collected in the great hall, where they fell to dancing. As I looked upon them, it seemed to my fancy an image of a people's lost liberty – an all but extinguished light throwing out a flickering gleam once a year, amid the shows of a saint's day.

Almost exactly three hundred years later, in 1858, Nathaniel Hawthorne was depressed, rather than impressed, by the same festival:

The Feast of St John, like the Carnival, is but a meagre semblance of festivity, kept alive factitiously, and dying a lingering death of centuries. It takes the exuberant mind and heart of a people to keep its holidays alive.

These already moribund festivities have long since been abandoned. The Feast of St John, the patron saint of Florence, is now celebrated on 24 June at the Piazzale Michelangelo with a public holiday and a fireworks display. A *calcio in costume* (football match in fancy dress) is also played three times during that week, in the Piazza Signoria, the Piazza S. Croce, and the Boboli Gardens.

In his autobiographical *A Voyage to Pagany* ('Pagany', the place of pagans), the result of a journey made in response to the urging of his friend Ezra Pound, 'You'd better come across [to Europe] and broaden your mind', William Carlos Williams has his forty-year-old American alter ego Dr Evans (Dev) arrive in Florence and eventually make his way into the Piazza della Signoria, to be confronted by Michelangelo's *David*. Dev has already gazed, in the course of his wandering about the city, at Donatello's depiction of the same subject and, inevitably, a comparison follows:

The false crudity of Angelo, the delicate torment drove him wild again. That's Christian, big with mental anguish, the genesis of which is the impossibility of fusing the old power with the new weakness. The pain, the weakening is the charm! Agh! He twisted the Greek; put the anguish of the soul into it. The Christian anguish. But why take *that* to torment the Greek, the quiet, the perfect, the lovely. No, no!

Evans could not frame it. He felt only the offence in the David. The too big hands, the over-anxious Jewish eyes. The neurasthenic size of the thing standing there in the courtyard with the Judith not far off turning her face away.

This is not Italy. The David meant nothing to him. It is lying. It leans on the Greek, which it bastardizes, to give it a kind of permission. Had to have something to lean on –

so it slimes the anguish over that, trying to unite two impossible themes.

Hazlitt, in 1821, was even less impressed by the *David*, remarking that it was 'as though a large mass of solid marble fell on one's head, to crush one's faith in great names. It looks like an awkward overgrown actor at one of the minor theatres, without his clothes; the head is too big for the body, and it has a helpless expression of distress.'

What William Carlos Williams's 'Dev' saw in the Piazza was not Michelangelo's original statue, long since removed to the Accademia di belle Arti, but a copy. Hazlitt saw the original.

There are other twentieth-century views of the Piazza della Signoria in D. H. Lawrence's *Aaron's Rod* and E. M. Forster's *A Room with a View*.

Lawrence's Aaron, a flautist, suddenly catches sight

of the long slim neck of the Palazzo Vecchio up above, in the air. And in another minute he was passing between massive buildings, out into the Piazza della Signoria. There he stood still and looked round him in real surprise and real joy. The flat, empty square with its stone paving was all wet. The great buildings rose dark. The dark sheer front of the Palazzo Vecchio went up like a cliff to the battlements, and the slim tower soared dark and hawk-like, crested, high above. And at the foot of the cliff stood the great naked David, white and stripped in the wet, white against the dark, warm-dark cliff of the building – and near, the heavy naked men of Bandinelli.

The first thing he had seen, as he turned into the square, was the back of one of these Bandinelli statues: a great naked man of marble, with a heavy back and strong naked flanks over which the water was trickling. And then to come immediately on the David, so much whiter, glistening skin-white in the wet, standing a little forward and shrinking.

He may be ugly, too naturalistic, too big, and anything else you like. But the David in the Piazza della Signoria, there under the dark great Palace, in the position

Michelangelo chose for him, there standing forward stripped and exposed and eternally half-shrinking, half-wishing to expose himself, he is the genius of Florence. The adolescent, the white, self-conscious, physical adolescent: enormous, in keeping with the stark, grim, enormous palace, which is dark and bare as he is white and bare. And behind, the big, lumpy Bandinelli men are in keeping too. They may be ugly – but they are there in their place, and they have their own lumpy reality. And this morning in the rain, standing unbroken, with the water trickling down their flanks and along the inner sides of their great thighs, they were real enough, representing the undaunted physical nature of the heavier Florentines.

Aaron looked and looked at the three great naked men. David so much white and standing forward, self-conscious: then at the great splendid front of the Palazzo Vecchio: and at the fountain splashing water upon its wet, wet figures; and the distant equestrian statue; and the stone-flagged space of the grim square. And he felt that here he was in one of the world's living centres, here, in the Piazza della Signoria. The sense of having arrived – of having reached a perfect centre of the human world: this he had.

And so, satisfied, he turned round to look at the bronze Perseus which rose just above him. Benvenuto Cellini's dark hero looked female, with his plump hips and his waist, female and rather insignificant: graceful, and rather vulgar . . .

The great naked men in the rain, under the dark-grey November sky, in the dark, strong, inviolable square! The wonderful hawk-head of the old palace! The physical self-conscious adolescent, Michelangelo's David, shrinking and exposing himself, with his white, slack limbs! Florence, passionate, fearless Florence had spoken herself out. Aaron was fascinated by the Piazza della Signoria. He never went into the town, never returned from it to his lodging, without contriving to pass through the square. And he never passed through it without satisfaction. Here men had been at their intensest, most naked pitch, here, at

the end of the old world and the beginning of the
new . . .

Just as Augustus Hare saw the Loggia dei Lanzi as a place of
men, so does Aaron see the whole of the Piazza della Signoria
and even the whole of Florence: 'He found the Piazza della
Signoria packed with men: but all, all men. And all farmers,
land-owners, land-workers. The curious, fine-nosed Tuscan
farmers, with their half-sardonic, amber-coloured eyes.'

On a day of warm sun in April 1887, Thomas Hardy sat
down for a long time on the steps of the Loggia dei Lanzi and,
as he put it, 'thought of many things'. His diary recorded:

It is three in the afternoon, and the faces of the buildings
are steeped in the afternoon stagnation. The figure of
Neptune is looking an intense white against the brown-
grey houses behind, and the bronze forms round the basin
[of the fountain] are starred with rays on their noses,
elbows, bosoms and shoulders . . .

In the caffè near there is a patter of speech, and on the
pavement outside a noise of hoofs. The reflection from
that statue of Neptune throws a secondary light into the
caffè.

Everybody is thinking, even amid these art examples
from various ages, that this present age is the ultimate
climax and upshot of the previous ages, and not a link in a
chain of them.

In a work of art it is the accident which *charms*, not the
intention; *that* we only like and admire. Instance the
amber tones that pervade the folds of the drapery in
ancient marbles, the deadened polish of the surfaces, and
the cracks and the scratches.

The scene in *A Room with a View* which E. M. Forster – of
whom Lawrence wrote, after a visit, 'his life is so ridiculously
inane, the man is dying of inanition' – sets in the Piazza is the
pivotal one of the novel:

'Nothing ever happens to me,' she [Lucy Honeychurch, the heroine] reflected, as she entered the Piazza
Signoria and looked nonchalantly at its marvels, now

fairly familiar to her. The great square was in shadow; the sunshine had come too late to strike it. Neptune was already unsubstantial in the twilight, half god, half ghost, and his fountain plashed dreamily to the men and satyrs who idled together on its marge. The Loggia showed as the triple entrance of a cave, wherein dwelt many a deity, shadowy but immortal, looking forth upon the arrivals and departures of mankind. It was the hour of unreality – the hour, that is, when unfamiliar things are real. An older person at such an hour and in such a place might think that sufficient was happening to him, and rest content. Lucy desired more.

She fixed her eyes wistfully on the tower of the palace, which rose out of the lower darkness like a pillar of roughened gold. It seemed no longer a tower, no longer supported by earth, but some unobtainable treasure throbbing in the tranquil sky. Its brightness mesmerised her, still dancing before her eyes when she bent them to the ground and started towards home.

Then something did happen.

Two Italians by the Loggia had been bickering about a debt. 'Cinque lire,' they had cried, 'cinque lire!' They sparred at each other, and one of them was hit lightly upon the chest. He frowned; he bent towards Lucy with a look of interest, as if he had an important message for her. He opened his lips to deliver it, and a stream of red came out between them and trickled down his unshaven chin.

That was all. A crowd rose out of the dusk. It hid this extraordinary man from her and bore him away to the fountain. Mr George Emerson [the man whom, at the close of the novel, Lucy marries] happened to be a few paces away, looking at her across the spot where the man had been. How very odd! Across something. Even as she caught sight of him he grew dim; the palace itself grew dim, swayed above her, fell onto her softly, slowly, noiselessly, and the sky fell with it.

She thought: 'Oh, what have I done?'

'Oh, what have I done?' she murmured and opened her eyes.

'You fainted.'

Later, as she is recovering, 'In the distance, she saw creatures with black hoods, such as appear in dreams.' Although she does not know it, these are members of the Misericordia, whose business it still is, in case of accident or sudden death, to assemble and render what assistance may be necessary.

In Anatole France's *Le Lys Rouge* (The Red Lily), set in Florence at almost exactly the same time as *A Room with a View*, there is also a description of the Misericordia:

> Just then they saw lights and heard mournful songs approaching them out of the darkness. And then, like phantoms, driven by the wind, there appeared before them black-robed penitents. The crucifix was carried before them. They were the Brothers of the Misericordia. With their faces hidden by cowls they were holding lighted torches and singing psalms. They were bearing a corpse to the cemetery. It was the Italian custom for the funeral procession to take place at night and to pass along rapidly. On the deserted quay there appeared cross, coffin and banners. Jacques and Thérèse stood against the wall to let pass the crowd of priests, choristers and hooded figures, and, in their midst, importunate Death, whom no one welcomes on this pleasure-loving earth. The black stream had passed. Weeping women ran after the coffin borne by weird shapes in hob-nailed boots.
>
> Therese sighed: 'Of what avail is it to torment ourselves in this world?'

Dickens, having noted that the Grand Duke himself wore the black robe and hood as a member of this body, described its duties as follows:

> If an accident takes place, their office is to raise the sufferer, and bear him tenderly to the hospital. If a fire breaks out, it is one of their functions to repair to the spot and render their assistance and protection. It is also among their commonest offices to attend and console the sick; and they neither receive money, nor eat, nor drink, in any house they visit for this purpose. Those who are on

duty for the time are called together at a moment's notice, by the tolling of the great bell of the tower; and it is said that the Grand-Duke might be seen, at this sound, to rise from his seat at table and quietly withdraw to attend the summons.

W. D. Howells writes of the Misericordia in less matter-of-fact fashion in his *Tuscan Cities*:

While these brothers, 'black-stoled, black-hooded, like a dream,' continue to light the way to dusty death with their flaring torches through the streets of Florence, the mediaeval tradition remains unbroken, Italy is still Italy. They knew better how to treat death in the Middle Ages than we do now. These simple old Florentines, with their street wars, their pestilences, their manifold destructive violences, felt instinctively that he, the inexorable, was not to be hidden or palliated, not to be softened or prettified, or anyways made the best of, but was to be confessed in all his terrible gloom; and in this they found, not comfort, not alleviation, but the anaesthesis of a freezing horror. Those masked and trailing sable figures, sweeping through the wide and narrow ways by night to the long, wild rhythm of their chaunt, in the red light of their streaming torches, and bearing the heavily draped bier in their midst, supremely awe the spectator, whose heart falters within him in the presence of that which alone is certain to be.

Except that now the torches of its members do not flare or stream, that the bell which summons them tends to be that of a telephone, and that they usually sweep through the streets not on foot but in motorized vehicles, the Misericordia today is little different from what it has been over the centuries.

THE UFFIZI

On their first visit to the Uffizi, the Hawthornes enjoyed something unexpected. Their friend, Mrs Mountford, summoned them to the Great Court, where a flower-carpet was in process of being laid.

> . . . Twenty or more men were at work, weaving a wonderful tissue, composed of petals of flowers, and leaves of box. The pattern was carefully chalked upon the flat flag-stones, and the men were rapidly filling in the forms with separate colours. Each of their baskets contained petals of one hue, and they, being perfectly instructed in what they were to accomplish, moved about, scattering blue, or red, or purple, or yellow petals in each defined division, so quickly and accurately, that, like a vision, the gorgeous carpet soon was spread over the stones. Its life was preserved bright and fresh by the continual sprinkling of water from many watering-pots which also made the petals heavy, so that the breeze would not blow them out of place. The fragrance was delicious, and can anything be more preciously beautiful than such a carpet? for its evanescence in this case added to its beauty. Such prodigality of richness just for a few hours – at the expense of so much toil! It was like carving and painting for the Lord, with the single purpose of worship; for it was Corpus Christi day, and the body of the Saviour was to pass over it – and the procession would inevitably destroy all the cunning workmanship. Thousands of wax-candles, in prismatic chandeliers, and in candelabras, placed in front of mirrors, with crystal pendants, were to light up the scene. As these chandeliers, composed of prisms, vibrated, they reflected the crimson tints of the surrounding silk hangings, and so looked like rubies flashing, even in the daylight.'

Sophia Hawthorne has recorded how, on their last visit to the Uffizi, she and her husband were distracted by two Englishmen –

> one a tall red-faced squire and fox-hunter, I fancy, with a loud, lumbering voice, like a sledge-hammer, slightly modulated by a certain amount of civilisation: the other a small, slender, delicately organized, polished, trim,

regular-featured, conceited, cautious gentleman, with silver hair, resembling a shining little minnow in the wake of a porpoise. The porpoise was the introducer of the minnow to the wonders of art before them, and it was a rare spectacle to see how he managed it. He plainly had no perception of art at all, but he was quite sure he had, and that he was an accomplished connoisseur, as he knew the names and reputations of the pictures. He desired a large audience, or more exactly, he felt that he deserved one, and looked about to observe who heard his remarks, as much as to say, 'Listen all who can.' To all his dogmatical assertions in heavy sledgy voice, the silver minnow responded in thin tones of assent, with consummate skill and nicety. Such a precise, immaculate little nonentity of a person! for there was no intellect in his face – he was only well arranged; but the small parlor of his mind was in exact order, and all its minute objects of *vertu* laid out to best advantage. The two friends consulted together about going to the Pitti. The silver minnow said to the red porpoise, in his fine, wee voice, 'It confuses one to see too many things at once.' 'It DOES SO,' replied the other in heavy boulder-tones. They were extremely diverting, yet there was so much for us to see that I could not spend any more time observing them.

After a visit to the Uffizi, E. M. Forster commented in a letter to E. J. Dent:

. . . How flagrantly indecent are the statues in the Uffizi with their little brown paper drawers, I almost feel that the permanent plaster article of the Catholic reaction is preferable. It did know its own mind.

His reaction recalls that of Samuel Butler, a writer whom he much admired, to the prudery of a fig-leaf on a statue in the Montreal Museum ('O God, O Montreal!').

The horror of Saunders McMuckleman, a Scottish clergyman character in *Continental Adventures* by the now forgotten nineteenth-century novelist Charlotte A. Eaton, is very different: 'Gude Lord, why she's stark naked!' he exclaims of the *Venus de Medici*.

This statue, found in Hadrian's villa in Tivoli, has inspired a number of writers. Samuel Rogers, who spent long periods gazing in absorbed silence at it, declared:

> We must return, and once more give a loose
> To the delighted spirit – worshipping,
> In her small temple of rich workmanship,
> Venus herself, who, when she left the skies,
> Came hither . . .

Byron wrote of the same statue:

> We gaze and turn away, and know not where,
> Dazzled and drunk with beauty, till the heart
> Reels with its fulness; there – for ever there –
> Chain'd to the chariot of triumphal Art,
> We stand as captives and would not depart.

Even the usually phlegmatic Hawthorne was moved to enthusiasm:

Her modest attitude is partly what unmakes her as the heathen goddess and softens her into woman. One cannot think of her as a senseless image, but as a being that lives to gladden the world, incapable of decay or death; as young and fair as she was three thousand years ago, and still to be young and fair as long as a beautiful thought shall require physical embodiment.

Smollett – who in January 1765 'lodged at the Widow Vinini's, an English house delightfully situated on the bank of the Arno' – was less enthusiastic about the *Venus*. While admitting that 'the back parts . . . are executed so happily as to excite the admiration of the most indifferent spectator,' he 'cannot help thinking that there is no beauty in the features . . . and that the attitude is aukward [sic] and out of character.' Leigh Hunt also admired 'the back parts' of the *Venus*, commenting:

It would be difficult nowadays to convey, in English, the impression of the Italian word *fianchi* (flanks) with the requisite delicacy, in speaking of the naked human figure. We use it only to mean the sides of an army, of a fortified place, or of a beast. Yet the words *rilevati fianchi* (flanks in relief) are used by the greatest Italian poets to express a beauty eminent among all beautiful females who are not pinched and spoilt by modern fashions . . .

But his final conclusion was even more severe than Smollett's:

I must make bold to say, that I think neither the gesture of the figure modest, nor the face worthy even of the gesture. . . . To my mind, the expression of the face (not to mince the matter, now I must come to it) is pert, petty, insolent, and fastidious. It is the face of a foolish young woman, who thinks highly of herself, and is prepared to be sarcastic on all her acquaintance.

Even in Madame de Staël's time the Uffizi was easily accessible to the public at large. In *Corinne* she comments approvingly: 'The fine arts are very republican in Florence. The statues and pictures are on show at all hours, with the utmost ease of entry. Attendants, trained and paid by the government, are on hand to explain the masterpieces.'

Few present-day visitors marvelling at the treasures of the Uffizi can be aware of the extent of their debt to the Archduke Pietro Leopoldo. Writing in the early nineteenth century, Antoine Laurent Castellan makes that debt clear in his *Letters on Italy*:

Under his directions, many more halls were built and a new flight of stairs to ascend them; and he added to the museum the most precious ornaments of the other palaces. He likewise sent to Rome for the statues from the Villa Medici, and more especially for those of Niobe and her children. By his exertions every class of objects had their distinct place, they were found without trouble, and classed so as to satisfy all tastes. He was rigorous in his selection, and admitted nothing that was not worthy of being preserved. The prince himself watched over the execution of his projects, and animated the workmen by his presence. One knows not which to admire most – the grandeur of the enterprise or the celerity of the execution. In 1780, in the space of one year, new buildings were added, and divided into halls; while, by this means, the communication was rendered more easy, and they were ornamented with stuccoes, gilding, paintings, and marbles; the tapestry and other drapery was renewed; the statues and pictures were placed in other situations, cleaned, or restored; whilst everything was ranged according to the system of a library, where every volume had its own separate and distinct place. And this metamorphosis was executed in so rapid a manner, that travellers, ere they had completed the tour of Italy, as they repassed through Florence, thought they beheld a new gallery, and were full of admiration at a change which almost appeared magical.

Via di San Martino to the Porta di San Piero

This street contains both the Casa di Dante, where an inscription records that Dante was born in 1265, and the little church of S. Martino, founded in 786 by the Irish St Andrew, Archdeacon of Fiesole. It was in the church of S. Martino that Dante was married. Augustus Hare writes that the house – subsequently to become a wine-shop frequented by Michelangelo, Cellini, and other notabilities – 'was of great interest as late as 1877, but has since been completely "renovated", to the utter destruction of its value, not a stone of the house which Dante looked upon having been spared.'

Mrs Oliphant describes the Florence of Dante as follows:

The little Florence in which Dante was born was very much unlike the noble and beautiful Florence which is now, like Jerusalem, a joy of the whole earth . . . The high houses that rose in narrow lines closely approaching each other, with a continual menace, across the straight thread of the street, had not yet attained to the character-

istic individuality of Tuscan architecture. The beautiful
cathedral, which so many a traveller, thoughtless of
dates, has contemplated from the Sasso di Dante, with a
dim notion that Dante himself must have sat there many a
summer evening . . . had not, even in the lower altitude
given to it by Arnolfo, begun to be when the poet was
born. The old Bargello and the Palazzo Vecchio were still
in process of building. Santa Croce, Santa Maria Novella,
and Giotto's lovely Campanile were all in the future with
their riches. The ancient Badia, or Abbey of Florence, still
struck the hour, as the poet records, to all the listening
city; and though the bridges, curiously enough, had all
been built, there was scarcely as yet any Oltr' Arno. . . .
The Baptistery had not even got its coating of marbles,
but was still in flint, grey and homely, when the child of
the Alighieri was christened there; and little Santa Reparata, with its grave-yard around it, lay deep down as in a
well in the heart of the tall houses. The Baptistery, too,
was surrounded by graves, its square being filled up by
sarcophagi of a still older date, in which – a curious fancy
– many of the greater families of Florence buried their
dead. The tower of one of the great houses was called
Guarda-morte, 'watcher of the dead', so closely round that
little centre of the buried clustered the houses of the
living. But to the old church of the Baptist, the 'bel San
Giovanni' of the poet, every child of Florence was carried
then, as now, to be made a Christian. That great solemn
interior, still and cool and calm amid the blazing sunshine, remains alone unchanged amid all the alterations
around. The graves have been cleared away, the great
Duomo has been built, the tower of Giotto, airy fabric of
genius, defying all its tons of marble to make it less like a
lily born of dew and sunshine, has sprung up into the
heavens; but San Giovanni is still the same, and still the
new Florentines are carried into its serene solemnity of
gloom to be enrolled at once in the Church and in the
world by names which may be heard of hereafter – as was
the infant Durante, Dante, prince of poets . . .

At the corner where the Corso now joins the Via del
Proconsolo, there stands the Palazzo Salviati, on the site of the
house of Folco Portinari, father of Dante's Beatrice. In the
courtyard is the *Nicchia di Dante* (Dante's Niche), from which
he is said to have watched for his love. In his *Life of Dante*,
Boccaccio tells the story of that first encounter:

> It happened that Folco Portinari, a man of great honour in
> those times among the citizens, had assembled the neigh-
> bours in his house to entertain them [*festeggiare*], among
> whom was the young man called Alighieri, whom (since
> little children, especially in places of merrymaking, are
> accustomed to go with their parents) Dante, not having
> yet completed his ninth year, accompanied. And it hap-
> pened that, with others of his age, of whom both boys
> and girls there were many in the house, after he had
> served at the first tables as much as his tender age permit-
> ted, childishly with the others he began to play. There
> was among this crowd of children a daughter of the
> above-named Folco, whose name was Bice (though he
> always named her Beatrice, her formal name), who was
> about eight years old, gay and agreeable; with habits and
> language more serious and modest than her age war-
> ranted; and besides this with features so delicate and so
> beautifully formed, and full, beside mere beauty, of so
> much candid loveliness that many thought her almost an
> angel. This girl then, such as I describe her, and perhaps
> even more beautiful, appeared at the *festa* – not I suppose
> for the first time, but for the first time in power to create
> love – before the eyes of Dante, who, though still a child,
> received her image into his heart with so much affection
> that from that day henceforward, as long as he lived, it
> never again departed from him.

The *Vita Nuova* is, of course, the story of this strange love.
In it Dante himself describes that first meeting. Beatrice's dress
was 'of a most noble colour, a subdued and goodly crimson,
girdled and adorned in such sort as best suited with her very
tender age.' As soon as he had looked on her:

Love ruled my soul . . . and began to take such security of sway over me . . . that it was necessary for me to do completely all his pleasure. He commanded me often that I should endeavour to see this so youthful angel, and I saw in her such noble and praiseworthy deportment that truly of her might be said these words of the poet Homer – 'She appeared to be born not of mortal man but of God.'

In Dante's time the Porta di San Piero, long since vanished, lay just beyond the church of San Piero Maggiore, in the busy little piazza of that same name. Franco Sachetti (c. 1333–1400), best known for his *Trecentonovelle*, tales of Florentine life, recounts the following:

Passing by the Gate of San Piero, Dante saw a smith beating iron upon his anvil, and all the while he sang from Dante's poem, as one singeth a song, and he so jumbled the verses, clipping here and adding there, that he seemed to Dante to be doing him a very great injury. Dante said nothing, but he approached the smith's shop – there where he had many irons with which he plied his trade. And Dante took the hammer and flung it into the street; he took the scales and he threw them into the street; and thus he threw out many of his tools. The smith, turning upon him with a threatening gesture, cried:

'What the devil are you doing? Are you mad?'

Dante asked him: 'What art thou doing?'

'I am doing my own business,' answered the smith, 'and you are spoiling my tools, throwing them into the street.'

Said Dante: 'If thou desirest that I should not spoil thy things, do not thou spoil mine.'

Said the smith: 'What am I spoiling of yours?'

Dante answered: 'Thou art singing out of my book, and are not singing it as I wrote it. I have no other trade but this, and thou art spoiling it for me.'

The smith was taken aback, and knowing not what to reply, he gathered his things together and returned to his work. And now if he wisheth to sing, he singeth Tristan or Lancelot, and leaveth Dante alone.

THE BARGELLO

The Bargello (entrance in Via del Proconsolo) was originally built as the Palace of the Podestà, the chief criminal magistrate of Florence. After the abolition of the office of Podestà by Cosimo I, the palace became the headquarters of the Bargello or chief of police.

More than a century ago the Bargello became the Museo Nazionale – a change of which Henry James could not wholly approve:

> Beautiful and masterful though the Bargello is, it smells too strongly of restoration, and, much of old Italy as still lurks in its furbished and renovated chambers, it speaks even more distinctly of the ill-mannered young kingdom that has – as 'unavoidably' as you please – lifted down a hundred delicate works of sculpture from the convent-walls where their pious authors placed them. . . . The Bargello is full of early Tuscan sculpture, most of the pieces of which have come from suppressed religious houses; and even if the visitor be an ardent liberal, he is uncommonly conscious of the rather brutal process by which it has been collected. One can hardly envy young Italy the number of odious things she has had to do.

In his Journal for December 1895, André Gide describes a visit to the Bargello where he gazed, enraptured, at the *David*:

> Wonderful *David* of Donatello! Small bronze body! ornamented nudity; Oriental grace; shadow of the hat over the eyes, in which the source of his glance is lost and become immaterial. Smile on the lips; softness of the cheeks.
>
> His small delicate body with its rather frail and strained grace – hardness of the bronze – the figured armor-plate on the legs covering only the calf and permitting the thigh to rise from it more tender by contrast.
>
> The very strangeness of that immodest accoutrement, and the taut nervousness of the little arms, which hold either the stone or the sabre. I should like to call him up

before me at will. For a long time I observed – trying to memorize, to retain within me those charming lines, that fold of the abdomen immediately under the ribs hollowed out when he breathes, and even that leanness of the muscle joining the top of the breast to the right shoulder – and that somewhat broken fold at the top of the thigh – and that extraordinary flatness of the loins immediately above the sacrum . . .

The rich and elderly connoisseur, Eustace, one of the leading characters in Aldous Huxley's *Time Must Have A Stop* (1945), decides 'to pop into the Bargello for a moment after a visit to Vieusseux's Lending Library':

Ten minutes were enough to whizz around the Donatellos and, his head full of heroic bronze and marble, he strolled up the street in the direction of the bookshop [owned in the novel by a 'Bruno Rontini', based on the real-life Pino Orioli, friend of D. H. Lawrence, Norman Douglas, and many other English writers].

Yes, it would have been nice, he was thinking, it would have been very nice indeed if one's life had the quality of those statues. Nobility without affectation. Serenity combined with passionate energy. Dignity wedded to grace. But, alas, those were not precisely the characteristics that one's life had exhibited. Which was regrettable no doubt. But of course it had its compensating advantages. Being a Donatello would have been altogether too strenuous for his taste. That sort of thing was much more John's cup of tea [a left-wing journalist] – John who had always seen himself as the equivalent of a mixture between Gattamelata and the Baptist. Instead of which, his actual life was . . . what? Eustace cast about for the answer, and finally decided that John's life was best compared to a war picture by one of those deplorable painters who were born to be magazine illustrators but had unfortunately seen the Cubists and taken to High Art. Poor John! He had no taste, no sense of style . . .

SANTA CROCE

The church and cloisters of Santa Croce are often referred to as
the Westminster Abbey of Florence. Madame de Staël wrote:
'This church of Santa Croce contains the most brilliant
assembly of corpses in perhaps the whole of Italy.' Here,
among many other illustrious people, lie Lorenzo Ghiberti,
Michelangelo, Galileo, and Alfieri. It was in reference to such
as these that Leigh Hunt wrote: 'The church of Santa Croce
would disappoint you as much inside as out, if the presence of
great men did not always cast a mingled shadow of the awful
and beautiful over our thoughts.'

In the fourth canto of *Childe Harold's Pilgrimage*, Byron
referred both to the illustrious Florentines who had found their
final resting place in Santa Croce and to those who, scandal-
ously, had failed to do so:

> But where repose the all-Etruscan three –
> Dante, and Petrarch, and scarce less than they,
> The Bard of Prose, creative spirit, he
> Of the Hundred Tales of love – where did they lay
> Their bones, distinguished from our common clay
> In death as life? Are they resolved to dust,
> And have their country's marbles nought to say?
> Could not her quarries furnish forth one bust?
> Did they not to her breast their filial earth entrust?

> Ungrateful Florence! Dante sleeps afar,
> Like Scipio, buried by the upbraiding shore:
> The factions, in their worse than civil war,
> Proscribed the bard whose name for evermore
> Their children's children would in vain adore
> With the remorse of ages; and the crown
> Which Petrarch's laureate brow supremely wore,
> Upon a far and foreign soil had grown,
> His life, his grave, though rifled – not thine own.

> Boccaccio to his parent earth bequeathed
> His dust, – and lies it not her great among,
> With many a sweet and solemn requiem breathed

O'er him who formed the Tuscan siren's tongue,
That music in itself, whose sounds are song,
The poetry of speech? No; even in his tomb
Uptorn must bear the hyaena bigot's wrong,
No more amidst the meaner dead find room,
Nor claim a passing sigh, because it told for *whom*!

One of the most interesting tombs is that of the great Italian poet and dramatist Alfieri (1749–1803), erected by Canova at the behest of Alfieri's lover, the Countess of Albany. Alfieri had declared that the love of fame first came to him as he was walking among the tombs of the illustrious dead in this church. The Countess herself sat to Canova for the figure of bereaved Italy. Her story is told with dry irony by E. V. Lucas:

This curious and unfortunate woman became, at the age of nineteen, the wife of the Young Pretender, twenty-seven years after the '45, and led a miserable existence with him (due chiefly to his depravity, but a little, she always held, to the circumstance that they chose Good Friday for their wedding day) until Alfieri fell in love with her and offered her his protection. Together she and the poet remained, apparently contented with each other and received by society, even by the English Royal Family, until Alfieri died in 1803, when after exclaiming that she had lost all – 'consolations, support, society, all, all!' – and establishing this handsome memorial, she selected the French artist Fabre to fill the aching void in her fifty-years-old heart; and Fabre not only filled it until her death in 1824, but became the heir to all that had been bequeathed to her by both the Stuart and Alfieri. Such was the Countess of Albany. She herself is buried close by, in the chapel of the Castellani.

Of Alfieri's monument Sophia Hawthorne wrote: 'It is not good for anything to me.' Now it is regarded as one of Canova's greatest works.

In the Palazzo Masetti (Castelbarco), now the home of the British Consulate, on the Lung' Arno, the Countess and Fabre maintained a *salon*, frequented by such literary celebrities as

Chateaubriand, Foscolo, and Von Platen. But increasingly dissatisfied with each other and therefore with life, they became a sour, gloomy couple. One of their writer guests, Massimo d'Azeglio, gave an amusing account of a visit paid to them. Arriving late, he heard the Countess exclaim to Prince Borghese: 'What an hour to arrive!' Overcome, d'Azeglio hurried over to the buffet, to help himself to an ice. The ices on offer were those especially hard ones called *mattonelle* ('little bricks'), on this occasion modelled into the shape of peaches. D'Azeglio takes up the story:

> While I was vainly striving to make an impression on my ice with the spoon, what does it do but slip off from under it, like a cherry-stone that is snapped? I see it now, bounding against the minister's diamond cross (the Sardinian Minister in Tuscany was standing by him), falling to the floor, and rolling straight to the Countess of Albany's feet. I felt as if I should never leave off running. That was my last visit.

It was in the Palazzo Masetti that Alfieri died in 1803. Delirious, his hand in that of the mistress who had finally become his wife, he miraculously recited one hundred verses of Hesiod, read only once in his youth, before he expired. It is a wonder that, during the recitation, the Countess did not herself expire of boredom.

Another interesting monument in Santa Croce is that by Bernardo Rossellino to Leonardo Bruni, known as Aretino. Unlike many of the others in this church, it is contemporary, dating from Aretino's death in 1444. Described by John Addington Symonds as 'the nearest approach to a really great figure in the Florentine literary world of the first half of the fifteenth century', Aretino was the translator of Plato and Aristotle, the author of a Latin history of Florence, and the first biographer of Dante.

In E. M. Forster's *A Room with a View*, the heroine Lucy Honeychurch and her companion Miss Lavish, a novelist who is constantly saying that she knows her Florence 'by heart', lose their way to Santa Croce, as many tourists have done both before them and since. Miss Lavish cries out:

'Lost! Lost! My dear Miss Lucy, during our political diatribes we have taken a wrong turning. How those horrid Conservatives would jeer at us! What are we to do? Two lone females in an unknown town. Now, this is what *I* call an adventure.'

Lucy, who wanted to see Santa Croce, suggested as a possible solution that they should ask the way there.

'Oh, but that is the word of a craven! And no, you are not, not, *not* to look at your Baedeker. Give it to me; I shan't let you carry it. We will simply drift.'

Accordingly they drifted through a series of those gray-brown streets, neither commodious nor picturesque, in which the eastern quarter of the city abounds. Lucy soon lost interest in the discontent of Lady Louisa, and became discontented herself. For one ravishing moment Italy appeared. She stood in the Square of the Annunziata and saw in the living terra cotta those divine babies whom no reproduction can ever stale. There they stood, with their shining limbs bursting from the garments of charity, and their strong white arms extended against circlets of heaven. Lucy thought she had never seen anything more beautiful; but Miss Lavish, with a shriek of dismay, dragged her forward, declaring that they were out of their path now by at least a mile.

The hour was approaching at which the continental breakfast begins, or rather ceases, to tell, and the ladies bought some hot chestnut paste out of a little shop, because it looked so typical. It tasted partly of the paper in which it was wrapped, partly of hair oil, partly of the great unknown. But it gave them strength to drift into another Piazza, large and dusty, on the farther side of which rose a black-and-white facade of surpassing ugliness. Miss Lavish spoke to it dramatically. It was Santa Croce. The adventure was over.

But before the two women can enter, Miss Lavish catches a glimpse of what she calls 'my local colour-box' – an old man with white whiskers – and hurries off in pursuit. Abandoned,

Lucy awaits her return; then, after ten minutes, enters the church alone.

Of course, it must be a wonderful building. But how like a barn! And how very cold! Of course, it contained frescoes by Giotto, in the presence of whose tactile values she was capable of feeling what was proper. But who was to tell her which they were? She walked about disdainfully, unwilling to be enthusiastic over monuments of uncertain authorship or date. There was no one even to tell her which, of all the sepulchral slabs that paved the nave and transepts, was the one that was really beautiful, the one that had been most praised by Mr Ruskin.

Then the pernicious charm of Italy worked on her, and instead of acquiring information, she began to be happy. She puzzled out the Italian notices – the notice that forbade people to introduce dogs into the church – the notice that prayed people in the interest of health and out of respect to the sacred edifice in which they found themselves, not to spit. She watched the tourists; their noses were as red as their Baedekers, so cold was Santa Croce. She beheld the horrible fate that befell three Baptists – two he-babies and a she-baby – who began their career by sousing each other with the Holy Water, and then proceeded to the Machiavelli memorial, dripping but hallowed. Advancing toward it very slowly and from immense distances, they touched the stone with their fingers, with their handkerchiefs, with their heads, and then retreated. What could this mean? They did it again and again. Then Lucy realised that they had mistaken Machiavelli for some saint, hoping to acquire virtue. Punishment followed quickly. The smallest he-baby stumbled over one of the sepulchral slabs so much admired by Mr Ruskin, and entangled his feet in the features of a recumbent bishop. Protestant as she was, Lucy darted forward. She was too late. He fell heavily upon the prelate's upturned toes.

Ruskin did indeed admire some of the sepulchral slabs; but there was much that he did not admire, haranguing his readers:

See those huge tombs on your right hand and left, with their alternate gables and round tops, and the paltriest of all possible sculpture, trying to be grand by bigness, and pathetic by expense.

During the course of the section entitled *Le Séjour à Florence*, the eponymous heroine of Madame de Staël's *Corinne* visits Santa Croce. Corinne is a woman of such a variety of talents – poet, musician, dancer, actress – that it is hardly surprising that a young Englishman called Oswald, travelling in Italy for his health, should fall in love with her, and extremely surprising that he should later abandon her for her half-sister, Lucile.

The sight of this church, adorned with so many noble memorials, reawakened Corinne's enthusiasm. Whereas the faces of the living had discouraged, so now the silent presence of these dead reanimated in her the craving for glory with which she had formerly been seized. She walked with a firmer tread through the church, and thoughts from the past once more traversed her spirit. She saw appear under the vault some young priests, who were chanting in deep voices even as they moved at a slow pace round the choir. She asked one of them what was the meaning of their ceremony. 'We are praying for our dead,' he answered her. 'Yes, you are right to remember your dead,' Corinne thought to herself. 'They make up the only glorious possession left to you. . . . Oh, why has Oswald snuffed out those gifts which I received from heaven, and which I ought to use to awake enthusiasm in souls in tune with mine? Oh, my God!,' she cried out, as she threw herself on her knees, 'it is not at all in empty pride that I beg you to return to me those talents with which you originally blessed me. Undoubtedly the most superior of all beings are those obscure saints who know how to live and die for You and You alone. But the path for ordinary mortals is different, so that the spirit which dedicates itself to generosity and goodness, to all that is noble, humane and true, can surely be admitted at least into the outer courts of heaven.' Corinne's eyes were lowered as she uttered this prayer, and it was thus that she was struck by the inscription on the tomb on which she was kneeling. It ran as follows: 'Alone at my dawn, alone at my setting, I am again alone here.'

'Ah!' Corinne cried out to herself, 'here is the answer to my prayer! What ambition can one feel when one is alone on the earth? Who would share in my success, if I was able to achieve it? Who would be concerned in my fate? What feeling would encourage my spirit to labour? I must have Oswald's approval for reward.'

Another epitaph caught her eye. 'Do not grieve for me,' enjoined a man who had died in his youth. 'If only you knew how much pain this tomb has spared me.' 'What a detachment from life these words inspire!' thought Corinne, shedding tears. So close to all the bustle of the town, there is this church, which teaches people the secret of everything, if only they have ears to hear it. But they pass by without entering, and the marvellous illusion of forgetfulness keeps the world turning.'

The cloister, in which can be found monuments of minor Florentine celebrities, has always appealed to visitors. W. D. Howells wrote of it in his *Tuscan Cities*:

There is nothing more Florentine in Florence than these old convent courts into which your sight-seeing takes you so often. The middle space is enclosed by sheltering cloisters, and here the grass lies green in the sun the whole winter through, with daisies in it, and other sympathetic little weeds or flowers; the still air is warm, and the place has a climate of its own.

Most visitors would regard Santa Croce as a monument both to the Christian faith and to the cultural greatness of Florence. But perversely the hero, Evans (Dev), of William Carlos Williams's 1928 *Voyage to Pagany* finds in it chiefly 'a resurgent paganism'.

Having pushed upon the church's soiled red leather inner doors and then let them close behind him, he is

overtaken by an emotional reaction, striking back upon him across that rolling floor, that lifted him into an enchantment he would never cease to recall thereafter as long as he should live – nor to enjoy.

He escaped wholly at that first moment the feeling of a church. A double row of widely spaced hexagonal columns held up the flat beamed middle ceiling painted with crude colours, a dark and intricate design of blue and red and gold, orange and green and red; it might have been the flat roof of an old temple. But the floor of worn mosaics, uneven, undulant, irregular, the tomb of saints over whose effigies in bronze and marble he walked; and in the side walls other famous tombs – of Dante, the Medici; the Pantheon of Florence; it seemed all to him a savage, spacious present; direct, puissant – overwhelming, free, free somehow of all that which he hated.

Viewing the altar and the chapels on either side of it, Dev – who is, the author tells us, 'unable to tell the Giotto from the Cimabue' – is 'carried away by awe and antiquity,' and feels, exultantly, 'a beauty that by its simplicity, not softened, reached back truly outside of church into a sunlight which he identified by his earliest uncaptured instincts.'

Being so huge, the Piazza Santa Croce has always been a centre for festivities and ceremonies: tournaments, jousts, and games of *calcio* (football) on the one hand, penitential processions of the victims of the Inquisition on the other. In his *Letters on Italy* (1820), the French painter and writer Antoine Laurent Castellan (1772–1838) has left us an account of the celebration there of the annual Carnival:

. . . We have descriptions of many of these festivals; and amongst others, of a magnificent masquerade given by Cosimo I in the carnival of 1565; the carnival of 1615 has been engraved by Callot, and many others have exercised the gravers of La Bella. The taste for these amusements was so great that during the reign of Ferdinand II and in the space of five months, six fetes of different kinds were given, each more magnificent than the preceding.

The square of Santa Croce is surrounded with a boundary of chains, which leave sufficient space for the passage of carriages before the houses. On certain occasions

amphitheatres are raised, round which also carriages can
drive. The square was thus laid out in 1738 for the last
festival of the *Calzio* or foot-ball, which has been engraved by Gioseppe Zocchi. This print gives a good idea
of the masquerades of Florence. Besides the harlequins
and punchinellos, which the French have in such numbers, the other characters are very various and well kept
up.

All ranks, without exception, are turned into ridicule.
A carriage filled with porters has a judge dressed in a long
robe and large wig, for a coachman. A physician is
mounted on a lean ass, with panniers and cages filled with
cats, and carrying a long staff, from which some large
dead rats are suspended, while a scroll on the top of it
bears the words *Remedi di topi*, 'antidotes against rats:' to
these may be added doctors with asses' heads. The spectators themselves form a spectacle; the windows of the
houses, and the balconies of the palaces, are all
ornamented with rich tapestry, and graced with brilliant
company. The people cover the tiles of the houses, and on
these aerial theatres engage in games, from which Italian
confidence and address take away all danger, and which
afford a very diverting appearance.

The spectacle which we ourselves saw was very agreeable. The carriages, which throng the road, give great
brilliancy to the scene; they are filled with masks who
answer the joy and acclamations of the multitude by
throwing them cakes and *confetti*, and by sprinkling
showers of perfumed water from little syringes towards
the spectators who line the windows and the balconies:
some of the carriages contain musicians, and others are in
the shape of triumphal cars, ornamented with different
symbols.

In 1874 Henry James was far less impressed with what he
called 'that languid organism known as the Florentine Carnival':

I encountered the line of carriages in the square before
Santa Croce, of which they were making the circuit.

They rolled solemnly by, with their inmates frowning at each other in apparent wrath at not finding each other more amusing. There were no masks, no costumes, no decorations, no throwing of flowers or sweetmeats. It was as if each carriageful had privately resolved to be inexpensive, and was rather discomfited at finding that it was getting no better entertainment than it gave. The middle of the piazza was filled with little tables, with shouting mountebanks, mostly disguised in battered bonnets and crinolines, offering chances in raffles for plucked fowls and kerosene lamps. I have never thought the huge marble statue of Dante, which overlooks the scene, a work of the least refinement; but, as it stood there on its high pedestal, chin in hand, frowning down on all this cheap foolery, it seemed to have a great moral intention.

In his *Ilex and Olive* Michael Swan, then in his early twenties, gives an account of a visit to Santa Croce in 1947:

It was half-past two and the sun was glaring in the piazza . . . In the shadow on the top step of the church a young man was asleep with his head slumped on his shoulder and his mouth wide open. I tried to open the enormous door but it was locked, so I sat in another shadow and waited for the sacristan to open it. Just as I had fallen into a doze I was woken by the drawing of bolts and through the door peered a young, smiling, bespectacled monk. I got up and he politely ushered me into the church; I had gone only four steps before he spoke to me, asking if I were German. I told him I was English and he pointed to my hair, which had been bleached by the sun, and said, 'You look like a German, tee-hee-hee' – his laugh was like a zany's. I was wearing short trousers to reduce the fatigue of sightseeing in the intense heat, and he looked at my legs. I looked down, too, as he did so, to see what extraordinary thing he had seen in them and as I did so he suddenly bent down and plucked at a bunch of hair on my left calf. Before I could say anything and by way of explanation he pulled up his cassock and revealed a pair of white and quite hairless legs. 'Look,' he said, 'I have no

hair at all on my legs.' I was, however far more interested
in the fact that he supported his socks with a pair of
inferior and secular suspenders. 'You're lucky,' he went
on, 'you have hair on your legs – I don't,' and his red face
beamed benevolently. Suddenly his right index finger
was stuck in my stomach with a little noise and a laugh.
He talked for a little in French, attempted to pull a few
more hairs from my legs and then offered me a historical
leaflet. His salesmanship was eccentric but successful. I
left him to examine the church which is vast and, immediately, of little interest. The wooden beams which
support the roof are barbarous. It is the First Church of
the Franciscans and has a Franciscan simplicity; no side
chapels, except in the chancel, little ornamentation. Apart
from the Giottos and the stained glass it is the tombs
which are of most interest. Michelangelo lies here, on a
spot chosen by himself because from it he might see,
through the open door, the cupola of the Cathedral. But
the interest of the tombs is sentimental rather than aesthetic, and soon I was in the little Capella Peruzzi looking
at the miraculous Giotto frescoes. It was, however, a
pleasure too exquisite to last; suddenly I felt an index
finger between my third and fourth rib and a little sound
accompanied it.

'You like Giotto, tee-hee-hee?' inquired the sacristan.

'Yes,' I replied, simply and sharply.

He asked me if he might take me for a tour round the
gallery – a circumambulation which I did not relish and
managed to refuse. Then he noticed my camera. Bless-
edly he seemed never to have seen a similar camera; I
handed it to him and he examined it most earnestly. '*Magnifico! Magnifico!*' he mumbled to himself and while he
continued to examine it I returned to Giotto. When I
had finished he asked me very seriously if he might take
a photograph and beamed when I agreed. We went into a
chapel and he reverently placed me on the first step of the
altar with a Virgin and Child by Andrea della Robbia
behind me. Unfortunately the photograph turned out a
complete blank.

The North-eastern Quarter

OR SAN MICHELE

The church of Or San Michele, originally San Michele in Orto or San Michele in the orchard, was erected in 1380. There is dispute as to its architect, with Taddeo Gaddi, Orcagna and Francesco Talenti and his son Simone all having claims to have built it. Richard Lassels describes a visit:

> Going from the Piazza towards the Duomo, we were presently stopped by the church of St Michael, a square flat church, whose outside is adorned with rare statues, if not of gold, yet worth their weight in gold. The best are, that of S. Matthew in brass made by Laurentius Cion; that of S. Thomas in brass touching the side of our Saviour, with great demonstrations of diffidence in his looks, is of Andrea Verrocchio's hand. That of S. George in marble is compared to the best in Rome, and hath been praised both in prose and verse.

Some two hundred years later, Hawthorne was to describe his own visit:

> We went into the church of San Michele, and saw in its architecture the traces of its transformation from a market into a church. In its pristine state it consisted of a double row of three great open arches, with the wind blowing through them, and the sun falling aslantwise into them,

while the bustle of the market, the sale of fish, flesh or
fruit went on within, or brimmed over into the streets
that enclosed them on every side. But, four or five
hundred years ago, the broad arches were built up with
stone-work; windows were pierced through and filled
with painted glass; a high altar, in a rich style of pointed
Gothic, was raised; shrines and confessionals were set up;
and here it is, a solemn and antique church, where a man
may buy his salvation instead of his dinner . . .

It appears that a picture of the Virgin used to hang
against one of the pillars of the market-place, while it was
still a market, and in the year 1292, several miracles were
wrought by it, insomuch that a chapel was consecrated
for it. So many worshippers came to the shrine that the
business of the market was impeded, and ultimately the
Virgin and St Michael won the whole space for themselves. The upper part of the edifice was at that time a
granary, and is still used for other than religious purposes.
This church was one spot to which the inhabitants betook
themselves much for refuge and assistance during the
great plague described by Boccaccio.

Ouida's *Pascarel* contains a characteristically overwrought
but perceptive passage about the church and about one of its
chief glories, Donatello's statue of *St George* – in complete
armour but without sword or lance, bare-headed, and leaning
on his shield, which displays the cross.

Or San Michele would have been a world's wonder had it
stood alone, and not been companioned with such wondrous rivals that its own exceeding beauty scarce ever
receives full justice.

Surely that square-set strength, as of a fortress, tower-
ing against the clouds, and catching the last light always
on its fretted parapet, and everywhere embossed and
enriched with foliage, and tracery, and figures of saints,
and the shadows of vast arches, and the light of niches
gold-starred and filled with divine forms, is a gift so
perfect to the whole world, that, passing it, one should
need say a prayer for the great Taddeo's soul.

Surely nowhere is the rugged, changeless, mountain force of hewn stone piled against the sky, and the luxuriant, dream-like, poetic delicacy of stone carven and shaped into leafage and loveliness, more perfectly blended and made one than where Or San Michele rises out of the dim, many-coloured, twisting streets, in its mass of ebon darkness and of silvery light.

The other day under the walls of it I stood, and looked at its Saint George, where he leans upon his shield, so calm, so young, with his bared head and quiet eyes.

'That is our Donatello's,' said a Florentine beside me – a man of the people, who drove a horse for hire in the public ways, and who paused, cracking his whip to tell his tale to me. 'Donatello did that, and it killed him. Do you know that? When he had done that Saint George he showed it to his master. And the master said, "It wants one thing only." Now, this saying our Donatello took gravely to heart, chiefly of all because his master would never explain where the fault lay; and so much did it hurt him, that he fell ill, and came nigh to death. Then he called his master to him. "Dear and great one, do tell me before I die," he said, "what is the one thing my statue lacks." The master smiled, and said, "Only – speech." "Then I die happy," said our Donatello. And he – died – indeed, that hour.'

Now, I cannot say that the pretty story is true; it is not in the least true; Donatello died when he was eighty-three, in the street of the Melon; and it was he himself who cried, 'Speak, then – speak!' to his statue, as it was carried through the city. But whether true or false the tale, this fact is surely true, that it is well – nobly and purely well – with a people, when the men amongst it who ply for hire on its public ways think caressingly of a sculptor dead five hundred years ago, and tell such a tale standing idly in the noonday sun, feeling the beauty and the pathos of it all.

'Our Donatello' still for the people of Florence – 'Our own little Donatello' still, as though he were living and working in their midst today, here in the shadow of the

Stocking-Makers' street, where his Saint George keeps watch and ward.

Because of the ravages of the weather, *St George* no longer keeps watch and ward in his original position but is now in the Bargello. A bronze copy of the marble is now in the niche.

The Cathedral, the Baptistery, the Campanile of Giotto

Florence at the end of the thirteenth century was a city of growing commercial and political importance – and swelling civic pride. Santa Reparata, the cathedral deemed sufficient at the time of Dante's birth in 1265, was now held by the Signoria to be 'crudely built and too small for such a city.' Such a city as Florence had become plainly needed a new cathedral, one to rival those at Siena and Pisa, one which would, in the words of the Signoria, 'possess the utmost and most sumptuous magnificence.' With this hyperbolic mandate as his guide, the master architect Arnolfo di Cambio conceived an enormous new cathedral rising, according to the French model, from clover-leaf foundations. Arnolfo, who died in 1302, just as those foundations were being laid and the courses rising upon them, did not live to see his plans brought to fruition. But then no one involved in the planning did. The present façade, by Emilio de Fabris, dates only from 1887, a part of its cost having been born by Thomas Trollope's friend Stanley Sloane, who had first arrived in Italy as tutor to the Russian Bourtourlin family and had subsequently made a fortune out of copper mines near Volterra.

An early view of the Duomo is given in Richard Lassels's *The Voyage of Italy* (1670):

> On the top of it stands mounted a fair cupola (or *tholus*) made by Brunelleschi, a Florentine. This was the first cupola in Europe; and therefore the more admirable for having no idea after which it could be framed; and for being the idea of that of St Peter's in Rome, after which so many young cupolas in Rome, and elsewhere, have been

made since. Hence it is said that Michael Angelo coming
now and then to Florence (his native country) while he
was making the cupola in Rome of St Peter's church, and
viewing attentively this cupola of Florence, used to say of
it: *Come te non voglio, meglio di te non posso.* [Similar to thee
I will not; better than thee I cannot]. It's said also that
Brunelleschi, making this cupola, caused taverns, cook
shops and lodgings to be set in it, that the workmen might
find all things necessary there, and not spend time in
going up and down . . .

Near the close of the eighteenth century, William Beckford
made the observation, repeated by many writers after him,
that 'The architect seems to have turned his building inside
out; nothing in art being more ornamented than the exterior,
and few churches so simple within.' He continues:

> The nave is vast and solemn, the dome amazingly
> spacious, with the high altar in its centre, inclosed by a
> circular arcade near two hundred feet in diameter. There
> is something imposing in this decoration, as it suggests
> the idea of a sanctuary, into which none but the holy
> ought to penetrate. However profane I might feel myself,
> I took the liberty of entering, and sat myself down in a
> niche. Not a ray of light reaches this sacred inclosure, but
> through the medium of narrow windows, high in the
> dome and richly painted.

Viewing the Duomo and its surroundings in 1860, George
Eliot wrote in her diary:

> Apart from its venerable historical glory, the exterior of
> the Duomo is pleasant to behold when the wretched
> unfinished facade is quite hidden. The soaring pinnacles
> over the doors are exquisite; so are the forms of the
> windows in the great semi-circle of the apsis; and on the
> side where especially the white marble has taken on so
> rich and deep a yellow, that the black bands cease to be felt
> as a fault. The entire view on this side, closed in by
> Giotto's tower, with its delicate pinkish marble, its deli-
> cate Gothic windows with twisted columns, and its tall

lightness carrying the eye upward, in contrast with the mighty breadth of the dome, is a thing not easily to be forgotten . . .

One of the most vivid scenes in *Romola* takes place in the Duomo, with Savonarola preaching to a crowded and rapt congregation. Having escaped from prison and seeking sanctuary, old Baldassare enters the Duomo:

He had expected to see a vast nave empty of everything but lifeless emblems – side altars with candles unlit, dim pictures, pale and rigid statues – with perhaps a few worshippers in the distant choir following a monotonous chant. That was the ordinary aspect of churches to a man who never went into them with any religious purpose.

And he saw, instead, a vast multitude of warm, living faces, upturned in breathless silence towards the pulpit, at the angle between the nave and the choir. The multitude was of all ranks, from magistrates and dames of gentle nurture to coarsely-clad artisans and country people. In the pulpit was a Dominican friar, with strong features and dark hair, preaching with the crucifix in his hand.

The Dominican friar is Savonarola; and he exhorts his congregation in the style, no doubt familiar to George Eliot from her youth, of some non-conformist preacher of mid-Victorian times. Seemingly as much intoxicated with his eloquence as the crowds ranged before him, Savonarola reaches his peroration:

'Listen, O people, over whom my heart yearns, as the heart of a mother over the children she has travailed for! God is my witness that but for your sakes I would willingly live as a turtle in the depths of the forest, singing low to my Beloved, who is mine and I am his. For you I toil, for you I languish, for you my nights are spent in watching, and my soul melteth away in very heaviness. O Lord, thou knowest I am willing – I am ready. Take me, stretch me on thy cross: let the wicked who delight in blood, and rob the poor, and defile the temple of their bodies, and harden themselves against thy mercy – let

them wag their heads and shoot out the lip at me: let the
thorns press upon my brow, and let my sweat be anguish
– I desire to be made like thee in thy great love. But let me
see the fruit of my travail – let this people be saved! . . .
Come, O blessed promise; and behold, I am willing – lay
me on thy altar: let my blood flow and the fire consume
me; but let my witness be remembered among men, that
iniquity shall not prosper for ever.'

Baldassare, the victim of an oppressive tyranny, thrills to
Savonarola's denunciation of it:

Among all the human beings present, there was perhaps
not one whose frame vibrated more strongly than his to
the tones and words of the preacher; but it had vibrated
like a harp of which all the strings had been wrenched
away except one. That threat of a fiery inexorable
vengeance – of a future into which the hated sinner might
be pursued and held by the avenger in an eternal grapple,
had come to him like the promise of an unquenchable
fountain to unquenchable thirst.

Baldissare feels at one with the speaker, as he cries out
within him: 'Let my blood flow; let the fire consume me!'
Then he too, along with everyone else in the vast cathedral,
bursts into sobs.

W. D. Howells was little impressed by the Duomo, calling
it 'a temple to damp the spirit, dead or alive, by the immense
impression of stony bareness, of drab vacuity, which one
receives from its interior, unless it is filled with people.' Mark
Twain was even less impressed, his natural egalitarianism
outraged by the contrast between the poverty of the average
Florentine and the richness of the church:

Look at the grand Duomo of Florence – a vast pile that has
been sapping the purses of her citizens for five hundred
years and is not nearly finished yet. Like all other men, I
fell down and worshipped it, but when the filthy beggars
swarmed around me the contrast was too striking, too

suggestive, and I said, 'O, sons of classic Italy, *is* the spirit of enterprise, of self-reliance, of noble endeavour, utterly dead within ye? Why don't you rob your church?' Three hundred happy, comfortable priests are employed in that cathedral.

Ruskin was appalled by the contrast between the sublimity of the buildings which make up the Piazza and the squalor of the daily life within it:

Of living Greek work there is none after the Florentine Baptistery; of living Christian work, none so perfect as the Tower of Giotto; and, under the gleam and shadow of their marbles, the morning light was haunted by the ghosts of the Father of Natural Science, Galileo; of Sacred Art, Angelico, and the Master of Sacred Song, Dante. Which spot of ground the modern Florentine has made his principal hackney coach stand and omnibus station. The hackney coaches, with their more or less farmyard-like litter of occasional hay, and smell of variously mixed horse-manure, are yet in more permissible harmony with the place than the ordinary populace of a fashionable promenade would be, with its cigars, spitting, and harlot-planned fineries: but the omnibus place of call being in front of the door of the tower, renders it impossible to stand for a moment near it, to look at the sculptures of the eastern or southern side; while the north side is enclosed with an iron railing, and usually encumbered with lumber as well: not a soul in Florence ever caring now for sight of any piece of its old artist's work; and the mass of strangers being on the whole intent on nothing but getting the omnibus to go by steam; and so seeing the cathedral in one swift circuit, by glimpses between the puffs of it.

On these comments Henry James took issue with Ruskin, as he was often to do:

This fact [that 'the little square in front of the Cathedral . . . is now the resort of a number of hackney-carriages and omnibuses'] is doubtless lamentable, and it would be a hundred times more agreeable to see among people who have been made the heirs of as priceless a work of art as the sublime campanile some such feeling about it as would keep it free even from the danger of defilement. A cab-stand is a very ugly and dirty thing, and Giotto's tower should have nothing in common with such conveniences. But there is more than one way of taking such things, and the sensitive stranger who has been walking about for a week with his mind full of the sweetness and suggestiveness of a hundred Florentine places may feel at last in looking into Mr Ruskin's little tracts that, discord for discord, there isn't much to choose between the importunity of the author's personal ill-humour and the incongruity of horse-pails and bundles of hay.

When Dickens visited the piazza of the Duomo, he noticed 'an irregular kind of market' being held there, with 'stores of old iron and other small merchandise set out on stalls.' He also noticed, set into the pavement, the *Sasso di Dante* or 'Stone of Dante', marking the place where legend has it that Dante sat and gazed at the Cathedral. He puts a jocular reference to the *Sasso* in *Little Dorrit*: '. . . Dante – known to that gentleman [Mr Sparkler] as an eccentric man in the nature of an Old File, who used to put leaves round his head, and sit upon a stool for some unaccountable purpose, outside the cathedral at Florence.'

The *Sasso di Dante* inspired several English poets, among them Wordsworth, who, visiting Florence with Crabb Robinson in 1837, sat on the *Sasso* and then wrote a sonnet about the experience:

> Under the shadow of a stately Pile,
> The dome of Florence, pensive and alone,
> Nor giving heed to aught that passed the while,
> I stood, and gazed upon a marble stone,
> The laurelled Dante's favourite seat. A throne,
> In just esteem, it rivals; though no style
> Be there of decoration to beguile
> The mind, depressed by thought of greatness flown.
> As a true man, who long had served the lyre,
> I gazed with earnestness, and dared no more.

But in this breast the mighty Poet bore
A Patriot's heart, warm with undying fire.
Bold with the thought, in reverence I sate down,
And, for a moment, filled that empty Throne.

The *Sasso* is now let into a nearby wall, to prevent undue obstruction of the pavement. Beside it is a café, much frequented by tourists in search of restoration and relief, called *Il Sasso di Dante*.

Still in Ouida's day (*Pascarel*, 1873), as in Dickens's, the piazza of the Duomo was a centre not merely for reverential tourists but for the day-to-day life of a populous and busy city:

About the Duomo there is stir and strife at all times; crowds come and go; men buy and sell; lads laugh and fight; piles of fruit blaze gold and crimson; metal pails clash down on the stones with shrillest clangour; on the steps boys play at dominoes, and women give their children food, and merry-makers join in carnival fooleries; but there in the midst is the Duomo all unharmed and undegraded, a poem and a prayer in one, its marbles shining in the upper air, a thing so majestic in its strength, and yet so human in its tenderness, that nothing can assail and nothing equal it.

On the flank of the Duomo stands the Campanile of Giotto – compared by Hippolyte Taine, 'erect, isolated', to the Tour Saint Michel in Bordeaux and the Tour St Jacques in Paris. When George Eliot visited it in 1860, tourists were still permitted to climb to its top: 'This evening we have been mounting to the top of Giotto's tower – a very sublime getting-upstairs indeed – and our muscles are much astonished at the unusual exercise . . .' [George Eliot to Charles L. Lewes, 27 May 1861].

Originally it had been planned that the tower, already 250 feet high, should have a 30-foot spire. It was to the lack of this spire that Longfellow alluded when he wrote:

In the old Tuscan town stands Giotto's tower,
    The lily of Florence blossoming in stone, –
    A vision of delight, and a desire,

The builder's perfect and centennial flower
That in the night of ages bloomed alone,
But wanting still the glory of the spire.

Browning also alluded to the lack of a spire in his philo-
sophic commentary on Vasari, 'Old Pictures in Florence':

Then one shall propose in a speech (curt Tuscan,
    Expurgate and sober, with scarcely an '*issimo*,')
To end now our half-told tale of Cambuscan,
    And turn the bell-tower's *alt* to *altissimo*:
And fine as the beak of a young beccaccia
    The Campanile, the Duomo's fit ally,
Shall soar up in gold full fifty braccia,
    Completing Florence, as Florence Italy.

Shall I be alive that morning the scaffold
    Is broken away, and the long-pent fire,
Like the golden hope of the world, unbaffled
    Springs from its sleep, and up goes the spire
While 'God and the People' plain for its motto,
    Thence the new tricolour flaps at the sky?
At least to foresee that glory of Giotto
    And Florence together, the first am I!

Ruskin thought that the Campanile was 'the model and
mirror of perfect architecture,' and instructed readers of his
Mornings in Florence: 'Of representations of human art under
heavenly guidance, the series of bas-reliefs which stud the base
of this Tower of Giotto must be held certainly the chief in
Europe . . . Read but these inlaid jewels of Giotto's once with
patient following, and your hour's study will give you
strength for all your life.'

The spirit of Dante haunts the Baptistery, as it does no other
building in Florence: '*il mio bel San Giovanni*' he calls it, and in
the fifteenth canto of *Il Paradiso* his ancestor Cacciaguida tells
him: '. . . in your ancient Baptistery Christian and Cacciaguida I became' (i.e. like Dante himself and countless other
Florentines, he had been baptized there). In Canto XXV of *Il
Paradiso*, Dante makes a reference to his own baptism:

If ever it happen that the sacred song
   Whereto both heaven and earth have set a hand,
   Whereby I am lean these many years and long,
O'ercome the cruelty which keeps me banned
   From the fair sheepfold where I slept, a lamb,
   Foe to the wolves that raven through the land,
With different voice now, nor with fleece the same,
   Shall I return, poet, and at the font
   Of my baptizing shall the chaplet claim
Because into the faith that makes the account
   Of souls to God I won then . . .

It was in the Duomo that, in 1817, the fourteen-year-old Harriet Charlotte Beaujolais, then in Florence with her widowed mother, Lady Charlotte Campbell, attended the wedding of the second daughter of the Grand Duke to the Prince de Carignan – who later became the luckless King Carlo Alberto of Sardinia. This is the account – her misspellings retained – that this precocious girl wrote in her journal:

We went with Miss de la Chaux [her Swiss governess, nicknamed 'Tiranna'] to see what we could. As we were very early nothing had even begun and we chose excellent places upon a temporary platform which had been erected for the occasion around the choir. Opposite the alter there were placed two large arm chairs with cushions at their feet and a table opposite all covered with red velvet. On the right were placed three other chairs one of which was placed on a raised step. On the left there was a small throne. Beyond these seats were ranged rows of benches leaving a space in the middle. Some of these for the court were covered with red cloth. Several English soon came in all dressed or attempting to be dressed in full feathers – such a vulgar representation of our nation I never saw. Mamma and Lady Octavia Law were the only decent ones. Presently the whole of the choir was illuminated with an innumerable quantity of wax tapers. The italian Ladies who sat on the benches placed in front were particularly well dressed with a great profusion of jewels and very good taste. They disgraced the English.

In front of both the alters there were seated a numerous band of musicians who played for a short time. Suddenly a general silence prevailed and the Prince de Carignan followed by several aid de camps &c entered the church. Behind them was the Princess holding her brother's arm and behind them the Grand Duke and his elder daughter who is deformed. The Prince and Princess seated themselves on the chairs opposite the alter, the Grand Duke upon one of those placed on the right, his son at his side and the hunch back daughter next to him. In a few minutes the arch Bishop of Florence entered and seated himself on an arm chair placed on the upper step of the alter. The Prince and Princess placed themselves kneeling at his feet. After a few ceremonies which it was impossible to distinguish the Princess rose and made a curtesy to her father as an indication of asking his leave to marry the Prince. There was then a ring given I could not distinguish by whom and they both rose the ceremony being over. Immediately a Sardinian Princess got up and in the most goodnatured smiling manner began to remove a large fine veil from the Princesses head to mark that she was no longer a damsel. The Archbishop retired for a few minutes and the Prince and Princess retired to their seats. High Mass was then performed during all which time the Princess and her sister remained kneeling and seemed to follow the service with great attention. The Prince looked very uneasy and his new spouse cried all the time although she did her utmost to appear calm. I felt moved at the whole scene and what must have been the feelings of so young a person being only 16 upon so imposing an occasion. Being united for life to a man must ever be an awful step but particularly when every circumstance was united to add to these feelings. The immense crowds who were assembled to gaze upon the scene, the dead silence which prevailed at intervals only interrupted by the trembling voice of the Archbishop, and next the stunning peals of the organ beside the general effect of the Catholic rites were indeed enough to move the hearts of any one. I was extremely delighted when it was over for during the

ceremony I was too much overpowered to enjoy it
thoroughly. I do not think I shall easily forget so striking a
scene.

To anyone who might question the right of this youthful
but far from artless young writer to be included in this book, I
can only reply that her *Journey to Florence in 1817* seems to me to
have as much right to be classified as a work of literature
as Daisy Ashford's *The Young Visiters*, which it so much
resembles in its ardour, its innocence, its snobbery, and the
sharpness of its perceptions.

SAN LORENZO

On June 19, Nathaniel Hawthorne recorded in his Journal:

This forenoon we have been to the church of St Lorenzo,
which stands on the site of an ancient basilica, and was
itself built more than four centuries ago. The facade is still
an ugly height of rough brickwork . . .

His wife Sophia has described the same visit:

The church is undergoing repairs within and without,
and heaps of rubbish were all around. Upon entering I
was very much disappointed in the general effect of the
interior. Indeed it is difficult to be reconciled to the plain
walls, after being accustomed to the magnificent mosaics
of marbles in all Roman churches.

Like most visitors, however, the Hawthornes were pro-
foundly impressed by the new sacristy. Hawthorne wrote of
the statue of Lorenzo de' Medici:

The statue that sits above these two later allegories
[Morning and Evening] is like no other that ever came
from a sculptor's hand. It is the one work worthy of
Michel Angelo's reputation, and grand enough to vindi-
cate for him all the genius that the world gave him credit
for. And yet it seems a simple thing enough to think of or

to execute; merely a sitting figure, the face partly over-shadowed by a helmet, one hand supporting the chin, the other resting on the thigh. But after looking at it a little while, the spectator ceases to think of it as a marble statue; it comes to life, and you see that the princely figure is brooding over some great design, which, when he has arranged his own mind, the world will be fain to execute for him. No such grandeur and majesty have elsewhere been put into human shape. It is all a miracle; the deep repose, and deep life within it. It is as much a miracle to have achieved this as to make a statue that would rise up and walk. The face, when one gazes earnestly into it, beneath the shadow of its helmet, is seen to be calmly sombre; a mood which, I think, is generally that of the rulers of mankind, except in moments of vivid action.

Samuel Rogers wrote twice about this statue of Lorenzo, once in verse and once in prose:

> Nor then forget that Chamber of the Dead,
> Where the gigantic shapes of Night and Day,
> Turned into stone, rest everlastingly;
> Yet still are breathing, and shed round at noon
> A twofold influence – only to be felt –
> A light, a darkness, mingling each with each;
> Both, and yet neither. There, from age to age,
> Two ghosts are sitting on their sepulchres.
> That is the Duke Lorenzo. Mark him well.
> He meditates, his head upon his hand.
> What from beneath his helm-like bonnet scowls?
> Is it a face, or but an eyeless skull?
> 'Tis lost in shade; yet, like the basilisk,
> It fascinates and is intolerable.
> His mien is noble, most majestical!
> Then most so when the distant choir is heard
> At morn or eve – nor fail thou to attend
> On that thrice-hallowed day, when all are there;
> When all, propitiating with solemn songs,
> Visit the Dead. Then wilt thou feel his power.

In prose Rogers wrote:

I am no longer my own master. I am become the slave of a demon. I sit gazing, day after day, on that terrible phantom, the Duke Lorenzo in M. Angelo's chapel. All my better feelings would lead me to the Tribune and the lovely forms that inhabit there. I can dwell with delight on the membra formosa of the Wrestlers, the Fawn and the Apollo, on the sunshine of Titian, the soul of Raphael; but the statue loses none of its influence. He sits, a little reclining from you, his chin resting upon his left hand, his elbows on the arm of his chair. His look is calm and thoughtful, yet it seems to say a something that makes you shrink from it, a something beyond words. Like that of the Basilisk it fascinates – is intolerable.

. . . The visage of Lorenzo under the shade of that scowling and helmet-like bonnet is scarcely visible. You can just discern the likeness of human features; but whether alive or dead, whether a face or a skull, that of a mortal man or a Spirit from heaven or hell, you cannot say. His figure is gigantic and noble, not such as to shock belief or remind you that it is but a statue. It is the most real and unreal thing in stone that ever came from the chisel.

A comparison of these two passages shows how Rogers worked up a spontaneous record in prose into a highly artificial piece of verse. Who would deny that the prose version is far more effective?

Mark Twain, who almost invariably viewed things from a human, not an artistic, standpoint, was less impressed:

They have a grand mausoleum in Florence, which they built to bury our Lord and Saviour and the Medici family in. It sounds blasphemous, but it is true, and there they *act* blasphemy. The dead and damned Medicis who cruelly tyrannised over Florence and were her curse for over two hundred years, are salted away in a circle of costly vaults, and in their midst the Holy Sepulchre was to have been set up. The expedition sent to Jerusalem to seize it got into trouble and could not accomplish the burglary, and so the centre of the mausoleum is vacant now. They say the entire mausoleum was intended for the Holy Sepulchre, and was only turned into a family burying place after the Jerusalem expedition failed – but you will excuse me. Some of those Medicis would have smuggled themselves in sure. – What *they* had not the effrontery to do was not worth doing. Why, they had their trivial, forgotten exploits on land and sea pictured out in grand frescoes (as also did the Doges of Venice) with the Saviour and the Virgin throwing bouquets to them out of the clouds, and the Deity himself applauding from his throne in Heaven! And who painted these things? Titian, Tintoretto, Paul Veronese, Raphael – none other than the world's idols, the 'old masters.'

Andrea del Sarto glorified his princes in pictures that must save them for ever from the oblivion they merited, and they let him starve – a thing by no means to be regretted. Raphael pictured such miscreants as Catherine de Medicis seated in heaven and conversing familiarly with the Virgin Mary and the angels (to say nothing of higher personages), and yet my friends abuse me because I am a little prejudiced against the old masters – because I fail sometimes to see the beauty that is in their productions. I cannot help but see it, now and then, but I keep on protesting against the grovelling spirit that could persuade those masters to prostitute their noble talents to the adulation of such monsters as the French, Venetian, and Florentine princes of two and three hundred years ago, all the same.

I am told that the old masters had to do these shameful things for bread, the princes and potentates being the only patrons of art. If a grandly gifted man may drag his pride and his manhood in the dirt for bread rather than starve with the nobility that is in him untainted, the excuse is a valid one. It would excuse theft in Washingtons and Wellingtons, and unchastity in women as well.

But somehow I cannot keep that Medici mausoleum out of my memory. It is as large as a church; its pavement is rich enough for the pavement of a King's palace; its great dome is gorgeous with frescoes; its walls are made of – what? Marble? – plaster? – wood? – paper? No. Red porphyry – verde antique – jasper – oriental agate – alabaster – mother-of-pearl – chalcedony – red coral – lapis lazuli! All the vast walls are made wholly of these precious stones, worked in, and in and in together in elaborate patterns and figures, and polished till they glow like great mirrors with the pictured splendours reflected from the dome overhead. And before the statue of one of these dead Medicis reposes a crown that blazes with diamonds and emeralds enough to buy a ship-of-the-line almost – if they are genuine. These are the happy things the Government has its evil eye upon, and a happy thing it will be for Italy when they melt away in the public treasury.

And now – . However, another beggar approaches. I will go out and destroy him, and then come back and write another chapter of vituperation . . .

Byron's robust view of the Medici Chapel was that it consisted of 'fine frippery in great slabs of various expensive stones, to commemorate fifty rotten and forgotten carcases.'

For aesthetic, and not political or humanitarian reasons, Augustus Hare also withheld his admiration, in a judgement of astonishing perversity:

The want of architectural power in Michelangelo is no-where more definitely shown than in these monuments. The narrow niches in which the Medici are confined would make it impossible for them to stand upright, and the disproportionate figures below are slipping off the pitiable pedestals which support them.

Of the figure of *Night*, Giovanni Battista Strozzi wrote:

> Carved by an Angel, in this marble white
> Sweetly reposing, lo, the Goddess
>   Night!
> Calmly she sleeps, and so must living be:
> Awake her gently; she will speak to thee.

To this Michelangelo replied with a quatrian of his own:

> Grateful is sleep, whilst wrong and shame survive;
> More grateful still in senseless stone to live;
> Gladly both sight and hearing I forego;
> Oh, then awake me not! Hush! – whisper low.
>
> [Trans. J. C. Wright]

Swinburne devoted a whole poem to San Lorenzo. In his lines on the figure of *Night* he echoed both Strozzi and Michelangelo:

> Is not thine hour come to wake, O slumbering Night?
> Hath not the Dawn a message in thine ear?
> Though thou be stone and sleep, yet shalt thou hear
> When the word falls from heaven – Let there be light.
> Thou knowest we would not do thee the despite
> To wake thee while the old sorrow and shame were
> near;
> We spake not loud for thy sake, and for fear
> Lest thou shouldst lose the rest that was thy right,
> The blessing given thee that was thine alone,
> The happiness to sleep and to be stone:
> Nay, we kept silence of thee for thy sake
> Albeit we knew thee alive, and left with thee
> The great good gift to feel not nor to see;
> But will not yet thine Angel bid thee wake?
>
> [In San Lorenzo]

William Wetmore Story (1819–95), the American sculptor and writer, who was long resident in Italy and whose personality was such that it attracted to him every foreign visitor of note, has left an account of the exhumation of the royal bodies which, in 1791, Ferdinand III had had 'piled together pell-mell in the subterranean vaults of the chapel, caring scarcely to distinguish one from another.' There they remained, uncared for and protected from invasion only by two wooden doors.

> . . . But shame then came over those who had custody of the place, and it was determined to put them in order. In 1818 a rumour was current that the Medicean coffins had been violated and robbed of all the articles of value which

they contained; but it was not until thirty-nine years afterwards, in 1857, that an examination into the fact was made. It was then found that the rumour had been well founded.

The forty-nine coffins containing the remains of the family were taken down one by one, and a sad state of things was exposed. Some of them had been broken into and robbed, some of them were the hiding-places of rats and every kind of vermin; and such was the nauseous odour they gave forth, that at least one of the persons employed in taking them down lost his life by inhaling it. In many of them nothing remained but fragments of bones and a handful of dust; but where they had not been stolen, the splendid dresses, covered with jewels, the wrought silks and satins of gold embroidery, the helmets and swords, crusted with gems and gold, still survived the dust and bones that had worn them in their splendid pageants and ephemeral days of power; and in many cases, where everything that bore the impress of life had gone, the hair remained, almost as fresh as ever.

Some, however, had been embalmed, and were in a fair preservation; and some were in a dreadful state of putre-faction. Ghastly and grinning skulls were there, adorned with crowns of gold. Dark and parchment-dried faces were seen, with thin golden hair, rich as ever, and twisted with gems and pearls and golden nets. The cardinals still wore their mitres and red cloaks and splendid rings. On the breast of Cardinal Carlos [son of Ferdinand I] was a beautiful cross of white enamel, with the effigy of Christ in black, and surrounded with emeralds, and on his hand a rich sapphire ring. On that of Cardinal Leopold, the son of Cosimo II, over the purple pianeta was a cross of amethysts, and on his finger a jacinth set in enamel. The dried bones of Vittoria della Rovere Montefeltro were draped in a dress of black silk of beautiful texture, trim-med with black and white lace, with a great golden medal on her breast, and the portrait of her as she was in life lying on one side, and her emblems on the other; while all that remained of herself was a few bones.

1. Pianta della Catena (detail). The first topographical plan of
Florence by Stefano Bonsignori, 1554. Museo di Firenze com'era.

2. *(above)* Piazza della Signoria. Savonarola being burnt at the stake, by Ignoto Fiorentino, 16th century. Museo di San Marco, Florence.

BELVEDER CON PITTI

4. *(right)* Walter Savage Landor (1755–1864) by William Fisher. National Portrait Gallery.

5. *(below)* Charles James Lever (1806–72) by Mayall. National Portrait Gallery.

3. *(opposite)* View of the Pitti Palace and Boboli Gardens by Giusto Utens, 1599. Museo di Firenze com'era.

6. *(left)* Elizabeth Barrett Browning (1806–61) by Field Talfourd. National Portrait Gallery.

7. *(right)* Robert Browning (1812–89) by Field Talfourd. National Portrait Gallery.

8. *(right)* George Eliot (1819–80) by Sir Frederick William Burton. National Portrait Gallery.

9. *(left)* Ouida (1839–1908) by Adolphe Beau. National Portrait Gallery.

10. *(left) David* by Donatello (1386–1466). Museo Nazionale, Florence.

11. *(right) David* by Michelangelo (1475–1564). Galleria dell'Accademia, Florence.

12. *(left) Venus of Medici*, 3rd century, artist unknown. The Uffizi, Florence.

13. *(right)* Monument to Lorenzo de'Medici by Michelangelo. Medici Chapel, Florence.

14. Monument to Vittorio Alfieri by
Antonio Canova. Chiesa di Santa Croce,
Florence.

16. *The Ponte Vecchio* by William Holman Hunt. The Victoria &
Albert Museum.

15. *(above) Arno with Fireworks* by Thomas Patch. The Royal Collection.

17. *(right)* Tomb of Elizabeth Barrett Browning in the Protestant cemetery, Florence.

18. *(right)* Henry
James (1843–1916) by
John Singer Sargent.
National Portrait
Gallery.

19. *(below)* The
Cascine.

20. *(above left)* D. H. Lawrence (1885–1930) by P. Juley & Son. National Portrait Gallery.

21. *(above right)* Aldous Huxley (1894–1963) by Man Ray. National Portrait Gallery.

22. *(right)* Norman Douglas with Osbert Sitwell, Ian Greenlees and Pino Orioli *(behind)* in Florence, 1933.

23. Hotel New York on the Lung'Arno Corsini.

24. *Piazza del Carmine* by Rosai. Galleria Arte Moderna, Florence.

Anna Luisa, the Electress Palatine of the Rhine, daughter of Cosimo III, lay there, almost a skeleton, robed in a rich violet velvet, with the electoral crown surmounting a black, ghastly face of parchment – a medal of gold, with her name and effigy, on one side, and on her breast a crucifix of silver; while Francesco Maria, her uncle, lay beside her, a mass of putrid robes and rags. Cosimo I and Cosimo II had been stripped by profane hands of all their jewels and insignia; and so had been Eleonora de Toledo and Maria Christina, and many others, to the number of twenty.

The two bodies which were found in the best preservation were those of the Grand-Duchess Giovanna d'Austria, the wife of Francisco I, and their daughter Anna. Corruption had scarcely touched them, and they lay there fresh in colour as though they had just died. The mother, in her red satin, trimmed with lace, her red silk stockings and high-heeled shoes, the earrings hanging from her ears, and her blonde hair as fresh as ever; and equally well-preserved was the body of the daughter. And so, centuries after they had been laid there, the truth became evident of the rumour that ran through Florence at the time of their death, that they had died of poison. The arsenic which had taken them from their life had preserved their bodies. Giovanni delle Bande Nere was also there – the bones scattered and loose within his iron armour, and his rusty helmet with the vizor down.

Visiting San Lorenzo in October 1901, E. M. Forster confessed in a letter to the musicologist E. J. Dent: 'I got ready all the appropriate sentiments for the New Sacristy [the Medici Chapel], and they answered very well. More spontaneous perhaps were my feelings at seeing the cloisterful of starved and maimed cats.'

It was in the Piazza San Lorenzo that, in June 1860, while rummaging among the junk offered for sale at one of the many stalls, Browning came on the 'square yellow book' that was to provide the story of the murder which was to inspire what many would regard as the greatest of all his works, *The Ring and the Book*. Browning describes the book as follows:

> Small-quarto size, part print part manuscript:
> A book in shape but, really, pure crude fact
> Secreted from man's life when hearts beat hard,
> And brains, high-blooded, ticked two centuries since.

On 'that memorable day', having paid a lira for his purchase, Browning first

> . . . leaned a little and overlooked my prize
> By the low railing round the fountain-source
> Close to the statue, where a step descends

and then, absorbed

> Still read I on, from written title-page
> To written index, on, through street and street,
> At the Strozzi, at the Pillar, at the Bridge;
> Till, by the time I stood at home again
> In Casa Guidi by Felice Church,
> Under the doorway where the black begins
> With the first stone slab of the staircase cold,
> I had mastered the contents, knew the whole truth
> Gathered together, bound up in this book . . .

In his *Ilex and Olive* Michael Swan describes how in 1948, in the immediate aftermath of the war, he bought something very different in the same piazza:

Today in the market place in front of San Lorenzo, where Browning bought his yellow book, I bought a packet of Pall Mall cigarettes from a *ragazzo*, which seemed to symbolise modern Italy perfectly. The packet was red and shiny and neatly cellophaned with a U.S.A. guarantee label, but inside were twenty miserable weeds, smelling of everything save tobacco, though each was printed with the words 'Pall Mall.' I was told later that a factory in Bari manufactures this product, packet and all, and supplies the *ragazzi* from Venice to Calabria. The Government, knowing how little effective its measures would be against this racket, produces its own version of Camels and Pall Malls, with the agreement of the American Government, and sells them reasonably in the normal way. But anyway, there in a packet of cigarettes is the *bella figura* and the maggot of Italy today.

That was a period when the English could still patronize and despise the Italians.

San Marco

The Convent of San Marco is noted for two associations: one with Savonarola and the other with Fra Angelico.

'In heaven,' said Pius VII, 'I shall know the explanation of three great mysteries – the Immaculate Conception, the suppression of the Society of Jesus, and the death of Savonarola.'

In *Romola* George Eliot pictures Savonarola on his knees in the monastery of which he became the prior in 1490 and in which he preached with such success that even in winter the square was thronged for hours before its doors were opened:

It was an hour of relaxation in the monastery, and most of the cells were empty. The light through the narrow windows looked in on nothing but bare walls, and the hard pallet and the crucifix. And even behind that door at the end of the long corridor, in the inner cell opening from an ante-chamber where the Prior usually sat at his desk or received private visitors, the high jet of light fell on only one more object that looked quite as common a monastic sight as the bare walls and hard pallet. It was but the back of a figure in the long white Dominican tunic and scapulary, kneeling with bowed head before a crucifix. It might have been any ordinary Fra Girolamo, who had nothing worse to confess than thinking of wrong things when he was singing *in coro*, or feeling spiteful when Fra Benedetto dropped the ink over his own miniatures in the breviary he was illuminating – who had no higher thought than that of climbing safely into Paradise up the narrow ladder of prayer, fasting, and obedience. But

under this particular white tunic there was a heart beating
with a consciousness inconceivable to the average monk,
and perhaps hard to be conceived by any man who has not
arrived at self-knowledge through a tumultuous inner
life: a consciousness in which irrevocable errors and lapses
from verity were so entwined with noble purposes and
sincere beliefs, in which self-justifying expediency was so
inwoven with the tissue of a great work which the whole
being seemed as unable to abandon as the body was
unable to abandon glowing and trembling before the
objects of hope and fear, that it was perhaps impossible,
whatever course might be adopted, for the conscience to
find perfect repose.

Savonarola was not only in the attitude of prayer, there
were Latin words of prayer on his lips; and yet he was not
praying. He had entered his cell, had fallen on his knees,
and burst into words of supplication, seeking in this way
for an influx of calmness which would be a warrant to him
that the resolutions urged on him by crowding thoughts
and passions were not wresting him away from the
Divine support; but the previsions and impulses which
had been at work within him for the last hour were too
imperious; and while he pressed his hands against his face,
and while his lips were uttering audibly, '*Cor mundum crea
in me*' his mind was still filled with the images of the snare
his enemies had prepared for him, was still busy with the
arguments by which he could justify himself against their
taunts and accusations.

Fra Angelico was a very different sort of man. Taine wrote
of him:

Fra Angelico came to the convent before Savonarola, and
his frescoes adorn the chapter-house, the corridors and
the grey walls of the cells. He had lived aloof from the
world, and amid new perturbations and doubts still lived
the pure life absorbed in God inculcated by the *Fioretti* . . .
His art is as primitive as his life; he had begun it with
missal-work, which he really continued on these walls,

for gold, vermilion, the brightest scarlets and most brilliant greens – all the medieval art of the illuminator shines in his work as though it were an old parchment . . . Around him all action is meditative, and every object gentle in hue. Day after day the unvarying hours bring before him the same dark lustre of the walls, the same severe folds of cowl and frock, the same rustling steps going to and fro between the chapel and the refectory. Delicate, indecisive sensations vaguely rise in this monotony, while tender dreams are like the perfume of a rose sheltered from the bitter winds and blooming far from the great highway noisy with the tread of men. The magnificance of eternity becomes visible, and the effort of the painter is centred on its expression . . .

The spiritual here has mastery; ponderable matter becomes transfigured; it has lost its mass, its substance is etherialised, and nothing remains but a vapour floating in azure splendour. In one instance the blessed ones go towards paradise over luxuriant meadows strewn with flowers white and red underneath beautiful trees in bloom. They are led by angels, and in saintly brotherhood form a circle, hand in hand. The burden of flesh no longer weighs them down, and light radiates from their heads as they glide through the air up to the flaming gate from which bursts a golden illumination, while above Christ, within a triple row of angels bowing before him like flowers, smiles upon the blessed from beneath his halo . . .

Although beautiful and ideal, Angelico's Christ, even in celestial triumph, is pale, thoughtful and somewhat emaciated. He is the eternal friend, the almost melancholy consoler of the *Imitation*, the poetic Lord of Mercy as the grieving heart imagines Him: He is in no way the over-healthy figure of the Renaissance painters. His long curling tresses and blonde beard mildly surround His features; sometimes He smiles faintly, while His gravity is always associated with gentle benignity . . . Near Him the Virgin, kneeling with downcast eyes, seems to be a young maiden who has just communicated . . . The

painter . . . cannot find colours pure enough or ornaments precious enough for his saints. He forgets that his
figures are but painted: he bestows on them the fond
devotion of a believer, a worshipper. He embroiders their
robes as if they were real, covering their mantles with
filigree as fine as the best goldsmith's work. He paints on
their copes small but perfect pictures; he delights in
delicately drawing their comely fair hair, or arranging
their curls, and severely marking the circular tonsure of
the monk. He lifts them into heaven for love and service;
and his art is the last blossom of the age of mysticism.

In his *Foreign Parts*, Henry James describes how he went to

the suppressed Convent of San Marco, paid my franc at
the profane little wicket which creaks away at the door
(no less than six custodians, apparently, are needed to
turn it, as if it had a recusant conscience), passed along the
bright, still cloister, and went in to look at Fra Angelico's
'Crucifixion', in that dusky chamber in the basement. I
looked long; one can hardly do otherwise. The fresco
deals with the highly pathetic, and after perceiving its
meaning you feel as little at liberty to go away abruptly as
you would to leave church during the sermon.

Having 'sat out the sermon, and departed, I hope, with the
gentle preacher's blessing', he went 'into the smaller refectory,
near by, to refresh my memory of the beautiful Last Supper of
Domenico Ghirlandaio.'

It would be putting things roughly to say that I felt as if I
had adjourned from a sermon to a comedy; but one may
certainly say that Ghirlandaio's theme, as contrasted with
the blessed Angelico's, was the dramatic, spectacular side
of human life.

. . . The main idea with him has been the variety, the
brilliancy, the material charm of the scene, which finds
expression, with irrepressible generosity, in the access-
ories in the background. Instinctively he imagines an
opulent garden – imagines it with a good faith which

quite tides him over the reflection that Christ and his disciples were poor men and unused to sit at meat in palaces. Great full-fruited orange-trees peep over the wall before which the table is spread, strange birds fly through the air, and a peacock perches on the edge of the partition and looks down on the sacred repast. It is striking that, without any religious purpose at all intense, the figures, in their varied naturalness, have a dignity and sweetness of attitude which admits of numberless reverential constructions.

Having left the Ghirlandaio, James 'suddenly faltered and paused', as he was about to mount the stairs to 'the little painted cells of the Beato Angelico.' Then he decided: 'I wanted no more of him that day. I wanted no more macerated friars and spear-gashed sides.' He walked across the Piazza to the Accademia, where he looked at Botticelli's *Coronation of the Virgin*.

It was not one of the great works of art in San Marco which attracted the attention of Sophia Hawthorne but, as she was leaving the monastery,

a wooden image of Christ, sitting with bound hands, and the crown of thorns upon his head, from which blood was trickling over his figure. An expression of the utmost pain is in both face and form. A great many candles were burning around this distressing object, and a crowd of people were kneeling before it; and the whole chapel was filled with offerings from the devout – silver and gold hearts without number, chains and all kinds of trinkets; and watches (!) were hung round the neck and arms. It was the most extraordinary, repulsive, and even grotesque spectacle.

SPEDALE DEGLI INNOCENTI

The *Spedale degli Innocenti* (Foundling Hospital) in the Piazza della SS. Annunziata was founded in 1421. It contains a number of excellent pictures, among them an *Adoration of the*

Magi by Ghirlandaio. In his *Italian Hours* Henry James describes a copyist at work on this masterpiece. Museums used
once to be full of such copyists – Reggie Temple, friend of so
many writers of the first half of this century, at once comes to
mind. Now, when photographic reproduction has attained a
degree of accuracy surpassing even theirs, they have virtually
disappeared.

It [the *Adoration*] hangs in an obscure chapel, far aloft,
behind an altar, and though now and then a stray tourist
wanders in and puzzles awhile over the vaguely glowing
forms, the picture is never really seen and enjoyed. I
found an aged Frenchman of modest mien perched on a
little platform beneath it, behind a great hedge of altar-
candlesticks, with an admirable copy all completed. The
difficulties of his task had been well-nigh insuperable, and
his performance seemed to me a real feat of magic. He
could scarcely move or turn, and could find room for his
canvas but by rolling it together and painting a small piece
at a time, so that he never enjoyed a view of his *ensemble*.
The original is gorgeous with colour and bewildering
with decorative detail, but not a gleam of the painter's
crimson was wanting, not a curl in his gold arabesques. It
seemed to me that if I had copied Ghirlandaio in such
conditions I would at least maintain for my own credit
that he was the finest painter in the world. 'Very good of
its kind,' said the weary old man with a shrug of reply for
my raptures; 'but oh how far short of Raphael!' However
that may be, if the reader chances to observe this consummate copy in the so commendable Museum devoted in
Paris to such works, let him stop before it with a due
reverence; it is one of the patient things of art. Seeing it
wrought there, in its dusky nook, under such scant
convenience, I found no bar in the painter's foreignness to
a thrilled sense that the old art-life of Florence isn't yet
extinct. It still at least works spells and almost miracles.

Santissima Annunziata

The church of the Santissima Annunziata was founded in the thirteenth century, but has been constantly altered and modernized over the centuries. John Evelyn described his visit as follows:

After dinner we went to the church of the Annunciata [sic], where the Duke and his Court were at their devotions, being a place of extraordinary repute for sanctity; for here is a shrine that does great miracles, proved by innumerable votive tablets, covering almost the walls of the whole church. This is the image of Gabriel who saluted the Blessed Virgin, and which the artist finished so well that he was in despair of performing the Virgin's face, whereupon it was miraculously done for him while he slept; but others say it was painted by St Luke himself. Whoever it was, infinite is the devotion of both sexes to it. The altar is set off with four columns of oriental alabaster, and lighted by thirty great silver lamps. There are innumerable other pictures by rare masters. Our Saviour's passion in brasse tables inserted in marble is the work of John di Bologna and Baccio Bandinelli . . .

The huddle of indifferent memorial slabs in the cloisters caused Albert Camus (1913–60) to reflect as follows:

I remember how in Florence, in the cloister of the dead in Santissima Annunziata, I was transported by a feeling I believed to be dismay, but which was really only anger. I was reading the inscriptions on the tomb-stones and votive offerings. One had been a tender father and faithful husband; another, both the best of husbands and a shrewd businessman. A young woman, paragon of all virtues, spoke French 'like a native.' Then there was a young girl who was the future hope of her parents, 'but joy in this world is fleeting.' And yet I was not struck by any of this. According to the inscriptions, they were all resigned to the idea of death, and without any perplexities, seeing that they had accepted other duties. That day, some children had invaded the cloisters and played leapfrog on

the tombstones that were intended to perpetuate their
virtues. Night fell; I sat on the ground against a column.
A priest passing by smiled at me. The muffled playing of
an organ came from inside the church and the warm tone
of parts of the general tune emerged in between the
shouting of the children. Alone, leaning against the
column, I felt like someone gripped at the nape of the neck
shouting his faith as the last word. Everything inside me
rebelled against such resignation. 'It is necessary,' read the
inscription. But it is not and my rebellion was right. That
same joy that proceeded indifferent and enraptured like a
pilgrim wandering in the world; it was necessary to
follow it step by step. But for all the rest I did not want it. I
said no to it with all my strength.

The tombstones taught me that it was useless and that
life goes 'with sunrise and sunset.' But still today I cannot
see what uselessness my rebellion removes, and can see
perfectly well instead what it adds.

In the middle of the piazza stands Giambologna's statue of
the Grand Duke Ferdinand. This statue is interesting for a
reason additional to the eminence of its sculptor, since it is to it
that Browning refers in his poem 'The Statue and Bust.'
According to the poet, Ferdinand ordered the statue to be set
here so that it could gaze for all eternity at the della Robbia bust
of the woman whom he had loved in vain. The della Robbia
bust has now vanished. Here, in the poem, Ferdinand himself
is speaking of his commission to John of Douay (as Giambologna, a Belgian, was originally called):

> John of Douay shall effect my plan,
> Set me on horseback here aloft,
> Alive, as the crafty sculptor can,
>
> In the very square I have crossed so oft:
> That men may admire, when future suns
> Shall touch the eyes to a purpose soft,
>
> While the mouth and the brow stay in bronze –
> Admire and say 'when he was alive
> How he would take his pleasure once!'

In *Romola* George Eliot vividly evokes the Peasants' Fair which was held annually in the piazza:

At each of the opposite inlets he [Tito] saw people struggling into the piazza, while above them paper lanterns, held aloft on sticks, were waving uncertainly to and fro. A rude monotonous chant made a distinctly traceable strand of noise, across which screams, whistles, gibing chants in piping boyish voices, the beating of drums, and the ringing of little bells, met each other in confused din. Every now and then one of the dim floating lights disappeared with a smash from a stone launched more or less vaguely in pursuit of mischief, followed by a scream and renewed shouts. But on the outskirts of the whirling multitude there were groups who were keeping this vigil of the Nativity of the Virgin in a more methodical manner than by fitful stone-throwing and gibing. Certain ragged men, darting a hard sharp glance around them while their tongues rattled merrily, were inviting country people to game with them on fair and open-handed terms; two masquerading figures on stilts, who had snatched lanterns from the crowd, were swaying the lights to and fro in meteoric fashion, as they strode hither and thither; a sage trader was doing a profitable business at a small covered stall, in hot *berlingozzi* [ring-shaped cakes], a favourite farinaceous delicacy; one man standing on a barrel, with his back firmly planted against a pillar of the loggia in front of the Foundling Hospital [Spedale degli Innocenti], was selling efficacious pills, invented by a doctor of Salerno, warranted to prevent toothache and death by drowning; and not far off, against another pillar, a tumbler was showing off his tricks on a small platform; while a handful of 'prentices, despising the slack entertainment of guerrilla stone-throwing, were having a private concentrated match of that favourite Florentine sport at the narrow entrance of the Via de' Febbrai.

PORTA PINTI: THE PROTESTANT CEMETERY

Perhaps because its art and artefacts, its people and its palaces, proved to be a tonic to the soul, Florence came to be regarded as some sort of palliative for bodily ills as well. In this it could only disappoint, however, for the city's cruel climate – torrid in summer, dank in winter – carried off far more ailing visitors than it ever cured. With its tombstones recording the deaths of so many foreign visitors in their early years, the Protestant Cemetery provides a stark demonstration of this fact.

By all accounts it was once a lovely spot, sheltered by the old walls of the city. But these having long since been removed, it has now become little more than an outsize traffic-island, with buses, cars, and motor-bicycles roaring about it and its air acrid with exhaust fumes.

Here is the tomb of Elizabeth Barrett Browning, sculpted by Lord Leighton, its grey casket flanked by box-hedges. It is perhaps appropriate that Arthur Hugh Clough (1819–61), a victim of typhoid fever, should also be buried here, since he fretted himself to a shadow in unrequited love for Florence Nightingale and it was after the city, her birthplace, that she was named. Matthew Arnold wrote *Thyrsis* in commemoration of Clough's death, and some verses from it are inscribed on the stone. Shortly before his own death, Arnold, a frequent visitor to Florence, was thinking of retiring there – 'It is the most beautiful place I know,' he wrote to the American Minister, Charles K. Tuckerman.

The remains of Walter Savage Landor are also in the cemetery, the tomb engraved with Swinburne's:

> And thou, his Florence, to thy trust
> Receive and keep,
> Keep safe his dedicated dust,
> His sacred sleep.
>
> So shall thy lovers, come from far,
> Mix with thy name,
> As morning-star with evening-star,
> His faultless fame.

The North-western Quarter

VIA TORNABUONI

Arnold Bennett found the shops of the Via Tornabuoni –
which might be described as the Bond Street, Rue de Rivoli,
or Fifth Avenue of Florence – 'rather disappointing.' But
Augustus Hare called it 'the gayest and handsomest street in
Florence, where the best clubs and caffès are, and where the
most beautiful flowers are sold at the street corners'; and
W. D. Howells wrote of it:

> Via Tornabuoni is charming, and merits to be observed
> for the ensemble it offers of the contemporary Florentine
> expression, with its alluring shops, its confectioners and
> cafés, its florists and milliners, its dandies and tourists,
> and, ruggedly massing up out of their midst, the mighty
> bulk of the old Strozzi Palace, medieval, sombre, superb,
> tremendously impressive of the days when really a man's
> house was his castle. Everywhere in Florence the same
> sort of contrast presents itself in some degree, but
> nowhere quite so dramatically as here.

Of the Palazzo Strozzi in particular and of Florentine palazzi
in general Madame de Staël wrote in her novel of Italian life,
Corinne:

> The palaces of the leading families of Florence were built,
> in effect, like fortresses, from which they could defend

themselves; one can still see, on their outsides, the iron
rings from which each side could hang out its standards;
in short, everything is arranged with the object of maintaining individual forces, rather than of uniting them in
the common interest. One might say that the city has
been built for civil war.

Having commented on 'the Corinthian elegance of its cortile' and 'the massive strength of its facade, composed of what
the Italians call *"bozze di pietra forte"*' [blocks of rough-hewn
stone], Lady Morgan in her *Italy* goes on to declare that the

> great interest attached to this noble and ancient palace is
> that it was raised and inhabited by Filippo Strozzi, the
> Cato of his age, and by his strong-minded and ambitious
> wife, the famous Clarice de' Medici. When the rank, the
> wealth, the high consideration in which this illustrious
> citizen was held, induced the people to give him the title
> of *Messire*, he observed: 'My name is Filippo Strozzi; I am
> a Florentine merchant and no more: who gives me a title
> insults me.' Yet at the moment he held the Popes and
> Cardinals of the house of Medici at bay.

In the Via Tornabuoni stood Doney's Café, now recently,
sadly and inexplicably closed to make way for a shoe-shop.
Tourists had been frequenting it literally for centuries. Visiting Florence, the Goncourt brothers spent much of their time
there when not avidly sightseeing. It was where Herman
Melville, James Russell Lowell, and Ralph Waldo Emerson all
took their breakfasts when staying at the Hotel du Nord in the
Via delle Terme. Stendhal also often went there for breakfast.

In 1858, touring Europe for his health, the young American
dilettante writer J. De Forest described the café as then con-
sisting of three saloons, with cream-coloured columns and
marble-topped tables. He noted

> the white uniforms of Austrian officers, the easy travel-
> ling-coats of English tourists, and the noisy waiters,
> rushing about like incarnations of perpetual motion, and
> shouting the orders of the guests with the vehemence of
> sea captains in a hurricane.

The *fioraia* or flower-girl at Doney is, he comments, of a special species.

She drops a bouquet on your table, fixes it in your button-hole; then, with a quick glance in your eye and a flattering smile, she trips hastily away; but at your departure, while you are stepping into the railway station or the diligence office, thinking in the joy of a good conscience that all your creditors are satisfied, you suddenly see before you the *fioraia*, smiling, wishing you *Buon viaggio*, presenting her final bouquet, and awaiting the reward of her floral benevolence.

In *Aurora Leigh*, Elizabeth Barrett Browning describes Doney, at about the same period when de Forest was so frequent a customer:

> Underneath,
> The river, just escaping from the weight
> Of that intolerable glory, ran
> In acquiescent shadow murmurously:
> And up, beside it, streamed the festa-folk
> With fellow-murmurs from their feet and fans
> (With *issimo* and *ino* and sweet poise
> Of vowels in their pleasant scandalous talk)
> Returning from the grand-duke's dairy-farm
> Before the trees grew dangerous at night
> (For, 'trust no tree by moonlight', Tuscans say),
> To eat their ice at Doni's tenderly, –
> Each lovely lady close to a cavalier
> Who holds her dear fan while she feeds her smile
> On meditative spoonfuls of vanille,
> He breathing hot protesting vows of love,
> Enough to thaw her cream, and scorch his beard.

The English governess, Ellen, who is the heroine of Lettice Cooper's Florentine novel *Fenny* – its time-scheme straddles the last War – frequently meets friends, English or Italian, in the café. Early on in the novel, it is while she is strolling along the Via Tornabuoni that she makes the momentous decision – the year is 1933 – to have her hair bobbed:

This was the first time that Ellen had been alone in Florence. She had not brought her guide-book, and without it did not know how to find the things she wanted to see. She sauntered along the Via Tornabuoni looking in the shop windows. It was one of the fashionable hours. Elegant women – Italian, English, American – strolled on the pavement, shining cars nosed their way along the street. Elderly ladies in pairs, with elaborately veiled hats and antique summer dresses, tottered towards Doney's for their five o'clock cup of tea. It amused Ellen to watch this decorative world, but when she came opposite to a mirror in a shop window she was struck by the incongruity of her own sober figure, in the grey tweed coat and skirt, with her grey hat tipping forward as usual on her coils of hair. A few doors farther on she came to a hairdresser's, where there was a notice in the window that they spoke French and English. She went in and asked them to cut off her hair.

The first snips of the scissors seemed to denude her of a good deal of what had so far been her life . . .

Later, in 1937, an excursion to Doney's with her two charges, Shand and Donata, leads to Ellen (or Fenny, as her charges call her) seeing rampant Fascism at close quarters:

When they came out of the café, the police had cleared the street of cars, and the procession was passing, cheered by spectators packed on the pavements and in the shop doorways and the windows above. A group of young Fascists went by, military and smart in their uniform jackets and top boots. They were boys of Shand's age or less. Some of them looked very hot, the sweat rolled down their solemn young faces under the peaked caps, but they carried themselves proudly, their limbs swinging in perfect time, their heads erect under the swaying banners with their portraits of the Duce, the Roman wolf, the fasces and the ever-repeated inscription, '*Credere, obedire, combattere.*'

'How well they march!' Donata said with exaggerated

fervour and a mischievous glance at her governess's unsmiling face.

Ellen saw Shand on the opposite pavement. In his flannel trousers, sandals and open-necked shirt – clothes which he always wore untidily – he could not have looked a more complete contrast to his marching contemporaries. He was frowning at them with open hostility. Behind the marching boys there was a brief gap in the procession between their rear rank and the leaders and the foremost banners of the *squadristi*, who followed them. Through this gap, as the movement of the procession brought it opposite to him, Shand slouched coolly across the road.

Luckily there were at the moment no policemen nor Blackshirts outside the door of Doney's. A young man wearing a party badge shook his fist at Shand, and began to pour out a torrent of abuse. He evidently thought him English, for the word 'sanctions' kept on recurring. Two or three of the bystanders joined in, and there was a movement towards them from the back of the crowd. Ellen pushed Donata inside Doney's and pulled Shand after her.

As sad as the demise of Doney is that of the restaurant the Buca di Lapi, also in the Via Tornabuoni and also much frequented by writers. Arnold Bennett describes a visit with typical relish:

Here the cooking is done in full view of the audience. Each dish specially prepared for each client. All by one man. About 35, dark, personable, extraordinarily quick and graceful. If he left his recess for a moment to go upstairs he would slide down the rail to come back again. Charcoal stove. He blew it up constantly with a fan. Sparks fly. He puts on charcoal with his hand. Everything goes through that hand. He would fan with one hand and stir with the other. He made an omelette in a moment: very quick his gesture in turning it over like a pancake, in the pan. Very careful and slow in making our coffee. Orders called out in a loud voice by the landlord or the boy waiter – who was not dressed as a waiter. All professional conversation very loud and constantly going on. Things not in stock, such as ham, sent for and brought down in paper. When a dish is ready the chef would plank it down on a ledge and whistle, or call out its name. When we arrived the landlord was finishing his dressing in the further saloon which was darkened. Later the boy waiter – perhaps his son – took a pair of loose cuffs from a hat-hook and slipped them on, at once giving himself an air of grande toilette. Still later, the landlord, evidently bethinking himself, did the same from another hook. About 10 or 12 or 15 customers, and all cooked by one man.

Off the Via Tornabuoni runs the Borgo Santi Apostoli. No. 19 is the Palazzo Usimbardi (Acciaoli), the beautiful sixteenth-century façade of which was destroyed in the last War. During the nineteenth century the palazzo became the Grand Hotel Royal, where such literary figures as Dickens, Longfellow, and Swinburne put up.

SANTA MARIA NOVELLA

The chief Dominican church of Florence is Santa Maria Novella. The building was begun in 1278, on a site that before the erection of a third set of walls around Florence was actually outside the city boundaries. As a result the church was first known as Santa Maria tra le Vigne, or St Mary among the Vineyards. *La sposa* – the bride – was the nickname given to it by Michelangelo, who thus conveyed the radiant innocence of a supreme example of Tuscan Gothic architecture.

The chief literary interest of this church is that it is here that Boccaccio set the first scene of the *Decameron*. Longfellow referred to this connection when noting in his Journal:

At Florence I took lodgings in a house which fronts upon the Piazza Novella. In front of my parlour windows was the venerable Gothic church of Santa Maria Novella, in whose gloomy aisles Boccaccio has placed the opening scenes of his *Decamerone*. There, when the plague was raging in the city, one Tuesday morning after mass, 'the seven ladies, young and fair,' held council together, and resolved to leave the infected city and flee to their rural villas in the environs, where they might 'hear the birds sing, and see the green hills, and the plains, and the fields covered with grain and undulating like the sea, and trees of species manifold.'

Of all the pictures within the church, none in the nineteenth century excited a greater diversity of opinion than 'Cimabue's' *Madonna*. (Subsequently ascribed to Cimabue's pupil Duccio, it is now to be seen in the Uffizi.) Lady Morgan calls it 'a horrible monster.' Hawthorne is hardly more complimentary:

I could see no charm whatever in the broad-faced Virgin, and it would relieve my mind and rejoice my spirit if the picture were borne out of the church in another triumphal procession (like the one which brought it here) and reverently burnt.

Elizabeth Barrett Browning was far more complimentary:

Ascend the right stair from the farther nave
    To muse in a small chapel scarcely lit
By Cimabue's Virgin. Bright and brave
    That picture was accounted, mark, of old;
A king stood bare before its sovran grace,
    A reverent people shouted to behold
The picture, not the king, not even the place
    Containing such a miracle grew bold,
Named the glad Borgo from that beauteous face
    Which thrilled the artist, after work, to think
His own ideal Mary-smile should stand
    So very near him, – he, within the brink
Of all that glory, let in by his hand
    With too divine a rashness! Yet none shrink
Who come to gaze here now; albeit 'twas planned
    Sublimely in the thought's simplicity:
The Lady, throned in empyreal state,
    Minds only the young Babe upon her knee,

While sidelong angels bear the royal weight,
  Prostrated meekly, smiling tenderly
Oblivion of their wings; the Child thereat
  Stretching his hand like God. If any should,
Because of some stiff draperies and loose joints,
  Gaze scorn down from the height of Raphaelhood
On Cimabue's picture, – Heaven anoints
  The head of no such critic, and his blood
The poet's curse strikes full on and appoints
  To ague and cold spasms for evermore.
A noble picture! worthy of the shout
  Wherewith along the streets the people bore
Its cherub-faces, which the sun threw out,
  Until they stooped and entered the church door.

The Piazza of Santa Maria Novella provides the setting for two passages in Anatole France's *Le Lys Rouge* (The Red Lily). Reading this novel, one realizes how much influence both it and its author must have had on Aldous Huxley. Some of its passages are, indeed, hardly distinguishable from ones in Huxley's own novel about aristocratic, rich, and intellectual *émigré* life in Tuscany, *Those Barren Leaves*.

In each extract from *Le Lys Rouge*, a contrast is drawn between the simplicity of an Italian cobbler and the sophistication of the foreign visitors, to the disadvantage of the latter. The Choulette of the two passages is an elderly, drink-sodden poet, clearly modelled on Verlaine:

The next day, as they were coming out of Santa Maria Novella, and crossing the square, where, as in an ancient circus, stand two obelisks of marble, Madame Marmet said to Countess Martin: 'I think I see Monsieur Choulette.'

Sitting in a cobbler's booth, pipe in hand, Choulette was gesticulating rhythmically, and appeared to be reciting verses. The Florentine shoemaker, as he worked with his awl, was listening with a good-natured smile. He was a little bald man, a favourite type in Flemish pictures. On the table, among the wooden lasts, nails, pieces of leather and balls of wax, was a basil plant. A sparrow with a false leg, made of a bit of match, was hopping gaily from the old man's shoulder to his head.

Delighted at such a sight, Madame Marmet stood on the threshold and called Choulette, who was reciting in a soft, singing voice, and asked him why he had not come with her to visit the Cappella degli Spagnuoli.

He rose and replied:

'Madame, you are occupied with vain imaginings. I am concerned with life and reality.'

He shook hands with the cobbler, and followed the two ladies.

'On my way to Santa Maria Novella,' he said, 'I saw this old man leaning over his work, holding the last between his knees as if in a vice, and stitching clumsy shoes. I felt that he was simple and good. I said to him in Italian, 'Father, will you drink a glass of Chianti wine with me?' He was quite willing. He went to fetch a bottle and glasses, while I minded his shop.'

And Choulette pointed to two glasses and a bottle standing on the stove.

'When he returned, we drank together; I repeated good words of obscure meaning, the music of which delighted him. I shall return to his booth. I shall learn from him how to make shoes and live a contented life. After that I shall never know sadness, which arises solely from discontent and idleness.'

Countess Martin smiled.

'Monsieur Choulette, I am not discontented and yet I am not gay. Must I also learn to make shoes?'

Choulette replied gravely:

'Not yet.'

When they reached the Oricellai Gardens, Madame Marmet dropped on to a seat. At Santa Maria Novella she had carefully examined the serene frescoes of Ghirlandajo, the choir-stalls, the virgin of Cimabue, and the pictures in the monastery. She had taken great pains in honour of her husband's memory, who was said to have loved Italian art. She was tired. Choulette sat down beside her and said:

'Could you tell me, Madame, if it is true that the Pope has his robes made by Worth?'

Countess Martin and Madame Marmet again visit Santa Maria Novella, on this occasion in the company of a spinster English writer, resident in Florence, called Vivian Bell – a character modelled on the real-life Vernon Lee, whom France had met and admired. Once again the cobbler is at work:

Coming out of the church, they passed the booth of the cobbler whom Choulette had adopted as his master. The good man was patching a countryman's boots. The pot of basil was at his side, and the sparrow with the wooden leg chirped close by.

Madame Marmet asked the old man if he were quite well, if he had enough work to do, and if he were happy. To all these questions he replied the charming Italian 'Yes,' the *Si* coming musically from his toothless mouth. She made him tell them his sparrow's story. One day the poor little creature had put his foot into the boiling wax.

'I made my little friend a wooden leg out of a match, and now he is able to perch on my shoulder as of old.'

'He is a kind old man,' said Miss Bell, 'who teaches M. Choulette wisdom. At Athens there was a cobbler, named Simon, who wrote works on philosophy and was a friend of Socrates. I have always thought M. Choulette resembled Socrates.'

Thérèse asked the shoemaker to tell them his name and story. His name was Serafino Stoppini, and he came from Stia. He was old. His life had been full of trouble.

He put back his spectacles on to his forehead, revealing his blue kindly eyes, growing dim beneath their reddened lids.

'I had a wife and children, now I am alone. I have known things, which now I have forgotten.'

. . . 'His tools, a handful of nails, the tub in which he soaks the leather, and a pot of basil are all he has in the world,' thought Thérèse, 'and yet he is happy.'

'This plant smells sweet, and soon it will flower,' she said.

'If the poor little thing flowers, it will die,' he replied.

There is a reference both to Michelangelo's *la sposa* and to France's 'two obelisks of marble' in Elizabeth Barrett Browning's *Aurora Leigh*, in which she writes of:

> Maria Novella's Place
> In which the mystic obelisks stand up
> Triangular, pyramidal, each based
> On a single trine of brazen tortoises,
> To guard that fair church, Buonarotti's Bride,
> That stares out from her large blind dial-eyes,
> Her quadrant and armillary dials, black
> With rhythms of many suns and moons, in vain
> Inquiry for so rich a soul as his . . .

These 'mystic obelisks' were erected to mark the goals of the chariot races held in the piazza under Cosimo I and his successors on the Eve of St John. Fenimore Cooper has left us a description of these races in his *Gleanings in Europe*:

The games are called the *corsi dei cocchi*. There are two small obelisks on opposite extremities of the square, and the temporary circus is constructed by their means. A cord is stretched from one to the other; a sort of amphitheatre is formed by scaffoldings around the whole, the royal and diplomatic boxes being prepared near the goal. As there is much scenic painting, a good parade of guards both horse and foot, a well-dressed population, and a background of balconies garnished by tapestry and fine women, to say nothing of roofs and chimneys, the general effect is quite imposing.

The falling off is in the chariots. The ancient vehicle was small and had but two wheels; whereas these were large and clumsy, had four wheels, and unusually long and straggling perches, – an invention to keep them from upsetting. In other respects the form was preserved, and the charioteers were in costume.

Four chariots, to use the modern language, entered for the race. The start was pretty fair, and the distance twice round the obelisks. If you ask me for the effect, I shall tell you that, apart from the appliances – such as the court, the guards, the spectators and the dresses, and perhaps I might add the turns, – one may witness the same any fine evening in New York, between two drunken Irish cart-men who are on their way home. There was certainly a little skill manifested at the turns, and it was easy to see that betting should have been on the outside chariot; for those nearer to the obelisks were obliged to go consider-ably beyond them before they could come round, while the one farthest from the poles just cleared them. This outside chariot won the race, the charioteer having the sagacity not to make his push before the last turn.

After the chariot-races we had the *corso dei barberi* or a race between barbs. The horses were without riders, and the track was the longest street of the town. To this amusement everyone who could went in a carriage, and the *corso* of vehicles was much the most interesting part of the exhibition. Two lines are made, and the coaches move in opposite directions through the same street, on a walk. Of course, everybody sees everybody, – and pretty often the somebodies see nobodies, for the mania to make one on these occasions is so strong, that half the artisans are abroad in carriages, as well as their betters. The royal equipages moved in the line, the same as that of the milliner. When we were well tired of looking at each other, the grand duke went into a gallery prepared for him, and the race was run. The latter does not merit a syllable; but so strong is the rage for sporting, that I heard some Englishmen betting on the winner.

PIAZZA DELL' UNITÀ

Near Santa Maria Novella and the railway station lies the Piazza dell' Unità, in which is situated the Hotel Baglioni. Having categorized this hotel as Expensive, the Fodor entry continues 'Large, comfortable rooms; Renaissance decor in public room; roof garden.' It is in the lift of the Hotel Baglioni that, in Mario Soldati's 1955 *The Confession*, there occurs an incident which is to cause the hero, Clemente Perrier, four-teen-year-old pupil at a Jesuit school in Turin, to agonize over his vocation for the priesthood. Clemente is obsessed with a remembered image:

of a plump, blonde woman, with rounded eyes, pouting lips, and that sad, jaded expression which, much more effectively than any other, stimulates the imagination and arouses the desire. Clemente had seen the woman only once, and then only for a few minutes. The autumn before, in Florence, he had found himself alone with her in a lift in the Hotel Baglioni. But afterward, thinking every day of what happened – for ten minutes in the morning as he lazed in the warmth of his bed, for ten minutes in the afternoon during the initial stupor of his siesta, and for ten minutes each night before falling off to sleep – he had passed that single, swift impression in slow motion before his eyes and had ended by increasing its duration. The blonde woman had made a long journey with him. Shut up, just the two of them, in that tepid and isolated lift as in the compartment of an old-fashioned train, standing close to each other, without fear of wit-nesses, they had risen mile after mile, hour after hour, in the tallest of skyscrapers. Once again Clemente saw that white pudgy hand, with scarlet sharply pointed nails and on one finger a huge pearl ring, place itself on the panel and push the button which would make the lift start to go up.

He seemed to remember that he had pretended a mo-ment's distraction and, as though he, too, wanted to push the button, had placed his hand over hers and felt its warm softness. But, as often happened to him in such fantasies, he was not completely sure whether he hadn't merely confined himself to desiring that contact and, having quickly conceived the trick by which to obtain it and yet lacking the courage to act, he had cherished it, afterwards, as something that had actually taken place, even to the point of deceiving his own memory.

Clemente saw again the black velvet dress that clung to

the woman's figure: the pinkish, plump legs that stood
out against the sharp black of the skirt's hem, the black
satin slippers with diamond buckles (it did not occur to
him to think, even about these gems on her slippers, that
they might be false), the naked arms, the deep slit down
her back – all that flesh which the velvet cloth, the pearl
necklace, and the other jewels endowed with the arcane,
heavy preciousness of an idol, an idol who stood very
close to him and in whom, he sensed, lived his happiness,
yet whom a superior and cruel will prohibited his hands
from even touching ever so lightly.

Clemente remembered the rise and fall of her breasts as
she breathed, and the faint pulsations that ran along the
folds of her velvet dress, at the waist and over the belly.

But, above all, he had been fascinated by her eyes, dark,
shining, and like a doll's. Now and then her heavy lids
would lower and her eyes would shut tightly; the skin all
around them would become wrinkled and the woman's
face then suggested the fulfilment of a pleasure, yet with
that almost ugly, almost sad grimace which comes
from great sensual experience and a knowledge of all its
refinements.

Even now when, returning to that scene for the
thousandth time, Clemente travelled up the woman's
body and at last saw again that exquisite, withered face,
those eyes that seemed closed in pleasure, his blood
would pound in his veins.

He would have liked to slake himself in that sweetness,
that sadness, that knowledge and enjoyment of life which
he felt he lacked. And he imagined finding himself again
in the lift and flinging himself without a word at the
woman's feet, embracing her legs, her knees, begging to
be taken, subjected, dominated, crushed.

He had thought of becoming her little servant and,
with the idea of greater humiliation and voluptuousness,
of wearing the absurd red uniform of the hotel bellboys.
No longer for anyone would he be Clemente Perrier, the
boy who studied with the Jesuits, the boy in whose
family's living-room among the lady friends and artillery

officers, on the seventh and the twenty-first of every month (the days of his mother's receptions), they would chat about, saying: 'He is very intelligent', 'shows a great deal of promise,' and 'will go far.' Yes, he could just hear them: 'But, my dear, you ought to have seen how excited he became, and at his age, in front of Michelangelo's *Moses* and the Duomo in Florence, during the trip he got as a reward last autumn,' and so on. No, he would vanish from the world. They'd search for him in vain. He'd go to that woman's country, which, he imagined, was either Hungary or Sweden. He'd become her servant for life. Nobody could ever track him down again. At the start he would forget everything, even his surname. Then at last he would feel annulled in her, sacrificed, her slave, and therefore happy.

PIAZZA DELLA REPUBBLICA

So that the present-day Piazza della Repubblica – originally the Piazza Vittorio Emmanuele – and the streets around it could be erected in all their empty grandeur, the accretions of two thousands years of history were swept away at the end of the last century and the beginning of this. The site of the Roman forum, later to become the site of the Mercato Vecchio, the Old Market, was transformed into an area of restaurants, cafés, shops, and hotels. The people who had lived in this area, once regarded as a slum, were relocated, usually against their will, in new housing especially built for them outside the Porta San Frediano.

George Eliot's *Romola* contains a description of the Mercato Vecchio as it was at the time of Savonarola:

This piazza, though it had been the scene of a provision-market from time immemorial, and may, perhaps, says fond imagination, be the very spot to which the Fesulean ancestors of the Florentines descended from their high fastness to traffic with the rustic population of the valley, had not been shunned as a place of residence by Florentine

wealth. In the early decades of the fifteenth century,
which was now near its end, the Medici and other power-
ful families of the *popolani grassi*, or commercial nobility,
had their houses there, not perhaps finding their ears
much offended by the loud roar of mingled dialects, or
their eyes much shocked by the butchers' stalls, which the
old poet Antonio Pucci accounts a chief glory, or *dignita*,
of a market that, in his esteem, eclipsed the markets of all
the earth beside. But the glory of mutton and veal (well
attested to be the flesh of the right animals; for were not
the skins, with the heads attached, duly displayed according to the decree of the Signoria?) was just now wanting
to the Mercato, the time of Lent not being yet over. The
proud corporation, or 'Art,' of butchers was in abeyance,
and it was the great harvest-time of the market-
gardeners, the cheese-mongers, the vendors of macaroni,
corn, eggs, milk, and dried fruits: a change which was apt
to make the women's voices predominant in the chorus.
But in all seasons there was the exceptional ringing of pots
and pans, the chinking of the money-changers, the
tempting offers of cheapness at the old-clothes stalls, the
challenges of the dicers, the vaunting of new linens and
woollens, of excellent wooden-ware, kettles and frying-
pans; there was the choking of the narrow inlets with
mules and carts, together with much uncomplimentary
remonstrance in terms remarkably identical with the
insults in use by the gentler sex of the present day, under
the same imbrowning and heating circumstances. Ladies
and gentlemen, who came to market, looked on at a
larger amount of amateur fighting than could easily be
seen in these later times, and beheld more revolting rags,
beggary, and rascaldom, than modern householders
could well picture to themselves. As the day wore on the
hideous drama of the gaming-house might be seen here
by any chance open-air spectator – the quivering eagerness, the blank despair, the sobs, the blasphemy, and the
blows . . .
    But still there was the relief of prettier sights: there
were brood-rabbits, not less innocent and astonished than

those of our own period; there were doves and singing-birds to be bought as presents for the children; there were even kittens for sale, and here and there a handsome *gattuccio*, or 'Tom,' with the highest character for mousing; and, better than all, there were young, softly-rounded cheeks and bright eyes, freshened by the start from the far-off *castello* at daybreak, not to speak of older faces with the unfading charm of honest goodwill in them, such as are never quite wanting in scenes of human industry. And high on a pillar in the centre of the place – a venerable pillar, fetched from the Church of San Giovanni – stood Donatello's statue of Plenty, with a fountain near it, where the good wives of the market freshened their utensils, and their throats also; not because they were unable to buy wine, but because they wished to save the money for their husbands.

The buildings now standing in and around the Piazza are of the kind described by Browning when he wrote:

They are stone-faced, white as a curd, there's something to
    take the eye!
Houses in four straight lines, not a single front awry!
Green blinds as a matter of course, to draw when the sun
    gets high,
And the shops with fanciful signs which are painted
    properly.

Writing in 1912, in his *A Wanderer in Florence*, E. V. Lucas commented:

In talking to elderly persons who can remember Florence forty and fifty years ago I find that nothing so distresses them as the loss of the old quarter for the making of this new spacious piazza; and probably nothing can so delight the younger Florentines as its possession, for having nothing to do in the evenings, they do it chiefly in the Piazza Vittorio Emmanuele. Chairs and tables spring up like mushrooms in the roadway, among which too few waiters distribute those very inexpensive refreshments which seem to be purchased rather for the right to the seat that they confer than for any stimulation. It is extraordinary to the eyes of the thriftless English, who are never so happy as when they are overpaying Italian and other caterers in their own country, to notice how long these wiser folk will occupy a table on an expenditure of fourpence.

If for 'very inexpensive refreshments' one substitutes 'very expensive refreshments', this passage has in no way dated.

In D. H. Lawrence's *Aaron's Rod*, set in the period immediately after the First World War, the piazza is described as 'the centre of Florence by night' – as, indeed, it still remains today. Aaron comes to a 'large, brilliantly-lighted café' on a Sunday evening, to find the place full.

Men. Florentines, many men sat in groups and in twos and threes at the little marble tables. They were mostly in dark clothes or black overcoats. They had mostly been drinking just a cup of coffee – others, however, glasses of wine or liquor. But mostly it was just a little coffee-tray with a tiny coffee pot and a cup and saucer. There was a faint film of tobacco smoke. And the men were all talking: talking, talking with that peculiar intensity of Florentines.

Aaron cannot find a table. But then Argyle – the character based on Norman Douglas – bobs up and suggests that Aaron join him and his friends. The little group of foreigners discuss the political unrest of the time and the likelihood that (as one of them puts it) 'Some form of Socialism is bound to come, no matter how you postpone it or try variations.'

Suddenly their erudite, sometimes rancorous discussion is literally blown apart:

CRASH!
There intervened one awful minute of pure shock, when the soul was in darkness.

Out of this shock Aaron felt himself issuing amid a mass of terrible sensations: the fearful blow of the explosion, the noise of glass, the hoarse howl of people, the rushing of men, the sudden gulf, the awful gurgling whirlpool of horror in the social life.

He stood in agony and semi-blindness amid a chaos. Then as he began to recover his consciousness, he found himself standing by a pillar some distance from where he had been sitting: he saw a place where tables and chairs were all upside down, legs in the air, amid debris of glass and breakage: he saw the cafe almost empty, nearly everybody gone: he saw the owner, or the manager, advancing aghast to the place of the debris: he saw Lilly standing not far off, white as a sheet, and as if unconscious. And still he had no idea of what had happened. He thought perhaps something had broken down. He could not understand.

Lilly began to look round. He caught Aaron's eye. And then Aaron began to approach his friend.

'What is it?' he asked.

'A bomb,' said Lilly.

The manager, and one old waiter, and three or four youths had now advanced to the place of debris. And now Aaron saw that a man was lying there – and horror, blood was running across the floor of the cafe. Men began now hastily to return to the place. Some seized their hats and departed again at once. But many began to crowd in – a black eager crowd of men pressing to where the bomb had burst – where the man was lying. It was rather dark, some of the lamps were broken – but enough still shone. Men surged in with that eager, excited zest of people, where there has been an accident. Grey carabinieri, and carabinieri in the cocked hat and fine Sunday uniform pressed forward officiously.

'Let us go,' said Lilly.

And he went to the far corner, where his hat hung. But Aaron looked in vain for his own hat. The bomb had fallen near the stand where he had hung it and his overcoat.

'My hat and coat?' he said to Lilly.

Lilly, not very tall, stood on tiptoe. Then he climbed on a chair and looked around. Then he squeezed past the crowd.

Aaron followed. On the other side of the crowd excited

angry men were wrestling over overcoats that were mixed up with a broken marble table-top. Aaron spied his own black hat under the sofa near the wall. He waited his turn and then in the confusion pressed forward to where the coats were. Someone had dragged out his, and it lay on the floor under many feet. He managed, with a struggle, to get it from under the feet of the crowd. He felt at once for his flute. But his trampled, torn coat had no flute in its pocket. He pushed and struggled, caught sight of a section and picked it up. But it was split right down, two silver stops were torn out, and a long thin spelk of wood was curiously torn off. He looked at it, and his heart stood still. No need to look for the rest.

He felt utterly, utterly overcome – as if he didn't care what became of him any further. He didn't care whether he were hit by a bomb, or whether he himself threw the next bomb, and hit somebody. He just didn't care any more about anything in life or death. It was as if the reins of his life slipped from his hands, and he would let everything run where it would, so long as it did run.

There is a parallel between this passage and that in E. M. Forster's *A Room With a View* in which the heroine, Lucy, witnesses the stabbing of a man. In each the act of violence takes place in a popular and crowded piazza; in each case it disrupts an atmosphere of happiness and relaxation; and in each case it transforms the protagonist's life.

It was in the Gambrinus, for a long time the café in the piazza most popular with writers, that in December 1895 André Gide met Gabriele d'Annunzio:

. . .d'Annunzio indulges with obvious greediness in little vanilla ices served in small cardboard boxes. He sits beside me and talks gracefully and charmingly without, it seems to me, paying any special attention to the role he is playing. He is short; from a distance his face seems ordinary or already familiar, so devoid is he of any exterior sign of literature or genius. He wears a little pointed beard which is pale blond and talks with a clearly articulated voice, somewhat cold, but supple and almost caressing. His eyes are rather cold; he is perhaps rather cruel, but perhaps it is simply the appearance of his delicate sensuality that makes him seem so. He is wearing a black derby, quite unaffectedly.

. . . I say to him laughingly: 'But you have read everything!' 'Everything,' he replies gracefully. 'I believe one has to have read everything. We read everything,' he continues, 'in the constantly renewed hope of finally finding the masterpiece that we are all awaiting so eagerly.' He does not much like Maeterlinck, whose language strikes him as too simple. Ibsen displeases him by 'his lack of beauty.' 'What do you expect?' he says, as though to excuse himself; 'I am a Latin.'

. . . When I expressed my amazement that his great erudition allows him so sustained and so perfect a literary production – or that his work as a writer allows him the time to read so much: 'Oh,' he says, 'I have my own method for reading quickly. I am a terrible worker; nine or ten months in the year without stopping I work twelve hours a day. I have already produced twenty books.'

Moreover he says this without boasting at all and quite simply. In this way the evening is prolonged without difficulty.

Some ten days later, Gide again met d'Annunzio at Gambrinus:

He tells me that he has never known insomnia, or at least never had to suffer from it. Fencing and riding keep him from it. He fences a great deal and often rides. Tomorrow he is to go to Vinci, Leonardo's village; it is a pilgrimage, he says, and invites me to accompany him. If I were not such a poor horseman, I should have taken pleasure in riding with him. Talking of irony, he says that he cannot endure it, that in using irony you oppose yourself to things whereas it is only through love that you penetrate them, and that is essential . . .

With his meals he drinks only water; this is a hard worker's practice. On the other hand, he says that he drinks ten or twelve cups of tea a day. This morning, excusing himself for coming to the table in riding-habit, his elegance, his suave assurance and his unselfconsciousness were charming.

Four years later, the electorate of Florence gave the *coup de grâce* to d'Annunzio's already ailing political career, when he stood for the San Giovanni district in a general election precipitated by the murder of King Umberto II by an anarchist called Bresci. In his biography of d'Annunzio, *The Poet as Superman*, Anthony Rhodes summarizes the situation as follows:

> The electors of the Via Tornabuoni and the Via Strozzi were suspicious of a man who went from the ultra-conservatism of the Right, to the ultra-radicalism of the Left, particularly as he had large outstanding accounts in their shops. His new adversary, Cambray-Digny, was quick to sense this and an attack was made on his private life. D'Annunzio was accused of adultery, polygamy, theft, incest, sodomy, simony, murder and cannibalism.

Not surprisingly, he was defeated.

THE CASCINE

English guide-books often call the Cascine the Hyde Park of Florence; French guide-books, its Bois de Boulogne. Before the First World War E. V. Lucas wrote of it: 'Here the wealthy Florentines drive, the middle-classes saunter and ride bicycles, the poor enjoy picnics, and the English take country walks.' Except that it is now not only the wealthy who drive their cars up and down its avenues, that the bicycles are all too often and all too noisily motor ones, that those who enjoy their picnics tend to bring transistor radios with them and leave an extraordinary amount of litter behind them, and jogging for many people has taken the place of walking, the Cascine has little changed.

In the seventeenth and eighteenth centuries, when Florence was still a small, compact city, to go out to the Cascine was similar to going out to Richmond Park or Wimbledon Common from London at the same period. This is how the Cascine in 1732 was described by Joseph Spence (1699–1768), chiefly now remembered for the bright, impartial light which his posthumously published *Andecdotes* throws on Pope, his circle, and his antagonists:

At a little way out of the gate that we live next to . . . is a place made for the pleasure of the Grand Duke and his good subjects. You go to it through a range of vast Scotch fir-trees: on your left hand is a long run of groves and pretty artificial islands full of arbours, and on the right lie the vineyards and cornfields interspersed, which is the manner all about Florence (as in Lombardy). This leads into a large beautiful meadow. The walk of firs is continued on, all the length of it; the groves and woods, with a variety of a thousand different walks on the left, beyond which, all along, runs the river Arno. These woods are at last brought rounding to join the fir-walk, and so terminate the meadow. This meadow all our autumn was almost as fresh a green as we have in England (a very uncommon thing here), and was all sprinkled with wild crocuses as thick as the stars in heaven. Many of the trees in the woody part wanted to show another crop of leaves, and the wild vines that are very frequent in it hung over your head from tree to tree with their glistening black bunches of grapes, that were left there for the happiness of the birds that inhabit those woods very plentifully . . .

Very different from this rural scene is that described by Charles Lever more than a hundred years later in 1856:

On one side the gentle river stealing past beneath the shadowing foliage; on the other, the picturesque mountains towards Fiesole, dotted with its palaces and terraced gardens. The ancient city itself is partly seen, and the massive Duomo and the Palazzo Vecchio proudly tower above the trees. What other people of Europe have such a haunt? What other people would know so thoroughly how to enjoy it?
. . . Although a choice military band was performing with exquisite skill the favourite overtures of the day, the

noise and tumult of conversation almost drowned their
notes. In fact, the Cascine is to the world of society what
the Bourse is to the world of trade. It is the great centre of
all news and intelligence, where bargains of intercourse
are transacted, the scene of past pleasures is revived, and
where the plans of future enjoyment are canvassed. The
great and wealthy are there to see and meet with each
other. Their proud equipages lie side by side, like great
liners; while phaetons, like fast frigates, shoot swiftly by,
and solitary dandies flit past in varieties of conveyance to
which sea craft can offer no analogies. All are busy, eager
and occupied. Scandal holds here its festival, and the
misdeeds of every capital of Europe are now being discussed. The higher themes of politics occupy but few: the
interests of literature attract still less. It is essentially of the
world they talk, and it must be owned that they do it like
adepts. The last witticism of Paris – the last duel at Berlin
– who has fled from his creditors in England – who has
run away from her husband at Naples – all are retailed
with a serious circumstantiality that would lead one to
believe that gossip maintained its own correspondent in
every city of the Continent. Moralists might fancy,
perhaps, that in the tone these subjects are treated there
might mingle a reprobation of the bad, and a due estimate
of the opposite if it ever occurred at all; but no. Never
were censors more lenient – never were critics so charitable. The transgressions against good breeding, the
gaucheries of manner, the solecisms in dress, language, or
demeanour, do indeed meet with sharp reproof and
cutting sarcasm; but in recompense for such severity,
how gently they deal with graver offences. For the fel-
onies they can always discover 'the attenuating circumstances'; for the petty larcenies of fashion they have
nothing but whipcord.

Lever himself was guilty of committing 'petty larcenies of
fashion' because of the boisterous and showy manner in which
he drove through the crowded avenues of the Cascine, with
his numerous children, brilliantly attired, accompanying him

on horseback. More than one onlooker remarked sarcastically that he must be Franconi, then famous as an equestrian in the Cirque Parisienne.

Elizabeth Barrett Browning provides a similar evocation of a place which, in the nineteeth century, was part Ranelagh and part Vauxhall:

> You remember down at Florence our Cascine
>> Where the people on the feast-day walk and drive,
> And through the trees, long-drawn in many a green way,
>> O'er-roofing hum and murmur like a hive,
>> The river and the mountains look alive.
>
> You remember the piazzone there, the stand-place
>> Of carriages alive with Florentine beauties,
> Who lean and melt to music as the band plays,
>> To smile and chat with some one who afoot is,
>> Or on horseback, in observance of male duties?
>
> 'Tis pretty, in the afternoons of summer,
>> So many gracious faces brought together!
> Call it rout, or call it concert, they have come here,
>> In the floating of the fan and of the feather,
>> To reciprocate with beauty and fine weather.

The 'carriages alive with Florentine beauties' could already be seen in the Cascine when Tobias Smollett visited it in 1765.

Here, in the summer evenings, the quality resort to take the air in their coaches. Every carriage stops and forms a little separate conversazione. The ladies sit within, and the *cicisbei* stand on the foot-boards, on each side of the coach, entertaining them with their discourse. It would be no unpleasant enquiry to trace this sort of gallantry to its original, and investigate all its progress. The Italians, having been accused of jealousy, were resolved to wipe off the reproach, and seeking to avoid it for the future, have run into the other extreme. I know that it is generally assumed that the custom of choosing *cicisbei* was calculated to prevent the extinction of families, which would otherwise often happen in consequence of marriages founded upon interest, without any mutual affection in the contracting parties. How far this political consideration may have weighed against the jealous and vindictive temper of the Italians, I will not pretend to judge; but certain it is, every married lady in this country has her *cicisbeo*, or *servente*, who attends her every where, and on all occasions; and upon whose privileges the husband dare not encroach, without incurring the censure and ridicule of the whole community. For my part I would rather be condemned for life to the gallies than exercise the office of *cicisbeo*, exposed to the intolerable caprices and dangerous resentment of an Italian virago. I pretend not to judge the national character from my own observation; but if the portraits drawn by Goldoni are taken from nature, I would not hesitate to pronounce the Italian women the most haughty, insolent, capricious, and revengeful females on the face of the earth. Indeed, their resentments are so cruelly implacable, and contain such a mixture of perfidy, that, in my opinion, they are very unfit subjects for comedy, whose province it is rather to ridicule folly than to stigmatize such atrocious vice.

Alexandre Dumas – who spent a year in Florence in 1840, renting the Villa Palmieri in Via Giovanni Boccaccio – also evokes a picture of easy-going dalliance in the Cascine:

Of their own accord, and without one telling them, the coachmen take the road to the Piazzale. They halt there without one's even being obliged to make them a sign.

The reason is that the Piazzale of Florence offers one something which perhaps no other town in the world can offer: a kind of open-air *salon*, in which everyone makes or receives visits. It goes without saying that the visitors are men. The women remain in their carriages, the men go from one to another and, some on foot, some on horseback and some, more familiar, standing on the pavement, converse at the carriage doors.

It is in the Piazzale that life is lived each evening, that glances are exchanged, that meetings are fixed.

Among all these carriages the flower-girls thread their

path, handing out bouquets of roses and violets. Next day the same flower-girls will turn up in the cafés to demand their payment. In doing so, they will present each gentleman with a carnation.

Visiting the Cascine on Ascension Day in 1912, Arnold Bennett noted:

I saw a number of people with little cages containing crickets or grasshoppers which, I am told, are on sale in hundreds or thousands in the Cascine on Ascension Day morning.

The Cascine as a place of popular celebration, of picnics and sport, of assignation and amorous intrigue is very different from the Cascine which, wild and deserted, inspired Shelley to write his *Ode to the West Wind*.

L'Oltrarno

Partly lying on the south bank of the Arno and partly climbing up the hill of San Giorgio, the quarter of Oltrarno was not originally part of the city itself. For long chiefly inhabited by the poor, it began to be settled in the thirteenth century by a few rich and noble families, among them the Bardi. At the junction of the Via dei Bardi, now a fashionable and much-frequented street, and the Ponte Vecchio used to stand the Casa Ambrogi, guest house of the British envoy Horace Mann, who there put up Horace Walpole and Gray in 1740. Sadly, this palazzo was among the buildings blown up by the retreating Germans in 1944.

VIA DE' BARDI

It is in the Via de' Bardi that the family of George Eliot's heroine Romola lives. The novelist writes of it as follows:

> The Via de' Bardi . . . extends from the Ponte Vecchio to the Piazza de' Mozzo at the head of the Ponte alle Grazie; its right-hand line of houses and walls being backed by the rather steep ascent which in the fifteenth century was known as the hill of Bogoli, the famous stone-quarry whence the city got its pavement – of dangerously un-stable consistence when penetrated by rains; its left-hand buildings flanking the river, and making on their

northern side a length of quaint, irregularly pierced facade, of which the waters give a softened, loving reflection as the sun begins to decline towards the western heights. But quaint as these buildings are, some of them seem to the historical memory a too modern substitute for the famous houses of the Bardi family, destroyed by popular rage in the middle of the fourteenth century.

They were a proud and energetic stock, these Bardi: conspicuous among those who clutched the sword in the earliest world-famous quarrels of Florentines with Florentines, when the narrow streets were darkened with the high towers of the nobles, and when the old tutelar god Mars, as he saw the gutters reddened with neighbours' blood, might well have smiled at the centuries of lip-service paid to his rival, the Baptist. But the Bardi hands were of the sort that not only clutch the sword-hilt with vigour, but love the more delicate pleasure of fingering minted metal: they were matched, too, with true Florentine eyes, capable of discerning that power may be won by other means than by rending and riving, and by the middle of the fourteenth century we find them risen from their original condition of *popolani* to be possessors, by purchase, of lands and strongholds, and the feudal dignity of Counts of Vernion, disturbing to the jealousy of their republican fellow-citizens. These lordly purchases are explained by our seeing the Bardi disastrously signalised a few years later as standing in the very front of European commerce – the Christian Rothschilds of that time – undertaking to furnish specie for the wars of our Edward the Third, and having revenues 'in kind' made over to them; especially in wool, most precious of freights for Florentine galleys. Their august debtor left them with an august deficit, and alarmed Sicilian creditors made a too sudden demand for the payment of deposits, causing a ruinous shock to the credit of the Bardi and of the associated houses, which was felt as a commercial calamity all along the coasts of the Mediterranean. But, like more modern bankrupts, they did not, for all that, hide their heads in humiliation; on the contrary, they seem to have held them higher than ever, and to have been amongst the most arrogant of those grandees . . . who drew upon themselves the exasperation of the armed people in 1343. The Bardi, who had made themselves fast in their street between the two bridges, kept these narrow inlets, like panthers at bay, against the oncoming gonfalons of the people, and were only made to give way by an assault from the hill behind them. Their houses by the river, to the number of twenty-two (*palagi e case grandi*), were sacked and burnt, and many among the chief of those who bore the Bardi name were driven from the city. But an old Florentine family was many-rooted, and we find the Bardi maintaining importance and rising again and again to the surface of Florentine affairs in a more or less creditable manner, implying an untold family history that would have included even more vicissitudes and contrasts of dignity and disgrace, of wealth and poverty, than are usually seen on the background of wide kinship.

The Pitti Palace and the Boboli Gardens

Arnold Bennett thought that the Pitti Palace looked like 'a rather expensive barracks'; but George Eliot described its architecture as 'a wonderful union of Cyclopean massiveness with stately regularity', and Taine wrote of it: 'I doubt if there is a more monumental palace in the whole of Europe; I have never seen one that left me with a comparable impression of grandeur and simplicity.'

Less than a hundred years after Ammannati had completed the building, originally the residence of Luca Pitti, for the Medici Duke Cosimo and his wife Eleonora of Toledo, John Evelyn visited it in the 1640s. Little has changed since his description:

> The Palace of Pitti was built by the family, but of late greatly beautified by Cosimo with huge square stones of the Doric, Ionic, and the Corinthian orders, with a terrace at each side having rustic uncut balustrades, with a fountain that ends in a cascade seen from the great gate, and so

forming a vista to the gardens. Nothing is more admirable than the vacant stayrecase, marbles, statues, urnes, pictures, courte, grotto, and waterworkes. In the quadrangle is a huge jetto of water in a volto of 4 faces, with noble statues at each square, especially the Diana of porphyrie above the grotto. We were here shew'd a prodigious greate load-stone.

Evelyn also toured the Boboli Gardens, which had been laid out for Duke Cosimo behind the palace:

The garden has every variety, hills, dales, rocks, groves, aviaries, vivaries, fountaines, especialy one of five jettos, the middle basin being one of the longest stones I ever saw. Here is everything to make such a paradise delightfull. In the garden I saw a rose grafted on an orange-tree. There was much topiary worke, and columns in architecture about the hedges. The Duke has added an ample laboratorye, over against which stands a Fort on a hill where they told us his treasure is kept. In this Palace the Duke ordinarily resides, living with his Swiss guards, after the frugal Italian way, and even selling what he can spare of his wines, at the cellar under his very house, wicker bottles dangling over even the chief entrance into the Palace, serving for his vinter's bush.

In that once immensely popular historical novel *John Inglesant*, J. H. Shorthouse (1834–1903) imagines the court of Evelyn's wine-merchant autocrat of a Duke in a hyperbolically romantic manner. Inglesant, an English Roman Catholic, arrives in Florence in 1651, on a secret errand for the Royalist cause, and is invited to the Pitti Palace:

The saloons were crowded and very hot, and when Inglesant left the supper room and came into the brilliant marble hall lighted with great lustres, where the Court was at play, he was more excited than was his wont. The Court was gathered at different tables – a very large one in the centre of the hall and other smaller ones around. The brilliant dresses, the jewels, the beautiful women, the reflections in the numberless mirrors, made a dazzling and mystifying impression on his brain. The play was very high and at the table at which Inglesant sat down especially so. He lost heavily and this did not tend to calm his nerves; he doubled his stake, with all the money he had with him, and lost again.

As he rises from the table, a page hands him a 'delicately perfumed note,' from an Italian woman, Lauretta, who needs his help and with whom he has already fallen in love. She summons him to the Grand Duchess's lodgings.

They [Inglesant and the page] passed through many corridors and rooms richly furnished until they reached the lodgings of the Grand Duchess. The night was sultry, and through the open windows above the gardens the strange odours that are born of darkness and of night entered the palace. In the dark arcades the nightingales were singing, preferring gloom and mystery to the light in which all other creatures rejoice; and in the stillness the murmur of brooks and the splash of the fountains oppressed the air with an unearthly and unaccustomed sound. Around the casements festoons of harmless and familiar flowers and leaves assumed wild and repulsive shapes, as if transformed into malicious demons who made men their sport. Inglesant thought involuntarily of those plants that are at enmity with man, which are used for enchantments and for poisoning, and whose very scent is death; such saturnine and fatal flowers seemed more at home in the lovely Italian night than the innocent plants which witness to lovers' vows, and upon which divines moralize and preach. The rooms of the Duchess were full of perfume of the kind that enervates and dulls the sense. It seemed to Inglesant as though he were treading the intricate pathways of a dream, careless as to what befell him, yet with a passionate longing which urged him forward, heedless of a restraining voice which he was even then half-conscious that at other times he should have heard. The part of the palace where he was seemed deserted, and the page led him through more than one anteroom without meeting any one, until they reached a curtained door, which the boy opened, and directed Inglesant to enter. He did so, and found himself at once in the presence of Lauretta, who was lying upon a low seat at the open window. The room was lighted by several small lamps in different positions, giving an ample, yet at the same time soft and dreamy light. Lauretta was carelessly dressed, yet, in the soft light, and in her negligent attitude, there was something that made her beauty the more attractive, and her manner to Inglesant was unrestrained and clinging. Her growing affection, the urgency of her need, and the circumstances of the hour, caused her innocently to speak and act in a way the most fitted to promote her brother's atrocious purpose.

'Cavaliere,' she said, 'I have sent for you because I have no friend but you. I have sent for you to help me against my own family . . .'

Although in 1785 Mrs Piozzi (Thrale) thought the Grand Duke's court informal she had little doubt that Leopold I was an autocrat:

Our Grand Duke lives with little state for aught I can observe here; but where there is least pomp, there is commonly most power . . . He tells his subjects when to go to bed, and who to dance with, till the hour he chooses they should retire to rest, with exactly that sort of old-fashioned paternal authority that fathers used to exercise over families in England before commerce had run her levelling plough over all ranks, and annihilated even the name of subordination. If he hear of any person living long in Florence without being able to give a good account of his business there, the Duke warns him to go away; and if he loiters after such warning given, sends him out. Does any nobleman shine in pompous equipage or splendid table; the Grand Duke enquires soon into his pretensions, and scruples not to give personal advice and add grave proofs with regard to the management of each individual's private affairs, the establishment of their sons, the marriage of their sisters etc. When they appeared to complain of this behaviour to me, I know not, replied

I, what to answer: one has always read and heard that the
Sovereigns ought to behave in despotic governments like
the *fathers of their family* . . . 'Yes, Madam,' replied one of
my auditors, with an acuteness truly Italian, 'but this
Prince is our *father-in-law* . . .'

By the time of Stendhal's visit in 1817, the Grand Duke of
the day, Ferdinand III, was a far less autocratic figure:

Grand-Duke Ferdinand, realising full well that he could
command neither enough soldiers nor enough courtiers
to live a happy life surrounded by the general execration
of his subjects, has chosen rather to become a most
familiar monarch, and you may meet him strolling un-
accompanied through the streets of Florence. His Highness the Grand-Duke has three Ministers, of whom one,
Prince Neri Corsini, is a dyed-in-the-wool reactionary,
whilst the other two, signor Fossombroni, a geometer of
noted reputation, and signor Frullani, are very reasonable
beings; His Highness foregathers with them but once a
week, and in fact takes little or no hand in the government
of his domain. Year by year it is his habit to commission
some thirty thousand francs' worth of pictures from the
studios of those excruciating painters whom the public
(which admires them) sees fit to designate for such an
honour; likewise, year by year, he purchases a fine estate
or two. Granted only that Heaven sees fit to preserve this
supremely *reasonable* being, whom it has thus pleased her
to bestow upon the Duchy, I am convinced that, in the
end, he will prosper to undertake the government of his
Tuscan subjects *free and for nothing*.

In 1817 the fourteen-year-old Charlotte Harriet Beaujolais
Campbell wrote in her journal of a visit of her mother and her
older sister Eleanor to the Grand Duke:

At 12 in the morning they were at the Palazzo Pitti and
with a few other English all of whom are really a disgrace
to the nation. Mr Dorkins [in fact, Dawkins, Secretary at
the British Legation] led them into the room where the
Grand Duke was standing. He spoke to nobody but

Mamma and the Miss Berries [two inseparable sisters,
intimates of Horace Walpole] whom he knew some years
ago. He merely said that he was glad that mamma was
come to Florence at the time of his daughter's marriage as
it would make every thing appear more gay to her. He
then bowed saying he would detain them no longer but
hoped· to see them very often. There are about twenty
other English who have the impudence to present themselves at this court because it is foreign whereas in England they would not dare to show their noses. This is a
disgusting forwardness and the Grand Duke scarcely
bowed to them . . .

Some dozen years later, James Fenimore Cooper was
presented at court:

Ten was the hour at which I presented myself at the Pitti,
in an ordinary morning-dress, wearing shoes instead of
boots. I was shown into an ante-chamber, where I was
desired to take a seat. A servant soon after passed through
the room with a salver, bearing a chocolate-cup and a bit
of toast, a proof that his imperial highness had just been
making a light breakfast. I was then told that the grand
duke would receive me.

The door opened on a large room, shaped like a
parallelogram, which had the appearance of a private
library, or cabinet. There were tables, books, maps,
drawings, and all the appliances of work. The library of
the palace, however, is another part of the edifice, and
contains many thousands of volumes, among which are
some that are very precious, and their disposition is one of
the most convenient, though not the most imposing as to
show, of any library I know.

The grand duke was standing alone at the upper end of
a long table that was covered by some drawings and plans
of the *Maremme*, a part of his territories in reclaiming
which he is said to be now much occupied. As I entered,
he advanced and gave me a very civil reception. I paid my
compliments, and made an offering of a book I had caused
to be printed in Florence. This he accepted with great

politeness; and then he told me, in the simplest manner, that 'his wife' was so ill, she could not see me that morning. I had a book for her imperial highness also, and he said that it might be left at Poggio Imperiale.

As soon as these little matters were disposed of, the grand duke walked to a small round table, in a corner, near which stood two chairs, and, requesting me to take one, he seated himself in the other, when he began a conversation that lasted near an hour. The prince was, as before, very curious on the subject of America, going over again some of the old topics. He spoke of Washington with great respect, and evidently felt no hostility to him on account of his political career. Indeed, I could not trace in the conversation of the prince the slightest evidence of a harsh feeling, distrust, or jealousy towards America; but, on the other hand, I thought he was disposed to view us kindly, – a thing so unusual among political men in Europe as to be worthy of mention. He left on my mind, in this interview, the same impression and integrity of feeling as the other. . . .

He observed that fewer Americans travelled now than formerly, he believed. So far from this, I told him, the number had greatly increased within the last few years. 'I used to see a good many,' he answered, 'but now I see but few.' I was obliged to tell him what is the truth, – that most of those who came to Europe knew little of courts, that they did not give themselves time to see more than the commoner sights, and that they were but indifferent courtiers. He spoke highly of our ships, several of which he had seen in Leghorn, and on board of one or two of which he had actually been. . . .

I found him better informed than usual on the subject of our history; though, of course, many of his notions had the usual European vagueness. He seemed aware, for instance, of the great difficulty with which we had to contend in the revolution, for the want of the commonest munitions, such as arms and powder. He related an anecdote of Washington connected with this subject, with a feeling and spirit that showed his sympathies were

on the right side of that great question, on whichever side
his policy might have been.

We had some conversation on the subject of the dis-
covery of America, and I took the occasion to compliment him on there having been a Florentine [Amerigo
Vespucci] concerned in that great enterprise; but he did
not seem disposed to rob Columbus of any glory on
account of his own countryman, though he admitted that
the circumstances in a degree connected his own town
with the event.

At length he rose, and I took my leave of him, after
thanking him for the facilities afforded me in Tuscany.
When we separated, he went quietly to his maps; and as I
turned at the door to make a parting salute, I found his
eyes on the paper, as if he expected no such ceremony.

Thomas Trollope and his indomitable mother attended the
weekly balls given by the Grand Duke. Florence at that period
was, as he remarked, 'an especially economical place for those
to whom it was pleasant to enjoy during the whole of the gay
season as many balls, concerts and other entertainments as
they could possibly desire, without the necessity, or indeed the
possibility, of putting themselves to the expense of giving
anything in return.' There were weekly balls at the club of the
Florentine aristocracy, the Casa dei Nobili; the foreign ministers were constantly giving balls; and from time to time some
wealthy grandee would also give one. But 'perhaps the
pleasantest of all these were the balls at the Pitti', since 'they
were so entirely *sans gêne.*'

No court dress was required save on the first day of the
year, when it was *de rigueur*. But absence on that occasion
in no way excluded the absentee from the other balls.
Indeed, save to a newcomer, no invitations to foreigners
were issued, it being understood that all who had been
there once were welcome ever after. The Pitti balls were
by no means concluded, but rather divided into two,
by a very handsome and abundant supper, at which, to
tell tales out of school (but then the offenders have no

doubt mostly gone over to the majority), the guests used
to behave abominably. The English would seize the plates
of *bonbons* and empty the contents bodily into their coat
pockets. The ladies would do the same with their pocket-
handkerchiefs.

But the Duke's liege subjects carried on their depre-
dations on a far bolder scale. I have seen large portions of
fish, sauce and all, packed up in a newspaper, and
deposited in a pocket. I have seen fowls and ham share the
same fate, without any newspaper at all. I have seen jelly
carefully wrapped in an Italian countess's laced *mouchoir*! I
think the servants must have had orders not to allow
entire bottles of wine to be carried away, for I never saw
that attempted, and can imagine no other reason why. I
remember that those who affected to be knowing old
hands used to recommend one to specially pay attention
to the Grand Ducal Rhine wine, and remember, too,
conceiving a suspicion that certain of these connoisseurs
based their judgement in this matter wholly on the knowledge that the Duke possessed estates in Bohemia!

Apparently the Americans behaved better than the other
nationalities: 'I never saw an American pillaging the supper
table; though I may add that American ladies would accept any
amount of *bonbons* from English blockade-runners.'

More than a century before, in 1740, Horace Walpole had
commented on the manner in which even the most affluent
and elegant people were not above filching food from the table
of their host.

. . . A large palace finely illuminated; there were all the
beauties, all the jewels, and all the sugar-plums of
Florence. Servants loaded with large chargers full of
comfits heap the tables with them, the women fall on
with both hands, and stuff their pockets and every creek
and corner about them.

In his *Life of Charles Lever*, Lever's first biographer, W. J.
Fitzpatrick quotes a Mrs M — 's account of Lever's behaviour as
a guest at these balls at the Pitti:

In one part of the palace card-playing would be going on, while the intoxicating whirl of the dance held sway in another. When deep in his game of whist and with me as his partner, he often, on hearing some favourite air struck up, flung down his cards, saying, 'I must give my little wife a turn;' which having done, he rapidly resumed his place at the table. The polka was the dance of which he was most fond. Mrs Lever was so small and he so fat that in heeling and toeing it he cut a rather comical figure, but all admired his abiding love for her; and he certainly looked supremely happy in her companionship. As his too solid belt of flesh increased, he gradually relinquished dancing, and remarked that nothing short of an Irish jig could tempt him to the effort.

Mrs Trollope was the only person in these gatherings before whom 'he seemed to collapse', so that he would transparently manoeuvre not to have her as his partner at whist, while she no less transparently coveted this position.

Of the treasures on show in the Pitti Palace, writers have been impressed by a variety of pictures and statues. For Swinburne the supreme painter here was Andrea del Sarto. Remarking that 'his life was corroded by the poisonous solvent of love, and his soul burnt into ashes' – this was clearly intended as a recommendation – he added that 'At Florence only can one trace and tell how great a painter and how various Andrea was. There only, but surely there, can the spirit and presence of the things of time on his immortal spirit be understood.' Hawthorne was drawn to a picture, *The Fates*, then ascribed to Michelangelo; 'As regards the interpretation of this, or of any other profound picture, there are likely to be as many interpretations as there are spectators. Each man interprets the hieroglyphic in his own way; and the painter perhaps had a meaning which none of them have reached; or possibly he put forth a riddle without himself knowing the solution.' Sophia Hawthorne was particularly taken by Titian's *Portrait of Ippolito de' Medici*, describing it as 'superb'. She goes on:

He is in a Hungarian dress, buttoned up to the throat, which is very becoming, when a handsome head and face are shut off in that way. He stands with a wonderful dignity and grace, and his features and style of head are of fascinating beauty, though I am sure he is not a good man. He looks dark and treacherous, with a princely state, worthy of a higher character.

While the Hawthornes were going round the palace, a military band struck up in the piazza, as it used to do each afternoon, and so 'glorified the common day and added life to the painted forms and faces. We came down and went into the magnificent Cortile . . . and walked round it, listening to the music.'

John Addington Symonds was rhapsodic about Giorgione's *Concert of Music*:

Of the indisputed pictures by Giorgione, the grandest is the *Monk at the Clavichord* [as he called it]. The young man has his fingers on the keys; his head is turned away towards an old man standing near him. On the other side of the instrument is a boy. These two figures are but foils and adjuncts to the musician in the middle; and the whole interest of his face lies in its concentrated feeling – the very soul of music, passing through his eyes.

For Henry James, viewing a dozen Titian portraits 'of unequal interest', the best was that of

that formidable young man in black, with the small compact head, the delicate nose and the irascible blue eye. Who was he? What was he? '*Ritratto virile*' [male portrait] is all the catalogue is able to call the picture. 'Virile! Rather!' you vulgarly exclaim. You may weave what romance you please about it, but a romance your dream must be. Handsome, clever, defiant, passionate, danger-ous, it was not his fault if he hadn't adventures and to spare. He was a gentleman and a warrior, and his adven-tures balanced between camp and court. I imagine him the young orphan of a noble house, about to come into mortgaged estates. One wouldn't have cared to be his guardian, bound to paternal admonitions once a month over his precocious transactions with the Jess or his scandalous abduction from her convent of such and such a noble maiden.

William Beckford (1759–1844) – who spent October 1780 in Florence in the course of a sumptuous Grand Tour – described a visit to the Boboli Gardens as follows:

I walked to one of the bridges across the Arno, and surveyed the hills at a distance, purpled by the declining sun. Its mild beams tempted me to the garden of Boboli which lies behind the Palazzo Pitti, stretched out on the side of the mountain. I ascended terrace after terrace, robed by a thick underwood of bay and myrtle, above which rise several nodding towers, and a long sweep of venerable wall, almost entirely covered by ivy. You would have been enraptured with the broad masses of shade and dusky alleys that opened as I advanced, with white statues of fauns and sylvans glimmering amongst them; some of which pour water into sarcophagi of the purest marble, covered with antique relievos. The capitals of columns and ancient friezes are scattered about as seats.

On these I reposed myself, and looked up at the cypress groves spiring above the thickets; then, plunging into their retirements, I followed a winding path, which led me by a series of steep ascents to a green platform overlooking the whole extent of wood with Florence deep beneath, and the tops of the hills which encircle it, jagged with pines; here and there a convent, or villa, whitening in the sun. This scene extends as far as the eye can reach.

Still ascending I attained the brow of the mountain, and had nothing but the fortress of Belvedere, and two or three open porticoes above me. On this elevated situation, I found several walks of trellis-work, clothed with luxuriant vines, that produce to my certain knowledge the most delicious clusters. A colossal statue of Ceres, her hands extended in the act of scattering fertility over the

prospect, crowns the summit, where I lingered to watch
the landscape fade, and the bright skirts of the western sun
die gradually away,

Then descending alley after alley and bank after bank, I
came to the orangery in front of the palace, disposed in a
grand amphitheatre, with marble niches relieved by dark
foliage, out which spring tall aerial cypresses. The spot
brought the scenery of an antique Roman garden full into
my mind. I expected every instant to be called to the table
of Lucullus hard by, in one of the porticoes, and to stretch
myself on his purple triclinias; but waiting in vain for the
summons till the approach of night, I returned delighted
with a ramble that had led me so far into antiquity . . .

Shelley was hardly less rhapsodic. Florence, seen from the
eminence of the Belvedere, was for him 'a smokeless city' –
which it certainly is not today. He remarked on 'a Babylon of
palaces and gardens', making up another city outside the then
narrow confines of the city itself; on 'the etherial mountain-
line, hoary with snow and intersected by clouds'; on 'the
cypress groves whose obeliskine forms of intense green pierce
the grey shadow of the wintry hill that overhangs them'; on
the cypresses of the garden, which 'form a magnificent foreground of accumulated verdure' – 'pyramids of dark leaves
and shining cones rising out of the mass, beneath which are
cut, like caverns, recesses which conduct into walks.'

The narrator of Henry James's early tale (1879) *The Diary of a
Man of Fifty* visits the Boboli Gardens and the Pitti Palace on
the day after his arrival in Florence. His previous visit, when
he fell in love with an Italian aristocrat, long since dead, was
twenty-seven years before; but, contrary to what everyone has
warned him, he finds 'Everything is so perfectly the same that
I seem to be living in my youth all over again; all the forgotten
impressions of that enchanting time come back to me.'

I wandered for an hour in the Boboli Gardens; we [he and
the Italian girl] went there several times together. I remembered all those days individually; they seem to me as
yesterday. I found the corner where she always chose to
sit – the bench of sun-warmed marble, in front of the

screen of ilex, with that exuberant statue of Pomona just beside it. The place is exactly the same, except that poor Pomona has lost one of her tapering fingers. I sat there for half-an-hour, and it was strange how near to me she seemed. The place was perfectly empty – that is, it was filled with *her*. I closed my eyes and listened; I could almost hear the rustle of her dress on the gravel. Why do we make such an ado about death? What is it after all but a sort of refinement of life? She died ten years ago, and yet, as I sat there in the evening stillness, she was a palpable, audible presence. I went afterwards into the gallery of the palace, and wandered for an hour from room to room. The same great pictures hung in the same places and the same dark frescoes stretched above them. Twice, of all, I went there with her; she had a great understanding of art. She understood all sorts of things. Before the Madonna of the Chair I stood a long time. The face is not a particle like hers, and yet it reminded me of her. But everything does that. We stood and looked at it together once for half-an-hour; I remember perfectly what she said.

Of Raphael's *La Madonna della Seggiola* – a tondo – George Eliot wrote that it 'leaves me, with all its beauty, impressed only by the grave gaze of the infant.'

It was at the back of the Pitti Palace that, in 1644, John Evelyn inspected 'the Prince's Cavalarizzo', moved there, some years previously, from the back of the Signoria.

. . . The Prince has a stable of the finest horses of all countries, Arabs, Turks, Barbs, Gennets, English, &c, which are constantly exercised in the *manège*.

Near the 'Cavalarizzo' was a place where he kept several wild beasts, as wolves, catts, beares, tygers and lions. They are loose in a deep wall'd court, and therefore to be seen with more pleasure than at the Tower of London, in their grates. One of the lions leaped to a surprising height to catch a joynt of mutton which I caused to be hung downe.

Visiting the same place a few years later, Richard Lassels recorded how the Grand Duke and his court would amuse

themselves by leaning over the pit and watching the animals
scrapping among themselves. When they had become bored
with the contest, the lions would be driven back to their lairs
by 'a fearful machine of wood made like a great Green Dragon
which a man within it rowles upon wheels, and holding out
two lighted torches at the eyes of it, frights the fiercest beast
thereby into his den.'

THE NATURAL HISTORY MUSEUM

The Museo di Fisica e di Storia Naturale (now the Museo
Zoologico 'La Specola'), situated at 17 Via Roma, beyond the
Pitti Palace, exercised on visitors of the nineteenth century a
fascination which it has lost for modern ones. We tend either
boldy to outface death or else to avert our eyes from it; they
tended morbidly to flirt with it.

Longfellow chiefly noticed 'the representation in wax of
some of the appalling scenes of the plague'. The artist, he
noted, was a Sicilian by the name of Zumbo. Zumbo, he
decided,

> must have been a man of the most gloomy and saturnine
> imagination, and more akin to the worm than most of us,
> thus to have revelled night and day in the hideous mys-
> teries of death, corruption, and the charnel-house. It is
> strange how this representation haunts one. It is like a
> dream of the sepulchre, with its loathesome corpses, with
> 'the blackening, the swelling, the bursting of the trunk –
> the worm, the rat, and the tarantula at work.' You
> breathe more freely as you step out into the open air again;
> and when the bright sunshine, and the crowded, busy
> streets next meet your eye, you are ready to ask, is this
> indeed a representation of reality? Can this pure air have
> been laden with pestilence? Can this gay city have ever
> been a city of the plague?

Dickens remarks that the Natural History Museum is

> famous throughout the world for its preparations in wax;
> beginning with models of leaves, seeds, plants, inferior

animals; and gradually ascending, through separate organs of the human frame, up to the whole structure of that wonderful creation, exquisitely presented, as in recent death. Few admonitions of our frail mortality can be more solemn and more sad, or strike so home upon the heart, as the counterfeits of Youth and Beauty that are lying there, upon their beds, in their last sleep.

Sophia Hawthorne found much at which to marvel: the 'wax models of rare exotics and fruits'; the collection of stuffed birds – 'the parrots in a corner looked like a fierce autumnal sunset'; the 'two real pearls still upon an oyster where they grew, more beautiful than any in the British Museum'; the skeletons of animals, the models of their interiors 'very curious and very horrid.' Above all, she was impressed by the relics of Galileo, among them 'one of his fingers, pointing upward.' Another finger, she records, is in the Laurentian Library, adding: 'How little he dreamed, when he sat in prison, that even his fingers would become precious relics for posterity! But I wish he had kept firm, and not denied the truth he had discovered. That is an endless grief to me.'

Santo Spirito

A visit to the Brunelleschi church of Santo Spirito – Luther preached there on his way to Rome as an Augustinian monk – caused Sophia Hawthorne to write some tart comments on the Italian priesthood at that period:

To rest, I went to the Church of Santo Spirito, so beautiful with its majestic colonnades and ruby lights forever burning at the superb altar of Florentine mosaic; and I sat there in peace and quiet for an hour. Meanwhile the priests came in, as once before when I was there, and chanted their evening service, but I could not see them from my seat. There were several persons, saying their prayers, with their rosaries, in the nave, and acolytes were crossing in the distance, with lamps and salvers and copes, but with no sound. All was still, except the voices

of the chanters, rising and falling like waves in a summer
sea. If there were always heart and truth in those monks
and prelates, real, religious worship, how deep would be
our emotions during those imposing functions! But I am
always sensible of hollowness and emptiness in every
ceremony I see; and especially with the ennui and inward
disgust of the priests themselves, who seem very anxious
to get through the endlessly repeated task, so as to go and
eat and drink and be merry. Yet there are doubtless many
among them truly devout. The appearance of the clergy
in Florence is almost invariably repulsive and gross, and
they are said to be peculiarly depraved. They are mostly
fat, with flabby cheeks, chins and throats, of very earthly
aspect. There is nothing to compare them to but hogs,
and they merely need to stoop upon their hands to be
perfect likenesses of swine, so that the encounter of one of
them in the street gives one a faint sensation. It is shocking
that such men are in holy garb, set apart from the constant
worship of God, and, under cover of superior sanctity,
becoming the most corrupt of human beings. Such blasphemy of the Holy Spirit seems to blot out the sun, and
poison the air; but I think there must be good persons
among them to bear witness – or how could these monasteries uphold themselves? 'A lie cannot stand,' says our
great philosopher.

To the immediate west of San Spirito lies the working-class,
once slummy but now rapidly improving district Borgo San
Frediano. It is in this district that many of the novels of Vasco
Pratolino (1913–   ), best of Florentine novelists of this
century, are set:

Sanfrediano is the unhealthiest section of the city; in the
heart of its streets, as densely populated as ant-hills, are
located the Central Refuse Dump, the public dormitory,
the barracks. The greater part of its slums is the home of
rag-pickers, and of those who cook the intestines of cattle
to make their living from them and from the broth that is
their product.
    . . . The houses are ancient because of their stones, and

even more because of their squalor. One banked up against another, they form an immense block . . . The happy, bickering clamour of the people brings these places to life: the sounds of the second-hand man and the rag-picker, the worker in the nearby repair shops, the office clerk, the artisan who works in gold, or in marble, or with furs. And even the women, most of them, have a job. Sanfrediano is a little republic of women who do work at home . . .

The Sanfrediani are sentimental and pitiless at once: their idea of justice is symbolized by the enemy's remains hung to a lamp-post; and their idea of Paradise, summed up in a proverb, is poetic and vulgar: a Utopian place where there is an abundance of millet and a shortage of birds.

Since Pratolini wrote these words in the 1950s, the Borgo San Frediano, like the East End of London, has undergone great changes. It now certainly contains more antique-dealers than rag-pickers and more restaurateurs than cookers of intestines.

San Miniato

Many people would claim that the Romanesque basilica of San Miniato al Monte is the most beautiful church in Florence, and some that it is the most beautiful church in the whole of Italy. Yet, when Oscar Wilde visited it in 1875, at the age of twenty-one, it induced in him not aesthetic delight but theatrical self-laceration:

> See, I have climbed the mountainside
> Up to this holy house of God,
> Where once the Angel-Painter trod
> Who saw the heavens opened wide,

> And throned upon the crescent moon
> The Virginal white Queen of Grace,
> Mary! Could I but see thy face,
> Death would not come at all too soon.

O crowned of God with thorns and pain!
Mother of Christ! O mystic wife!
My heart is weary of this life
And oversad to sing again.

O crowned by God with love and flame!
O crowned by Christ the Holy One!
O listen ere the setting sun
Show to the world my sin and shame!

The last quatrain is chillingly prophetic.

Nineteen years later, in May 1894, shortly before the libel action that was to precipitate his ruin, Wilde was once again in Florence, this time with Alfred Douglas. Gide, who constantly swung between discretion and recklessness, was disconcerted when, in a café, he ran into the famous English writer in the company of (as he wrote circumspectly to Paul Valéry) 'another poet of a younger generation'.

While in Florence on this second occasion, Wilde renewed an acquaintanceship with Vernon Lee and her brother, the poet Eugene Lee-Hamilton. Mary Berenson, who eight years before had been enchanted by 'the fair Oscar' – seated next to him at a dinner-party, she had 'simply revelled in his witty aphorisms about America and England and Art and Novels and all manner of subjects' – was the intermediary, taking Wilde to call with her. Next day she recorded of the visit:

> It was a great success. Oscar talked like an angel, and they all fell in love with him – even Vernon, who had hated him almost as bitterly as he had hated her. He, on his part, was charmed with her – he likes people without souls, or else with great peace in their souls, and when he met her before he found her restless and self-assertive. But yesterday he admitted that she had grown less strenous.

By now Mary Berenson's admiration of Wilde was no longer whole-hearted. 'Oscar says such extraordinarily clever and subtle things, I can't help liking to talk to him, but he is so untrustworthy, on the other hand, so utterly lacking in any kind of character with which I have sympathy, but it is a "mingled cup".'

The Environs

Leigh Hunt wrote that his almost daily walk was to Fiesole, through a path skirted with wild myrtle and cyclamen. There he could stop at the cloister of the Doccia, and sit 'on the melancholy platform behind it, reading or looking through the pines down to Florence.'

Milton and Galileo give a glory to Fiesole beyond even its starry antiquity: nor perhaps is there a name eminent in the best annals of Florence to which some connections cannot be traced with this favoured spot. When it was full of wood, it must have been eminently beautiful. It is at present full of vines and olives, but this is not wood, *woody*.

Hunt and his family were staying in the nearby village of Maiano, now subsumed into Fiesole itself. The ground floor of the villa which they had rented was occupied by 'a Hebrew family' of jewellers, 'who partook the love of music in common with their tribe.' The little girls 'declaimed out of Alfieri' in the morning; and in the evening the parents 'led concerts in the garden.' Often there were visits from the priest, who would play 'a Christian game at cards with his Hebrew friends.' Hunt recounts how

one evening all the young peasantry in the neighbour-hood assembled in the hall of the village, by leave of the proprietor (an old custom), and had the most energetic ball I ever beheld. The walls of the room seemed to spin round with the waltz, as though it would never leave off – the whirling faces all looking grave, hot, and astonished at one another. Among the musicians I observed one of the apprentices of my friend the bookseller, and evidence of a twofold mode of getting money not unknown in England. I recollected his face the more promptly, inasmuch as not many days previous he had accompanied me to my abode with a set of books, and astonished me by jumping on a sudden from one side of me to the other. I asked what was the matter, and he said, 'A viper, sir.' He seemed to think that an Englishman might as well settle the viper as the bill.

Of the panoramic view of Florence and the hills around it, Hunt said that it was 'a sight to enrich the eyes.' Charles Armitage Brown, Shakespearian scholar and friend of Keats, was a neighbour of Hunt's at the former convent of San Baldassare.

On the *Arx* (citadel) of the ancient city rests the church of S. Alessandro and Franciscan convent. To this Franciscan convent, the young American, Rowland Mallett, one of the leading characters of Henry James's *Roderick Hudson*, makes his way:

It was a day all benignant; the March sun felt like May, as the English poet [Browning] of Florence says; the thick-blossomed shrubs, the high-climbing plants that hung over the walls of villas and *podere* flung their odorous promise into the warm still air. He followed our friend, the winding, mounting lanes; lingered as he got higher beneath the rusty cypresses, beside the low parapets, where you look down on the charming city and sweep the vale of the Arno; reached the small square before the cathedral and rested a while in the massive, dusky church; then, climbing hither, pushed up to the Franciscan convent poised on the very apex of the great hill. He rang at the little gateway; a shabby, senile, red-faced brother admitted him, a personage almost maudlin with the milk of

human kindness. There was a dreary chill in the chapel
and the corridors, and he passed rapidly through them
into the delightfully steep and tangled old garden which
runs wild over the forehead of the mountain. He had been
there before, he came back to it as to a friend. The garden
hangs in the air, and you ramble from terrace to terrace
and wonder how it keeps from slipping down, in full
consummation of its dishonour and decay, to the nakedly
romantic gorge beneath. It was just noon at Rowland's
visit, and after roaming about a while he flung himself on
the sun-warmed slab of a mossy stone bench and pulled
his hat over his eyes. The short shadows of the brown-
coated cypresses above him had grown very long, later
on, and yet he had not passed through the convent. One
of the monks, in a faded snuff-coloured robe, came
wandering out into the garden, reading a greasy little
breviary. Suddenly he approached the bench on which
Rowland had stretched himself and paused for respectful
interest. Rowland was still in possession, but seated
himself now with his head in his hands and his elbows on
his knees. He seemed not to have heard the sandalled tread
of the good brother, but as the monk remained watching
him he at last looked up. It was not the ignoble old man
who had admitted him, but a pale, gaunt personage, of a
graver and more ascetic and yet of a charitable aspect.
Rowland's face might have borne for him the traces of
extreme trouble; something he appeared mildly to consider as he kept his finger in his little book and folded his
arms picturesquely across his breast. Was his attitude, as
he bent his sympathetic Italian eyes, the mere accident of
his civility or the fruit of an exquisite spiritual tact? To
Rowland, however this might have been, it appeared a
sort of offer of ready intelligence. He rose and approached
the monk, laying his hand on his arm.

'My brother,' he said, 'did you ever see the Devil in
person?'

The *frate* gazed gravely and crossed himself. 'Heaven
forbid, my son!'

'He was here,' Rowland went on, 'here in this lovely

garden, as he was once in Paradise, half an hour ago. But
have no fear; I drove him out.' And he stooped and picked
up his hat, which had rolled away into a bed of cyclamen
in vague suggestion of a positive scrimmage.

'You've been tempted, *figlio mio*?' asked the friar
tenderly.

'Hideously!'

'And you've resisted – and conquered!'

'I believe I've conquered.'

'The blessed Saint Francis be praised. It's well done. If
you like, we'll offer a mass for you.'

Rowland hesitated. 'I'm not of your faith.'

The *frate* smiled with dignity. 'That's a reason the
more.'

'But it's for you then to choose. Shake hands with me,'
Rowland added; 'that will do as well; and suffer me as I go
out to stop a moment in your chapel.'

They shook hands and separated. The *frate* crossed
himself, opened his book and wandered away in relief
against the western sky. Rowland passed back into the
convent and paused long enough in the chapel to look for
the alms-box. He had had what is vulgarly called a great
scare; he believed very poignantly, for the time, in Beel-
zebub and felt an irresistible need to subscribe to any
institution that might engage to keep him at a distance.

At the end of October 1950, Noël Coward stayed in Fiesole
with Derek Hill, in a villino which Bernard Berenson had put
at the then youthful painter's disposal on his estate of I Tatti.
On his arrival, Coward noted in his diary: 'Went to Derek's
little house which is a dear little ice-house and very horrid
indeed. It was pitch dark.' On the next day he recorded:

Cough not improved by freezing house. Woke feeling
lousy. Bathroom *frigorifico* and no hot water. Just my
dish. Derek took me over Berenson's villa. It is filled with
priceless *objets d'art* and pictures – a great number of
immensely famous Madonnas simpering in gold leaf. The
car broke down so it was hours before we could get away.
On arrival at Derek's house, I made my great decision

and told Derek in no uncertain terms that I was leaving his bed and board in favour of the Excelsior Hotel on account of not wanting to catch pneumonia. He was very sweet about it. I packed like lightning and was out of that beastly little ice-box for ever. Began to relax at the Excelsior. Retired to my warm bed in a warm room with infinite relief.

On the following day Coward had dinner with Derek Hill, at an expensive restaurant in Florence. During it, he expressed his disapproval of 'the prissy, self-conscious academic beauty of Florence'. Hill subsequently executed the most truthful portrait in existence of Coward. So far from being 'very horrid indeed', the Berenson villino was charming, albeit primitive in its comforts.

Below Fiesole lies San Domenico and the Valle delle Donne, beloved of Landor:

> Here by the lake, Boccaccio's fair brigade
> Beguiled the hours and tale for tale repaid.

At the end of the tenth novel of the *Decameron*, when the men settle themselves to gambling, Madonna urges the women to come on an afternoon excursion with her:

'Ever since we have been here I have wished to show you a place not far off where I believe none of you has ever been: it is called La Valle delle Donne, and till today I have not had a chance to speak of it. It is yet early; if you choose to come with me, I promise that you will be pleased with your walk.' And they answered that they were all willing: so without saying a word to the gentlemen, they called one of their women to attend to them, and after a walk of nearly a mile they came to the place which they entered by a strait path where there burst forth a crystal stream, and they found it so beautiful and so pleasant, especially in those hot still hours of afternoon, that nothing could excel it: and as some of them told me later, the little plain in the valley was an exact circle, as though it had been described by a pair of compasses, as though it was indeed rather the work of Nature than of Man. It was about half a mile in

circumference surrounded by six hills of moderate
height, on each of which was a palace built in the form of a
little castle . . . And then what gave them the greatest
delight was the rivulet that came through the valley
which divided two hills and, running through the rocks,
fell suddenly and sweetly in a waterfall seeming, as it was
dashed and sprinkled in drops all about, like so much
quicksilver. Coming into the little plain beneath this fall,
the stream was received in a fine canal, and, running
swiftly to the midst of the plain, formed itself in a pool not
deeper than man's breast and so clear that you might see
the gravelly bottom and the pebbles intermixed, which
indeed you might count: and there were fishes there
also swimming up and down in great plenty; and the
water that overflowed was received into another little
canal which carried it out of the valley. There the ladies all
came together, and after praising the place, seeing the
basin before them, that it was very private, they agreed to
bathe. Bidding the maid to keep watch and to let them
know if anyone came nigh by, they stripped off their
clothes and went in, and it covered the beauty of their
bodies as a crystal glass conceals a rose. After they had
diverted themselves there for some time, they dressed
themselves again and returned, softly talking all the way
of the beauty of the place.

On his Italian tour in 1887, Thomas Hardy was always far
more interested in the Roman and Etruscan remains than in the
architecture and art of subsequent centuries. It is not surprising
therefore that the only poem which Florence inspired him to
write should have been 'In the Old Theatre, Fiesole'. This
Roman theatre was built at the end of the first century BC
and subsequently enlarged by Claudius and Septimius
Severus.

> I traced the Circus whose grey stones incline
> Where Rome and dim Etruria interjoin,
> Till came a child who showed an ancient coin
> That bore the image of a Constantine.

She lightly passed; nor did she once opine
How, better than all books, she had raised for me
In swift perspective Europe's history
Through the vast years of Caesar's sceptred line.

For in my distant plot of English loam
'Twas but to delve, and straightway there to find
Coins of like impress. As with one half blind
Whom common simples cure, her act flashed home
In that mute moment to my opened mind
The power, the pride, the reach of perished Rome.

The Certosa

The Certosa (Charterhouse, or Carthusian monastery) di Val
d'Ema, reached until recently by tram through the suburbs of
Le Due Strade to Galluzzo, is now accessible by bus. But
Stendhal was obliged to go by other means:

> This morning I hired a *sediolo* [gig] in order to visit the
> famous Charterhouse which lies some two miles distant
> from the walls of Florence. This consecrated building
> stands upon a hill-top beside the highway to Rome; at
> first glance you might well mistake it for a *palazzo* or a
> gothic stronghold. As a structure, the mass is imposing;
> yet the impression is very different from that which is left
> upon the mind by the Grande Chartreuse, near Grenoble.
> There is nothing *holy* about this edifice; nothing sublime,
> nothing to exalt the spirit, nothing to fill the soul with
> involuntary religious awe; rather is this a satire against
> religion itself; the mind dwells willy-nilly upon the limit-
> less treasuries of gold poured out in order to afford some
> eighteen *fakirs* the grim satisfaction of mortifying the
> flesh. It would be simpler, all in all, merely to lock them
> away in a dungeon cell, and to convert this Charterhouse
> into a common gaol to serve the whole of Tuscany. And
> even so, with this new attribution, it might well still num-
> ber no more than eighteen inmates, so dispassionately
> do these people affect to calculate their interests, and so

little swayed are they by those surging tempests of the
heart which may send the most upright men headlong
toppling into the abyss.

Today Stendhal would certainly be even more disapprov-
ing. From the magnificent apartments in which Charles V,
Pius VI, and Pius VII were lodged, one now passes over to the
Farmacia, where postcards, chocolate, scent, and the liqueurs
of the place, many of them in majolica flasks, are on sale to
hordes of tourists.

The Certosa was the first stop on an energetic walk taken
by James Russell Lowell, with his friends Frank Shaw and
William Page, on the first of his three visits to Florence. From
the Certosa:

We took a roundabout course among the hills, going first
to Galileo's tower, and then to that of the Church of San
Miniato which Michelangelo defended. Thence we descended steeply towards the Arno, crossed it by a ferry-
boat, and then found ourselves opposite a *trattoria*. It was a
warm October day, and we unanimously turned in at the
open door. There were three rooms, one upstairs, where
one might dine 'more obscurely and courageously', the
kitchen, and the room in which we were. As I sat upon the
corner of the bench, I looked out through some grape-
trailers which hung waving over the door, and saw first
the Arno, then, beyond it a hill on which stood a villa
with a garden laid out in squares with huge walls of box
and a clump of tall black cypresses in the middle, then, to
the right of this, the ruined tower of San Miniato, and
beyond it that from which Milton had doubtless watched
the moon rising 'o'er the top of Fiesole.' This was my
landscape. Behind me was the kitchen. The cook in his
white linen cap was stirring alternately a huge cauldron of
soup and a pan of sausages, which exploded into a sudden
flame now and then, as if by spontaneous combustion. A
woman wound up at short intervals a jack which turned
three or four chickens before the fire, and attended a kind
of lake of hot fat in which countless tiny fishes darted,
squirmed, and turned topsy-turvy in a way so much more

active and with an expression of so much more enjoyment than is wont to characterize living, that you would
have said that they had now for the first time found their
element, and were created to revel in boiling oil. The
wine sold here was the produce of the vineyard which you
could see behind and on each side of the little *trattoria*. We
had a large loaf of bread, and something like a quart and a
half of pure cool wine for nine of our cents. During the
whole time I was in Florence, though I never saw anyone
drink water, I also never saw a single drunken man,
except some Austrian soldiers, and only four of these –
two of them officers . . .

THE PALACE OF PRATOLINO

Little now remains of the Palace of Pratolino, about 9 miles
from the Porta S. Gallo. It was built by Francesco de' Medici,
an outrageous voluptuary, for the beautiful Venetian, Bianca
Cappello, whom, having had her young husband murdered in
the street and having poisoned his own Duchess, Francesco
eventually married in 1578. Richard Lassels left an account of
the aquatic marvels to be found there:

> Here we saw in the garden excellent grots, fountains,
> water-works, shady-walks, groves and the like, all upon
> the side of the hill. Here you have the Grot of Cupid with
> the wetting-stools, upon which, sitting down, a great
> spout of water comes full in your face. The Fountain of
> the Tritons overtakes you too, and washeth you soundly.
> Then being led about this garden, where there are stores
> of fountains under the laurel trees, we were carried back
> to the grots that are under the stairs and saw there many
> *giuochi d'aqua*: as that of Pan striking up a melodious tune
> upon his mouth-organ at the sight of his mistress, appear-
> ing over against him: that where the Angel carries a
> trumpet to his mouth and soundeth it; and where the
> Country Clown offers a dish of water to a serpent, who
> drinks it and lifteth up his head when he hath drunk: that
> of the Mill which seems to break and grind olives: the

Paper Mill: the Man with the Grinding Stone: the
Saracen's Head gaping and spewing out water: the grot of
Galatea who comes out of a door in a sea-chariot with two
nymphs, and saileth awhile upon the water and so returns
again in at the same door: the curious Round Table
capable of twelve or fifteen men, with a curious fountain
playing constantly in the midst of it, and places between
every trencher, for every man to set his bottle of wine in
cold water: the Samaritan Woman coming out of her
house with her buckets to fetch water at the fountain, and
having filled her buckets, returns back again the same
way: in the meantime you see Smiths thumping, Birds
chirping in trees, Mills grinding: and all this is done by
water, which sets these little inventions awork, and
makes them move as it were of themselves: in the meantime an organ plays to you while you dine there in *fresco* at
that table, if you have meat. Then the neat bathing place,
the pillar of petrified water: and lastly, the great pond and
grotta before the house, with the huge Giant stooping to
catch at a rock, to throw it to heaven. This Giant is so big,
that within the very thigh of him is a great grot of water,
called the Grot of Thetis and Shell Fishes, all spouting
water.

At the beginning of the nineteenth century, Ferdinando of
Lorraine wantonly ordered that the villa, with its fountains
and *jeux d'eaux*, should be blown up. In 1872 the immensely
wealthy Russian Prince Demidoff bought the estate. The huge
park, eventually made over to the province, is now open to the
public.

BELLOSGUARDO

On the hill of Arcetri, south of Florence, rises the Torre del
Gallo, restored in 1904–6 in the style of the fourteenth century. From its tower Galileo made his observations; and it is
here that Milton is supposed to have visited him, subsequently
writing of

> . . . the moon, whose orb
> Through optic glass the Tuscan artist views
> At evening from the top of Fiesole,
> Or in Valdarno, to descry new lands,
> Rivers, or mountains in her spotty globe.

In his *Italy* Samuel Rogers has a passage about the meeting between the then aged and blind Galileo, forced by the Inquisition to live at Arcetri, outside the confines of the city, which he was only to reenter when his body was carried in for burial, and the still youthful and clear-sighted Milton:

> Nearer we hail
> Thy sunny slope, Arcetri, sung of old
> For its green vine; dearer to me, to most,
> As dwelt on by that great astronomer,
> Seven years a prisoner at the city-gate,
> Let in but in his grave-clothes. Sacred be
> His villa (justly it was called the Gem)!
> Sacred the lawn, where many a cypress threw
> Its length of shadow, while he watched the stars!
> Sacred the vineyard, where, while yet his sight
> Glimmered, at blush of morn he dressed his vines,
> Chanting aloud in gaiety of heart
> Some verse of Ariosto! – There, unseen,
> Gazing with reverent awe – Milton his guest,
> Just then come forth, all life and enterprise;
> *He* in his old age and extremity
> Blind, at noonday exploring with his staff;
> His eyes upturned as to the golden sun,
> His eyeballs idly rolling. Little then
> Did Galileo think whom he received:
> That in his hand he held the hand of one
> Who could requite him – who would spread his name
> O'er land and seas – great as himself, nay, greater;
> Milton as little that in him he saw,
> As in a glass, what he himself should be,
> Destined as soon to fall on evil days
> And evil tongues – so soon, alas! to live

> In darkness, and with dangers compassed round,
> And solitude.

The heroine of Ouida's *Pascarel* – a novel about the adventures of a troop of *commedia dell'arte* players – describes a visit to the Torre del Gallo, and in so doing evokes the life of the countryfolk around Florence in the age of Garibaldi:

> . . . He took me up to the Star Tower of Galileo amongst the winding paths of the hills, with the grey walls over-topped by white fruit blossoms, and ever and again, at some break in their ramparts of stone, the gleam of the yellow Arno water, or the glisten of the marbles of the City shining far beneath us, through the silvery veil of the olive-leaves.
>
> . . . The air was full of a dreamy fragrance; the bullocks went on their slow ways with flowers in their leather frontlets; the contadini had flowers stuck behind their ears or in their waistbands; women sat by the wayside, singing as they plaited their yellow curling lengths of straw; children frisked and tumbled like young rabbits under the budding maples; the plum-trees strewed the green landscape with flashes of white like newly fallen snow on Alpine grass slopes; again and again amongst the tender pallor of the olive woods there rose the beautiful flush of rosy almond-tree; at every step the passer-by trod ankle deep in violets.
>
> . . . About the foot of the Tower of Galileo ivy and vervain, and the Madonna's herb, and the white hexagons of the stars of Bethlehem grew amongst the grasses; pigeons paced to and fro, with pretty pride of plumage; a dog slept on the flags; the cool, moist, deep-veined creepers climbed about the stones; there were peach-trees in all the beauty of their blossoms, and everywhere about them were close-set olive-trees, with the ground between them scarlet with the tulips and the wild rose bushes.
>
> From a window a girl leaned out and hung a cage amongst the ivy-leaves, that her bird might sing his vespers to the sun.

Who will may see the scene today.

So little changed – so little, if at all, from the time when the feet of the great student wore the timber of the tower stairs, and the fair-haired scholar, who had travelled from the isles in the northern sea, came up between the olive stems to gaze thence on Vallombrosa.

The world has spoiled most of its places of pilgrimage, but the old Star Tower is not harmed as yet, where it stands amongst its quiet garden-ways and grass-grown slopes, up high amongst the hills, with sounds of dripping water on its court, and wild wood-flowers thrusting their bright heads through its stones.

. . . It is as peaceful, as simple, as homely, as closely girt with blossoming boughs and with tulip-crimsoned grasses now as then, when, from its roof, in the still midnights of far-off time, its master read the secret of the stars.

'The world has spoiled most of its places of pilgrimage.' Some hundred years after Ouida wrote this description, it has also spoiled much of the countryside around the Torre.

It was not far from the Torre, on the hill of Bellosguardo, that in the summer of 1858 Nathaniel Hawthorne rented what Henry James called

a picturesque old villa . . . a curious structure with a crenelated tower, which, after having in the course of its career suffered many vicissitudes and played many parts, now finds its most vivid identity in being pointed out to strangers as the sometimes residence of the celebrated American romancer.

The Villa Montauto was subsequently transformed into the castle of Monte Beni, the ancestral home of Donatello, the hero of *The Marble Faun* (or *Transformation*, as it was originally called in England).

Montegufoni

When, in 1909, Sir George Sitwell bought the estate of Montegufoni, he sent a letter to his eldest son Osbert, who was later

to guy and pillory his many oddities to such amusing effect in
his many-volumed autobiography *Left Hand, Right Hand*. It
began:

> My dearest Osbert,
> You will be interested to hear that I am buying in your
> name the Castle of Acciaiuoli (pronounced Accheeyawly)
> between Florence and Siena. The Acciaiuoli were a reign-
> ing family in Greece in the thirteenth century, and after-
> wards great Italian nobles. The castle is split up between
> many poor families, and has an air of forlorn grandeur. It
> would probably cost £100,000 to build today.

Sir George then gave a catalogue of the innumerable rooms,
including a picture-gallery with frescoed portraits of the
owners, a great saloon opening on to an interior courtyard, a
library, and a museum. He concluded:

> We shall be able to grow our own fruit, wine, oil – even
> champagne! I have actually bought half the castle for
> £2,200; the other half belongs to the village usurer, whom
> we are endeavouring to get out. The ultimatum expires
> today, but I do not yet know the result. The purchase,
> apart from the romantic interest, is a good one, as it
> returns five per cent. The roof is in splendid order, and the
> drains can't be wrong, as there aren't any. I shall have to
> find the money in your name, and I do hope, my dear
> Osbert, that you will prove worthy of what I am doing
> for you, and you will not pursue that miserable career of
> extravagance and selfishness which already once ruined
> your family. – Ever your loving father,
>   GEORGE R. SITWELL

In June 1926, D. H. Lawrence visited Montegufoni. He
wrote of the furnishings of the Castle in a letter to a friend,
Mrs Otway:

> Sir G. [Sir George Sitwell] collects *beds*. . . . Room
> after room, and nothing but bed after bed. I said 'but do
> you put your guests in them?' – Oh! he said. They're not
> to sleep in. They're museum pieces. Also gilt and wiggly-

carved chairs. I sat on one. Oh! he said. Those chairs are
not to sit in! – So I wiggled on the seat in the hopes that it
would come to pieces.

In subsequent years Osbert, his brother Sacheverell, and his
sister Edith were frequently to entertain their friends at
Montegufoni. But 'the rarest of all houseparties' (Osbert
Sitwell's own phrase) gathered there, in their enforced absence, in 1940. This consisted of such pictures, sent there from
Florence for safe-keeping from the possible ravages of war, as
Botticelli's *Primavera* and Uccello's *Battle of San Romano*.
Osbert Sitwell records that all were undamaged, with the
exception of Ghirlandaio's circular *Adoration of the Magi*,
greatly admired by Ruskin. 'The Germans used it face up-
wards, as a table-top (though the table beneath had a top of its
own), and it was stained in consequence with wine, food, and
coffee, and with marks which the soldiers made on it with
their knives.'

A Distant Retrospect

With rare exceptions – Byron was one – the love which nineteenth-century expatriate writers felt for Florence was passionate and unqualified. Of all the cities of Italy, it was the one which, lacking the religious oppressiveness of Rome and the hedonistic frivolity of Venice, they most favoured. With the coming of the twentieth century, however, a note of carping insinuated itself. Already in 1909 the Russian poet Alexander Blok (1880–1921) could address Florence with a mixture of disgust and pity:

> . . . Oh, laugh at yourself today, Bella,
> For your features have fallen in,
> Death's rotten wrinkles disfigure
> That once miraculous skin.
>
> The motorcars shout in your lanes,
> Your houses fill me with disgust;
> You have given yourself to the stains
> Of Europe's bilious yellow dust.

Although he and his wife spent so much time in Florence and its environs, Huxley could declare perversely that 'the spectacle of that second-rate provincial town with its repulsive Gothic architecture and its acres of Christmas card primitives made me almost sick.'

Dylan Thomas (1914–53), ensconced thanks to the generosity of his foolishly long-suffering patroness, the first wife of the historian A. J. P. Taylor, in the Villa del Beccaro in Scandicci in 1947, found Florence 'a gruelling museum' and eventually decided that he was 'sick . . . of drinking chianti in our marble shanty, sick of vini and contadini and bambini.'

Another English poet, Laurie Lee (1914–), also soon decided that he had had his fill of 'the lovely but indigestible city.' He had been tormented by the heat, in which 'the carved palaces quivered like radiators in the sun,' 'hot blasts of air, as from kitchen stoves, moved through the streets laden with odours of meat and frying oil' and 'in the cheaper cafés brick-faced British tourists sat sweating and counting their crumpled money.'

But despite such voices raised in irritation, exasperation, and even hatred, for most literary visitors the spell has remained as potent as it was for Ouida more than a hundred years ago:

> The beauty of the past goes with you at every step in Florence. Buy eggs in the market, and you buy them where Donatello bought those which fell down in a broken heap before the wonder of the crucifix. Pause in a narrow street and it shall be that Borgo Allegri, which the people so baptized for the love of the old painter [Cimabue] and the new-born art. Stray into a great dark church at evening-time, where peasants tell their beads in the marble silence, and you are where the whole city flocked, weeping, at midnight, to look their last upon the dead face of their Michelangelo. Pace up the steps of the palace of the Signoria, and you tread the stone that felt the feet of him [Savonarola] to whom so bitterly was known 'com' e duro calle lo scendere e lo salir per l'altrui scale.' Buy a knot of March anemones or April arum lilies, and you may bear them with you through the same city ward in which the child Ghirlandajo once played amidst the golden and silver garlands that his father fashioned for the young heads of the Renaissance. Ask for a shoemaker, and you shall find a cobbler sitting with his board in the same old twisting, shadowy street-way where the old man Toscanelli drew his charts that served a fair-haired sailor of

Genoa, called Columbus. Toil to fetch a tinker through
the squalor of San Nicolo, and there shall fall on you the
shadow of the bell-tower, where the old sacristan saved to
the world the genius of Night and Day. Glance up to see
the hour of the evening, and there, sombre and tragical,
will loom above you the walls of the communal palace on
which the traitors were painted by the brush of Sarto, and
the tower of Giotto, fair and fresh in its perfect grace as
though angels had built it in the night just past . . .

It is this interpenetration of past and present which – albeit
nowadays all too often a source of friction and therefore
of discomfort – gives to Florence its unique interest and
distinctive charm.

Bibliography

Acton, Harold and Chaney, Edward, *Florence: A Traveller's Companion*, London, 1986

Acton, Harold, *Spectator*, 23 September 1989

Addison, Joseph, *Remarks on Several Parts of Italy etc.*, London, 1705

Aldington, Richard, *Pinorman*, London, 1954

Arnold, Matthew, *Letters (1848–88)*, ed. G. W. E. Russell, London, 1901

Beckford, William, *Dreams, Waking Thoughts, and Incidents, in a series of letters from various parts of Europe*, London, 1783, revised 1834

Bennett, Arnold, *Florentine Journal*, London, 1967

Berenson, Mary, *A Self-Portrait from her Letters and Diaries*, ed. Barbara Strachey and Jayne Samuels, London, 1983

Biagi, Guido, *Men and Manner of Old Florence*, London, 1919

Blok, Alexander, *The Twelve and Other Poems*, trans. Jon Stallworthy and Peter France, London, 1974

Boccaccio, *Life of Dante*, trans. Mrs Oliphant in *The Makers of Florence*, London, 1883

Boynton, Henry Walcott, *James Fenimore Cooper*, New York, 1931

Browning, Elizabeth Barrett, *Aurora Leigh*, London, 1857

——, *Casa Guidi Windows*, London, 1851

—— and Robert, *Letters*, London, 1899

Browning, Robert, *The Ring and the Book*, London, 1868–9

—— *The Complete Works*, 2 vols., London, 1915

Byron, Lord George Gordon, *Letters and Journals*, ed. Leslie A. Marchand, London, 1973–81

—— *Poems*, Oxford, 1945

Campbell, Harriet Charlotte Beaujolais, *A Journey to Florence in 1817*, ed. G. R. de Beer, London, 1951

Camus, Albert, essay in *Reflections on Florence*, ed. Simone Bargellini and Alice Scott, Florence, 1984

Castellan, Antoine Laurent, *Letters on Italy*, London, 1820

Cooper, James Fenimore, *Gleanings in Europe*, Italy, 1838

Cooper, Lettice, *Fenny*, London, 1953.

Coward, Noel, *Diaries*, ed. Graham Payn and Sheridan Morley, London, 1982

Cunard, Nancy, *Grand Man*, London, 1954

Dante, *Il Paradiso*, trans. Laurence Binyon, London, 1943

Day Lewis, C., 'Florence: Works of Art' from *Collected Poems*, London, 1954

Dentler, Clara Louise, *Famous Foreigners in Florence*, Italy, 1964

Dickens, Charles, *Little Dorrit*, London, 1855–7

—— *Pictures from Italy*, London, 1846

Dostoevsky, Anna, *Dostoevsky: Reminiscences*, London, 1926

Dostoevsky, Fyodor, *Letters*, London, 1961

Dowden, Edward, *Browning*, London, 1904

Downey, E., *Charles Lever, his Life and Letters*, London, 1906

Dumas, Alexandre, *Une Année à Florence*, Paris, 1851 (author's translation)

Eaton, Charlotte A., *Continental Adventures*, London, 1826

Eliot, George, *Journals and Letters*, ed. J. W. Cross, London, 1885

—— *Romola*, London, 1863

Evelyn, John, *Diary*, London, 1818

Fields, Anna, *Harriet Beecher Stowe*, London, 1898

Fitzpatrick, W. J., *The Life of Charles Lever*, London, 1879

Forest, J. de, *European Acquaintances*, New York, 1858

Forster, E. M., *A Room with a View*, London, 1908

—— *Selected Letters*, Vol. I, ed. Mary Lago and P. N. Furbank, London, 1983

Forster, J., *Walter Savage Landor*, London, 1869

France, Anatole, *Le Lys Rouge*, trans. *The Red Lily*, Winifred Stephens, London, 1908

Gardner, Edmund G., *The Story of Florence*, London, 1902

Gide, André, *Journals*, trans. Justin O'Brien, London, 1947

Gray, Thomas, *Letters*, ed. Mason, London, 1835–40

Hardy, Florence Emily, *The Life of Thomas Hardy 1840–1928*, London, 1962

Hare, Augustus J. C., *Florence*, London, 1896

Hawthorne, Nathaniel, *The Marble Faun*, London, 1860

—— *Passages from the French and Italian Notebooks*, London, 1871

Hawthorne, Sophia, *Notes in England and Italy*, London, 1851

Hazlitt, William, *Notes of a Journey Through France and Italy*, London, 1826

Holloway, Mark, *Norman Douglas*, London, 1976

Howells, W. D., *Tuscan Cities*, London, 1891

Hunt, Leigh, *Autobiography*, London, 1850

Hutton, Edward, *Florence*, London, 1952

—— *Country Walks About Florence*, London, 1908

Hutton, Laurence, *Literary Landmarks of Old Florence*, London, 1897

Huxley, Aldous, *Letters*, ed. Grover Smith, London, 1969

—— *Time Must Have a Stop*, London, 1945

James, Henry, *Foreign Parts*, London, 1883

—— *Italian Hours*, London, 1909

—— *Letters*, ed. Leon Edel, London, 1975–80

—— *Portrait of a Lady*, London, 1881

—— *Roderick Hudson*, London, 1876

—— *The Diary of a Man of Fifty*, London, 1879

—— (ed.), *William Wetmore Story and His Friends*, London, 1903

Johnson, Samuel, *Miscellanies*, ed. George Birkbeck Hill, Oxford, 1897

Kjetsaa, Geir, *Fyodor Dostoevsky: A Writer's Life*, London, 1988

Landor, Walter Savage, *Complete Poems*, 4 Vols., ed. Stephen Wheeler, London, 1933–6.

Lassels, Richard, *The Voyage of Italy*, London, 1670

Lawrence, D. H., *Letters*, ed. Aldous Huxley, London, 1932

—— *Aaron's Rod*, London, 1922

Lawrence, Frieda, *Not I, But the Wind*, London, 1935

Lee, Elizabeth, *Ouida, a Memoir*, London, 1914

Lee, Laurie, *I Can't Stay Long*, London, 1975

Lewis, Sinclair, *World So Wide*, London, 1951

Longfellow, Henry Wadsworth, *Outre-mer: A Pilgrimage Beyond the Sea*, Boston, 1833–4

Lowell, James Russell, *Letters*, ed. C. E. Norton, New York, 1894

Lucas, E. V., *A Wanderer in Florence*, London, 1912

Macaulay, Thomas Babbington, *Life and Letters* by George Otto Trevelyan, London, 1877

Maugham, H. Neville, *The Book of Italian Travel*, London, 1903

Maugham, William Somerset, *Then and Now*, London, 1967

Meyers, Jeffrey, *D. H. Lawrence*, London, 1990

Montaigne, Michel de, *Journal du voyage en Italie*, trans. William Hazlitt, London, 1842

Moore, Harry T., *The Priest of Love: A Life of D. H. Lawrence*, London, 1974

Morgan, Lady Sydney, *Italy*, London, 1821

Oliphant, Margaret, *The Makers of Florence*, London, 1883

Origo, Iris, *Images and Shadows*, London, 1970

Ouida (Marie Louise de la Ramée), *Pascarel*, London, 1873

Piozzi, Mrs (Thrale, Hester Lynch), *Observations and Reflections made in the course of a Journey through France, Italy and Germany*, 1789

Pratolini, Vasco, *The Girls of San Frediano*, trans. William Weaver, London, 1950

Proust, Marcel, *À la recherche du temps perdu: Du côté de chez Swann* and *Le côté de Guermantes*, 1913, trans. C. K. Scott Moncrieff, *Remembrance of Things Past: Swann's Way* and *The Guermantes Way*, London, 1922 and 1925

Rhodes, Anthony, *The Poet as Superman*, London, 1957

Rogers, Samuel, *Italy*, London, 1836

—— *The Italian Journal*, ed. J. R. Hale, London, 1956

Ruskin, John, *Mornings in Florence*, Orpington, 1875–7

—— *Praeterita*, London, 1885–9

—— *The Diaries of John Ruskin*, selected and edited by Joan Evans and John Howard Whitehouse, Oxford, 1956

Shelley, Percy Bysshe, *Letters*, ed. Roger Ingpen, London, 1909

Shorthouse, J. H., *John Inglesant*, London, 1881

Sitwell, Osbert, *Great Morning*, London, 1948

Smollett, Tobias, *Travels through France and Italy*, London, 1766

Soldati, Mario, *The Confession*, trans. Raymond Rosenthal, London, 1958

Spence, Joseph, *Letters from the Grand Tour*, ed. Slava Klima, Montreal–London, 1975

Staël, Madame de, *Corinne*, Paris, 1807 (author's translation)

Steegmuller, Francis, 'A Letter from Florence' in *Stories and True Stories*, Boston, 1972

Stendhal (Henri Beyle), *Rome, Naples and Florence*, London, 1959

Stirling, Monica, *The Fine and the Wicked*, Gollancz, 1957

Strelsky, Katherine, *Dostoevsky in Florence*, *The Russian Review*, Vol. XXIII, No. 2, April 1964

Swan, Michael, *Ilex and Olive*, London, 1949

Swinburne, Algernon Charles, *Songs Before Sunrise*, London, 1871

Symonds, John Addington, *Renaissance in Italy*, London, 1898

Taine, Hippolyte, *Italy*, trans. J. Durand, New York, 1875

Taylor, Katherine Kressman, *Diary of Florence in the Flood*, New York, 1967

Tennyson, Hallam, *Tennyson and His Friends*, London, 1911

Thomas, Dylan, *Selected Letters*, London, 1965

Trefusis, Violet, *Don't Look Round*, London, 1952

Treves, G. Artom, *The Golden Ring*, London, 1956

Trollope, Anthony, *He Knew He was Right*, London, 1869

Trollope, Thomas, *What I Remember*, London, 1887

Twain, Mark, *The Innocents Abroad*, Hartford, Connecticut, 1869

Walpole, Horace, *Letters*, ed. P. Toynbee, London, 1903–5

Waterfield, Lina, *Castle in Italy*, London, 1961

Williams, William Carlos, *A Voyage to Pagany*, New York, 1928

Acknowledgements

Acknowledgement is due to the following for kindly giving permission to reproduce copyright material: Lettice Cooper, *Fenny*, Virago, 1987. Extract reproduced by permission of Lettice Cooper; Noel Coward, *Diaries*, G. Payn, 1983. Extract reproduced by permission of Macmillan Ltd.; C. Day Lewis, *Collected Poems*, 1954. Extract reproduced by permission of the Peters Fraser & Dunlop Group Ltd.; E. M. Forster, *A Room with a View*, 1908. Extract reproduced by permission of Edward Arnold Ltd.; Aldous Huxley, *Letters*, 1969. Extract reproduced by permission of Mrs Laura Huxley and Chatto & Windus Ltd; Sinclair Lewis, *World So Wide*, 1951. Extract reproduced by permission of William Heinemann Ltd.; Somerset Maugham, *Then and Now*, 1967. Extract reproduced by permission of William Heinemann Ltd.; Anthony Rhodes, *The Poet as Superman*, Weidenfeld & Nicolson, 1957. Extract reproduced by permission of A. M. Heath Ltd.; Osbert Sitwell, *Left Hand! Right Hand!*, Macmillan, 1945. Extract reproduced by permission of David Higham Associates Ltd.; Mario Soldati, *The Confession*, 1958. Extract reproduced by permission of André Deutsch Ltd.; Michael Swan, *Ilex and Olive*, Home & Van Thal, 1949. Extracts reproduced by permission of Anna P. Swan and Curtis Brown Ltd.; Violet Trefusis, *Don't Look Round*, 1952. Extract reproduced by permission of the Estate of Violet Trefusis and Hutchinson Ltd.; William Carlos Williams, *A Voyage to Pagany*. Copyright © 1970 New Directions Publishing Corp. Extract reproduced by permission of New Directions.

Index